I PLEDGE ALLEGIANCE

I PLEDGE ALLEGIANCE

*A Believer's Guide to Kingdom Citizenship
in Twenty-First-Century America*

David Crump

WILLIAM B. EERDMANS PUBLISHING COMPANY
GRAND RAPIDS, MICHIGAN

Wm. B. Eerdmans Publishing Co.
2140 Oak Industrial Drive N.E., Grand Rapids, Michigan 49505
www.eerdmans.com

Published 2018
Printed in the United States of America

27 26 25 24 23 22 21 20 19 18   1 2 3 4 5 6 7 8 9 10

ISBN 978-0-8028-7174-9

Library of Congress Cataloging-in-Publication Data

Names: Crump, David, 1956- author.
Title: I pledge allegiance : a believer's guide to kingdom citizenship in
    twenty-first-century America / David Crump.
Description: Grand Rapids : Eerdmans Publishing Co., 2018. | Includes
    bibliographical references and index.
Identifiers: LCCN 2017034277 | ISBN 9780802871749 (pbk. : alk. paper)
Subjects: LCSH: Christianity—United States. | Christian life—United States.
    | Christianity—21st century.
Classification: LCC BR526 .C78 2018 | DDC 261.70973—dc23
    LC record available at https://lccn.loc.gov/2017034277

Unless otherwise noted, Scripture quotations are taken from the
New International Version (NIV).

This book is dedicated to those among my former students at Calvin College who were intent about following Jesus as true disciples and conforming their lives to his upside-down, counterintuitive kingdom ethic. They are scattered now across this country and around the world. Their examples of obedience, passion, and idealism continue to inspire me.

Contents

Foreword

On election night 2016, I sat on our basement sofa awash with disbelief at what was unfolding before me. A narrative had been built over the course of the election cycle that indicated that the country would reassert the identity of America as a white nation and elevate its own sense of greatness, even if it went against the very tenets of Christianity. That narrative had been cemented in my mind on election night 2016 when 81 percent of white evangelicals voted for a non-Christian candidate of questionable moral character.

My wife had turned in early, anticipating a disappointing outcome. Close to midnight my daughter, who had been monitoring the election results online while doing her homework, came downstairs in tears. In her mind, the country had spoken. She felt that her country had informed her that, as a female of color, she would have no standing in the world. I tried to assure her that there were still many in the world, particularly her parents, who passionately disagreed with that statement. She went upstairs to bed, but I wasn't sure she was convinced.

Through a quirk of scheduling, my daughter's sixteenth birthday party was held the day after the 2016 elections. Twenty of my daughter's closest friends gathered at our home in Chicago. We live in a diverse neighborhood and our children have an extremely diverse group of friends. The twenty that gathered around our dining room table that evening represented the present and future demographic of the United States. Some wore their hijabs; some spoke in Spanish; they represented the range of hues in skin color; they represented the range of cultures. They would be the community that would restore dignity to my daughter who felt that the nation had rejected her.

When confronted with profound challenges, the church faces the option of giving up (running away and hiding from the challenge) or giving in (yielding to the ways of the world around us). Or we can seek a more biblical path, a path that leads to the church being the body of Christ and the living embodiment of our Savior here on earth. Rather than complaining about the latest election results or the message sent to us by the American people, I want my family to begin weaving a new narrative, one that more fully embodies the Scriptures and the narrative of the kingdom of God.

As an evangelical of color who made a deliberate choice to become a naturalized citizen of the United States and to claim it as my home and the homeland of our children, what I see developing in the American evangelical community is deeply troubling. I see a movement that seems to be abandoning our scriptural norms and embracing secular, cultural, political ones. Evangelicals have become equated with the empire. We seek first the greatness of the empire of the United States rather than embracing the task of proclaiming and demonstrating the kingdom of God.

I Pledge Allegiance by David Crump calls us back to a primary allegiance to the kingdom of God rather than a worldly empire. Crump recognizes the fallen nature of human systems, as is befitting an evangelical teacher in the Reformed tradition. As a biblical scholar, Crump carefully exegetes Scripture, revealing the best of an evangelical Christianity that takes seriously the authority of God's Word. As a resident alien in this world, Crump offers examples of living as God's representatives in a broken world.

As an evangelical of color, I see the need for this text to be devoured by those I would consider my enemies—those who would seek the American empire above the kingdom of God. As an act of love, I would implore them to read this text and be transformed by it. But I also see my own need to read through this book, that the kingdom of God may never be subsumed by the illicit allure of the empire in my own life. This book is not a partisan book. It is a political book in the best sense of the word. It is a book that calls the church to a scriptural standard that elevates the people of God in our moral standing without removing us from a world in need. May this text find its way before the eyes and hearts of those who wish to build a more biblical narrative for the church in the years to come.

SOONG-CHAN RAH
Milton B. Engebretson Professor of
Church Growth and Evangelism,
North Park Theological Seminary
Author of *The Next Evangelicalism* and
Prophetic Lament

Preface

I began my research for *I Pledge Allegiance* near the end of George W. Bush's presidency. I am finishing the book and writing this preface with Donald Trump's presidential inauguration only weeks away. According to the Pew Research Center, 58 percent of American Protestants (including "other Christian" groups) and 52 percent of Roman Catholics voted for Trump in the 2016 elections. But these figures pale in comparison to the 81 percent majority Trump garnered among people who identify themselves as white, evangelical, born-again Christians.[1] If there was ever any doubt, Trump's hearty embrace by US evangelicals demonstrates once and for all how completely the Republican Party has captured the American church.[2] How the descendants of Jerry Falwell's Moral Majority, long-standing advocates of "traditional family values," managed to convince themselves that a foul-mouthed, narcissistic real-estate mogul—accused of sexual assault (including rape) by dozens of women—could ever represent their moralizing Christian interests will surely occupy many sharp minds for years to come.

Remember, this is the same constituency that cheered for the Republican impeachment of President Clinton when he was found guilty of lying under oath while questioned about his relationship with Monica Lewinsky. Imagine the lurid, race-based caricatures these same Republican stalwarts would have hurled at our first African-American president if Barack Obama had walked on stage at the 2008 Democratic National Convention and introduced his five children by three different women. Yet Donald Trump, a serial philanderer who openly condoned violence at his campaign rallies and refused to release his tax forms or divest himself of his many financial holdings (as every previous president-elect before him had), received overwhelming support from conservative Christian voters. Clearly, the old insistence on admirable character, of viewing the president as a public role model, has fallen prey to a blind faith that any candidate will suffice as long as voters can convince themselves that he will implement their favorite Republican policies.

My goal is not to be another partisan harpy picking over the bones of our continuing political debates. My readers will discover that I am as happy to criticize Democrats as I am Republicans. If space allowed, I could explain why I believe that President Obama failed in as many ways as did his predecessor.[3] Instead, my point is to highlight the major theme of this book and the urgent need for a study such as this: *that every disciple of Jesus Christ, as a citizen of God's kingdom here on earth, must live out that citizenship by becoming more like Jesus, faithfully following his teaching and developing the character he exemplified.* I am afraid that, in the era of President Trump, the Christian church in America will have a greater need than ever to repent and to confess its long-standing disregard for the character and behavioral changes Jesus requires of anyone who claims to be a loyal citizen in the kingdom of God.

Tragically, for a large majority of the conservative American church, allegiance to the nation-state and their favored political party is more important than faithfulness to the kingdom of God and to the lordship of Jesus Christ. In fact, these two disparate arenas have become so thoroughly confused with each other as to become virtually indistinguishable in the minds of most "born-again" people. Remaining a patriotic American nationalist who is faithful to one's political party is now the sine qua non of Christian living. The overwhelming support given by the Christian church to Donald Trump and his refrain promising to "make America great again" is exhibit A in proving this point.

Of course, Christians, like everyone else, can always find a way to turn their choices into necessities, baptizing their ideological commitments as expressions of a Christian mind, defending their political positions as the inherent outworkings of faithful Christian living. On the surface, it appears that the family of God is no different from any other family obliged to sit together at holiday dinners heavily seasoned with half-baked pronouncements and peppery retorts, while everyone cringes over another endless round of he-said-she-said political argument.

My claim is that Christian people must shift their focus to another issue. For the litmus test determining the adequacy of any religious defense of a political or social policy is not its alignment with a political party's ideology but its coherence with biblical teaching. In saying this, I am not suggesting that everyone recite their favorite proof-texts as if the Bible were an odd assortment of Hallmark greeting cards—offering appropriate advice and consolation for life's special moments—which unfortunately is the most popular way for American churchgoers to use the Bible. I am talking about studying the Bible closely and holistically as the story of God's direction of salvation-history as it unfolded in the life of ancient Israel and was finalized in the life, teaching, and ministry of Jesus Christ. It turns out that Jesus has always had specific expectations for how his people should live their lives; expectations that extend well beyond fundamentalism's preoccupation with sex, alcohol, tithing, and Republican politics; expectations that include matters of social welfare, nonviolence, economic justice, and human equality.

Some readers will undoubtedly find a great deal to disagree with in this book. But if the disagreements are only sparked by shopworn policy disputes or differing philosophies about the size and role of government, then the arguments will remain sadly predictable and irrelevant, generating more heat than light. Any meaningful disagreement with the arguments presented here must begin by demonstrating how I have misunderstood—and therefore misapplied—the relevant biblical texts pertaining to God's aspirations for creation, its resources, the human family, and his chosen people. The debate must be rooted in thoughtful biblical interpretation, preferably among people who genuinely wish their opinions and their lives to be conformed to the mind and likeness of Christ. Those who disagree with me are obliged to offer a superior, more coherent set of interpretations that do greater justice to both the original intent and the practical application of God's word. Such Bible reading will meet the challenge offered by William Stringfellow when he rightly explained that "the task is to understand America biblically, *not* the other way around, *not* to construe the Bible Americanly."[4]

That kind of interpretive debate is well worth having, especially if all the participants remain prayerfully open to the Holy Spirit's transforming work, allowing God's living Word to teach, to rebuke, to correct, and to train us in righteousness, so that we will be thoroughly equipped for every good work (2 Tim. 3:16-17). We may never see eye to eye on every topic that I discuss in *I Pledge Allegiance*, but the process of studying the God-inspired Scripture with an open heart and mind is never a waste of time. I have changed my opinions at several points in the course of researching this book.

My academic training is in the field of New Testament studies, not ethics. However, I have always believed that ethics is an integral part of Christian theology (when properly understood); therefore, like any theology worth its salt, it will be firmly grounded in biblical interpretation. During my eighteen years of teaching college students about the New Testament and biblical theology at Calvin College, I have regularly included discussions about the ethical, behavioral significance of the texts we were studying in class. Those years of teaching and classroom discussion—conversations that sometimes continued in my office long after class was over—became the maternity ward for this book.

I realize that substantial volumes, even small libraries, have been devoted to all of the topics covered here in one or two short chapters. There is so much more that could be said. For that reason, I have concluded each chapter with a short bibliography for additional reading, as well as several questions to stimulate classroom or small-group conversation. I hope that my readers will continue their investigations. *I Pledge Allegiance* is merely an introduction to a Christian ethic that is firmly rooted in biblical teaching, but especially in Jesus's insistence that no one can follow after him who is not, first and foremost, a faithful citizen in the kingdom of God.

Acknowledgments

I want to thank the friends who patiently shared impassioned conversations discussing the material contained in *I Pledge Allegiance*. Some of them—Cameron, Jill, Herman, Kyle, Jeff, Richard, and Marla—have gone the extra mile in reading and responding to early drafts of various parts of the manuscript. Their thoughts and feedback have always been helpful.

I especially want to thank Chaplain (Colonel) Herman Keiser for his insights into military culture and his thoughts on being a Christian witness in the midst of war's brutality. I am happy to count Herman among my friends. We have had many lengthy conversations over the years, and he was kind enough to visit my senior seminar at Calvin College as we studied the topics of just war and pacifism in the spring of 2014. Chaplain Keiser continues an important ministry across the country as he counsels, lectures, and leads weekend seminars discussing the heartbreaking problems related to moral injury (discussed in chapter 9). Any church hoping to develop a meaningful ministry to the combat veterans in its congregation will find crucial resources available through Chaplain Keiser and his work in connection with the Soul Repair Center at Brite Divinity School in Fort Worth, Texas, and the Moral Injury Project associated with Syracuse University.

I also want to offer a special word of thanks to Jeff Brown, a former student at Calvin College, who shared his story with me of how he came to withdraw from Calvin's ROTC program and the personal price exacted from him by its military culture (also in chapter 9, below).

Finally, I cannot forget the ever-helpful labors of my editors at Eerdmans Publishing, Michael Thomson and Jenny Hoffman. Michael has become a true friend over the years. This is the second book we have worked on together, and they both have been the better for it.

Chapter One

Whom Would Jesus Torture?

Stationed at an American air base in Tal Afar, Iraq, Alyssa Peterson was one of the first female soldiers to die in the Iraq war. She was not the victim of a roadside bomb. She did not fall in a firefight. On the night of September 15, 2003, US Army Specialist Peterson positioned her loaded service rifle against her body at just the right angle—something she learned in a suicide-prevention course—and she pulled the trigger. She was twenty-seven years old.

A trained interrogator, conversant in Arabic, and well-versed in the various techniques traditionally used by military interrogators to obtain intelligence from enemy detainees, Alyssa had worked for only two nights in the unit known as "the cage." That was more than enough for her moral sensibilities to bear. Shocked by what she had seen and been forced to do, she reported to her superiors, refusing to participate in any more sessions that she believed constituted torture.

Records show that she was reprimanded for having undue empathy for the enemy. She was instructed to "compartmentalize" the different areas of her life, keeping the professional separate from the personal. The military investigation into her death makes this statement: "We told her that you have to be able to turn on and off the interrogation mode. . . . She said that she did not know how to be two people; she could not be one person in the cage and another outside the wire."[1]

Alyssa wanted to preserve both her humanity and a clear conscience everywhere—at all times. Neither of these aspects of her life was connected to an internal switch that she could flip on and off whenever she wished. The compassionate humanity that flourished in her personal friendships would not allow itself to be bound, gagged, and locked away in a back closet just because she had stepped into "the box"; neither would her memory of the horrible acts of dehumanization committed inside the box, vicious acts that assaulted her

1

moral sensibilities, be wiped away once she stepped out from behind the razor wire and returned home.

Before that fateful evening, Alyssa had sought the advice of a friend, another intelligence specialist named Kayla Williams. Kayla admitted that she had also been forced to participate in interrogation sessions where prisoners were blindfolded, beaten, burned with cigarettes, stripped and then confronted by a female interrogator. The subjects were also subjected to lengthy periods of cramped confinement, stress positions, sleep deprivation, and waterboarding. Like Alyssa, Kayla eventually refused to participate in any more sessions that used techniques she knew (because her training had taught her to know) constituted torture.[2]

Unfortunately, standing up for what is right in this world does not always lead to happy endings. Courageously saying "no" to injustice while resisting abusive, illegal authority—as vital and admirable as it was—had not fully satisfied Alyssa's troubled mind. Perhaps she was disillusioned over the prospects of continuing to serve a government that not only approved of but insisted that its citizens perform such atrocities against the image of God (Gen. 1:26-27). As brief and unwilling as her brush with torture may have been, it seemed to have stained her conscience indelibly with the inky blackness of guilt and shame. A good, honest, caring young woman came to believe that there was only one way to be cleansed.

Thinking back over the entire episode and remembering the friend she described as "deeply religious," Kayla Williams later wrote: "It made me think, what are we as humans, that we do this to each other? It made me question my humanity and the humanity of all Americans. . . . To this day I can no longer think I am a really good person."[3]

Ms. Williams asks a profound question about the nature of humanity at large—not only for Americans but for all people everywhere. Yet the implicit national question also demands an answer: Can anyone today honestly believe that America is a "really good" country? Where is the humanity of a country that loudly and proudly proclaims its historic, global exceptionalism—President Reagan once said that America was "the last best hope of man on earth"— while simultaneously institutionalizing torture as a matter of government policy?[4] What about the many citizens who insist that our nation's religiosity, its so-called Christian foundations, democratic principles, and free-market economy are all evidence of America's divinely ordained special-nation status? Does God condemn torture when it is used by other countries but condone it when practiced by Americans?[5]

I wonder whether the average American would be as shattered and repelled by witnessing such grotesque behavior as Alyssa Peterson and Kayla Williams were. Curiously enough, the answer to that question depends on precisely *how* a person is religious. In the spring of 2009, the Pew Research Center conducted a survey asking Americans if it was ever justifiable to torture a prisoner. The results show that Ms. Peterson was sorely out of step with her fellow "deeply religious" Americans. According to the Pew study, white religious conservatives, those who call themselves evangelicals—the deeply religious who emphasize the importance of being born again, having a conversion story and possessing the Holy Spirit, those who attend weekly church services, read the Bible, and protest against abortion and gay marriage—these are the people who, by a 60 percent margin, believe that it is "often or sometimes" acceptable to torture another human being. Only 16 percent of conservative Christian Americans said that they definitely would stand side by side with Alyssa Peterson and Kayla Williams in their refusal to have anything to do with torture.

What about the rest of America? Where do we have to look in order to discover a majority of Americans who object to torture? Finding the comparable six-in-ten Americans who believe that torture is rarely if ever allowable requires looking in the other direction, well away from the majority of born-again folks who call themselves conservative or evangelical Christians. In fact, we have to trek all the way to the opposite horizon, into the embrace of the catchall group labeled "religiously unaffiliated" before we unearth a majority of Americans who are opposed to torture. Here we discover the irreligious cross section of citizens who say they seldom or never attend religious services of any sort. Yet, even in this group, only 26 percent believe that torture is never justifiable under any circumstances. Apparently, citizens like Alyssa and Kayla, people of good conscious with the courage of their convictions, are a distinct minority in this "land of the free" and "home of the brave."

I have to confess that, when the results of the Pew torture survey were first published in 2009, I was completely dumbfounded—and not because I was ignorant of the use of enhanced interrogation techniques. I was well aware of the public controversy surrounding the revelations of torture at Bagram Airbase, Guantanamo Bay, Abu Ghraib, and various US "black sites" scattered around the world. My New Testament studies classes provided numerous opportunities for me to lead class discussions on the ethical questions surrounding America's use of torture. As a part of these discussions I occasionally mentioned the stories of Alyssa Peterson, Kayla Williams, and the handful of other courageous men and women who had taken a public stand against torture, usually at a significant cost to their careers. Although I was frequently startled by the unreflective "my country right or wrong" approach to patriotism expressed by some of my undergraduate students at a Christian liberal arts college, I was not at all prepared to learn that a sizable majority of professing Christians in this country actually approved of torture. Furthermore, my jaw dropped at the direct correlation the Pew researchers discovered between theological, religious conservatism and the willingness to endorse torture.

What had happened to my country? Where was America's conscience? More to the point, what had happened to the Christian church in this country? Where was its witness on behalf of justice? Where had God's people gone?

In case I need to be more explicit about where my sympathies lie, let me put a few of my ethical and theological cards on the table. It is my strong conviction that the Pew research data indicts large segments of the modern American church—especially those who claim the mantle of Bible-believing Christians—to be living in a state of apostasy. Only an imitation, bogus, pretend church, one that is completely out of step with its Lord and utterly unfamiliar with the tone and tenor of his living voice in the New Testament, could conscientiously harbor a 60 percent majority that condones the torture of a fellow human being. This is prima facie evidence that these weekly gatherings of men and women who call themselves Christian are, at best, a collection of spiritual schizophrenics and, at worst, wolves in sheep's clothing. Such people have forgotten, if indeed they ever truly knew, that the authentic church of Jesus Christ serves a tortured Savior who still bears the bodily scars of torn flesh inflicted by his Roman torturers. It is impossible to have genuinely appropriated a biblical vision of the crucified Lord hanging from a Roman cross while simultaneously approving the torturous abuses being inflicted on others by a new generation of executioners. The mere passage of time, whether two weeks or two thousand years, does not change the moral calculus involved in making this judgment. The American embrace of torture is a cardinal sign of the cataclysmic, ethical degeneration and continuing moral misdirection of the so-called church in this country, a degeneration facilitated by an appalling biblical and theological illiteracy.

My initial shock at the results of this survey eventually became the origin of this book. I have always tried to include an element of ethical reflection in my classroom teaching, because I believe that it is impossible to study the New Testament adequately without some consideration of what the biblical message means for today's reader. Over the years I have gathered a sizable collection of essays, excerpts, book chapters, and dozens of relevant video clips from YouTube and various online news outlets that I used to spark discussion on a wide variety of contemporary social issues: American militarism, endless warfare, drone strikes, warrantless surveillance, growing economic disparity, civic responsibilities, world hunger, global poverty, pollution, the ecological crisis and other concerns. Eventually, I began to set apart a portion of every Friday's class for group discussion in all but my 100 level courses, and I started searching for a supplementary ethics textbook that might facilitate such discussions in a biblical studies course.

I quickly discovered a wealth of fine literature available, but the majority of ethics texts I found took a more dogmatic/theological approach to the subject than would be useful in my teaching. The books that followed a biblical-theological approach, though more appropriate to my New Testament courses, were somewhat unwieldy for my undergraduate students. During lunch one afternoon with a friend and colleague, I talked about my unsatisfying search for a brief, undergraduate-level ethics book that rooted its analysis in biblical interpretation, addressed the social issues confronting today's church, and took the teaching of Jesus as its starting point.

Eventually, my friend broke into my lament and said, "Why don't you write it?" That thought had never occurred to me. So I did. Or at least I've tried. As I mentioned above, my goal has been to offer topical discussions of what I believe are pressing social issues in today's America, concerns that are related to our "citizenship" and rooted in an exegetical appraisal of the New Testament. At some time or other, I taught the full spectrum of New Testament literature: Paul's letters, the general letters, Acts, the Gospels, and the book of Revelation. I hope that, whichever area of New Testament literature interests the reader, my discussion here will create a point of contact between (a) studying the biblical literature, which I take to be the divinely inspired Word of God, (b) reflecting on its practical significance, and then (c) applying that significance to the way Jesus's disciples are called to think and act in their immediate social setting as citizens and political actors.

I realize that my focus on social setting may be a debatable demarcation. The line between social and individual responsibilities is blurry, to say the least. Personal matters such as sexual behavior and truth-telling are not addressed in this study, not because they are unimportant but because every study must limit itself in some reasonable way. My primary concern in this work revolves around the demands of *Christian citizenship*. Specifically, how does the disciple's citizenship in the kingdom of God, the personal allegiance that must come first and remain foremost for every Jesus follower (Matt. 6:33), bear on the secondary, more relative obligations of national citizenship? Every disciple has this dual identity. We live in two different realms simultaneously—an eternal kingdom and a temporal nation. Both place their own demands on us. Sorting out how those two realms should relate to each other is not easy, nor are there many universally accepted solutions. I suspect that most, if not all, professing Christians will at least pay lip service to the idea that a Christian's primary allegiance is to Christ and his kingdom. But what does that priority mean—practically speaking? What does that commitment require of a disciple when she confronts the numerous claims and obligations placed on her by the state? Some will insist that obedience to the state *is,* in and of itself, the obedience that God requires. Others will disagree—including me.

In 1942, the Swiss theologian Karl Barth was asked to answer several questions put to him by American church leaders about the church's role in the state (whether in Germany or the United States) during wartime, in this case World War II. Barth was one of the leaders of the Confessing Church movement, which resisted National Socialist interference in the German church. He was also the principal author of the Barmen Declaration, a German confessional statement reaffirming the lordship of Jesus Christ in the face of Nazi political demands. Barth insisted that every Christian must, "to the best of his ability, do his part to perfect and keep the national state as a righteous state." Whenever the state seeks only to serve its own national interests, "it ceases to be a righteous state . . . in this unrighteous state the Christian can show his civic loyalty only by resistance and suffering."[6]

I believe that on this point Barth was absolutely correct, which raises a few questions for the contemporary American church. How much resistance has the US church offered recently? How much suffering has the church in this country endured because it refused to remain silent in the face of flagrant human rights abuses planned, approved, executed, and rationalized by the leaders of this country as necessary to defend our national interests?

Many, if not most, American politicians boastfully pronounce the pursuit and protection of American national interests as *the* guiding principle governing their decision-making in foreign and domestic policy. They then use an unassailable belief in American exceptionalism to justify all manner of bullying and exploitation of other nations, peoples, races, religions, and, of course, inconvenient individuals—because American interests must trump all other interests.

In the heyday of the US auto industry it was said that "what's good for General Motors is good for America." Now US actions around the world are directed by an ominous expression of national hubris: what is right for America is right for the world. As always, this nationalist principle translates politically into an age-old pragmatic axiom: the ends justify the means. Whatever our political leaders decide is necessary for securing American interests (however minuscule, managed, manipulated, trivial, and underreported the so-called public debate has been), achieving those goals justifies any and all means that are required to achieve success, no matter the depths of criminality and moral repugnance to which the nation descends in the process. Nothing and no one can be allowed to stand in the way. After all, even if our actions momentarily appear blameworthy, we know that in the long run, if it is good for America (as goodness is defined by the American power brokers pursuing American interests), it must eventually be good for the rest of the world (even if, at the moment, the rest of the world is unable to grasp how good it will be for them). The United States, the lone global superpower, has assumed the title of international disciplinarian, telling those who labor under the weight of our actions—typically military actions—"Trust me, I am doing this for your own good. You will thank me one day."

So, on a Sunday morning not long after September 11, 2001, Vice President Dick Cheney told a nation at breakfast that it is time "for the gloves to come off" and that "we must begin to work on the dark side" in order to protect America and guard our interests. Some may have wondered, as I did, when America had ever avoided the dark side and protected itself with the gloves on, but the national conscience seemed unperturbed by his announcement.

Not long after that, the director of the CIA sat through a combative television interview in which he defended America's use of "enhanced interrogation techniques," the newly minted official euphemism for torture. (Actually, the phrase was first used by the Nazis to describe their creative methods of questioning prisoners. Now, with some indiscernible logic, the director of the CIA was insisting that techniques that had long been defined as torture and outlawed by our government were suddenly no longer acts of torture and were officially embraced by our government.) Once again, the voices of dissent were few and far between when compared to the uniformly outspoken wish for vengeance against Osama bin Laden and the rest of his al-Qaeda network. If torture was added to the approved repertoire of tools thought necessary to protect the national interests, then how could any true patriot object?

Perhaps it is understandable that nation-states and the leaders who have sacrificed their consciences to the gods of national interest will—or must—behave this way. Maybe this means that obedience to Jesus will rarely prove to be a successful political campaign strategy, nor will it ensure the popularity of one's policy platform. Maybe disciples aspiring for popular leadership can rarely, if ever, count on mass followings. Perhaps the Reformer Martin Luther was correct when he suggested that disciples need to distinguish their public from their private responsibilities, changing tactics from the one to the other. These are all possibilities that we will need to explore as this study unfolds. But one thing can be stated categorically right now: It is impossible for a Christian to obey Jesus Christ by embracing behaviors, policies, and solutions that are openly hostile to his incarnate character, the pattern of his life and teaching, as well as the guidance found in his eternal Word.

Consequently, the main premise of this book is that Christian ethics must begin with a proper understanding of Jesus. Many might think that this is an obvious point, but not everyone agrees with it. The earliest documents in the New Testament are the letters of Paul. The earliest Gospel, Mark, was not composed until well after the last of Paul's writings was completed. Given the observable influence of the Gospel writers and their communities in the final composition of each of the four Gospels, many have argued that Paul's writings offer the earliest, most reliable account of Christian morality. Fortunately, the tide has recently begun to shift in this debate, and several strong studies have been published in the past ten years that correctly argue for the reliability of the Synoptic Gospels in preserving the ethical substance of Jesus's teaching. I will not reproduce the historical arguments undergirding those works here; the curious reader can find those titles in the accompanying bibliography. Instead, we will simply move forward in faith, as all obedient disciples must, while trying to listen to the voice of Jesus as we hear him speak to us in Scripture. The subsequent apostolic voices will also get a hearing as we will see the consistency between the Lord's own words and the obedience of the apostles and the early church. But just as the earliest disciples and the post-Pentecost church patterned their behavior after the model and instructions of their Lord Jesus, so shall we begin by focusing on the life and message of Jesus.

I am not suggesting that the Christian only needs to ask "What would Jesus do?" in order to resolve every debate. But, as one of my students once reminded me, it certainly would not be a bad way to begin. Life is complicated, and there certainly may be times when we need to embrace the ambiguity, continue to pray for guidance, solicit the wise counsel of like-minded people, and risk launching out to do our best. But there are many more ways than we are willing to admit that the Holy Spirit has already given God's people more direction than they are willing to follow.

Where is the prophetic voice of the disciples of Jesus Christ who understand the Lord's command when he says that his followers are *never* to lead or rule or make decisions like the authoritarian, pagan leaders surrounding them (Mark 10:42-45)? How can it be that the community purporting to worship the Lord who taught us by his own example to love our enemies, to pray for those who curse us, to forgive those who abuse us, even to lay down our lives in sacrificial service to those who fail to appreciate us—how can such people ever approve of torture? How can the voice of protest from the Father's kingdom community perpetually remain so slight and pathetically ineffectual?

Redressing the balance in this moral, theological, and spiritual equation is one of the goals of this book. The American church is in desperate need of thoroughgoing renewal, not in the pietistic terms through which most people envision renewal, but through its saturation with the offensive word from Scripture as opposed to the flabby comfort of self-help books; in its grasp of against-the-grain Christian theology rather than business-as-usual pop psychology; and in its willingness to embrace the suffering of societal rejection, rather than selling its soul for an invitation to the next presidential ball.

I pray that this study, as inadequate as it may be, will make some small contribution to such renewal. We will know that the renewal is happening when the confessing church in this country unashamedly witnesses to the offensive foolishness of the gospel; and when God's people willingly embrace suffering as the normative, best evidence that they are following hard after their tortured, crucified, and resurrected Savior.

Discussion Questions

1. What social concerns might the author encourage the Christian church to engage today? (Set aside the debates over abortion and homosexuality, for the moment.) What leads you to suggest this/these additional issue(s)?

2. What biblical principles do you think are at stake in moving the church to address this/these social problem(s)?

3. Have you ever participated in any type of social action in the past? If so, what did you do? Did you believe that your activities were effective or made a difference? Explain.

4. What kinds of social involvements are open to you in the future as you study this book?

Additional Reading

Cavanaugh, William. *Torture and Eucharist: Theology, Politics, and the Body of Christ.* Cambridge, UK: Cambridge University Press, 1991.

Conroy, John. *Unspeakable Acts, Ordinary People: The Dynamics of Torture; An*

Examination of the Practice of Torture in Three Democracies. Berkeley: University of California Press, 2000.

Danner, Mark. *Torture and Truth: America, Abu Ghraib, and the War on Terror*. New York: New York Review of Books, 2004.

Gushee, David P., Jillian Hickman Zimmer, and J. Drew Zimmer, eds. *Religious Faith, Torture, and Our National Soul*. Macon, GA: Mercer University Press, 2010.

Hunsinger, George, ed. *Torture Is a Moral Issue: Christians, Jews, Muslims, and People of Conscience Speak Out*. Grand Rapids: Eerdmans, 2008.

Siems, Larry. *The Torture Report: What the Documents Say about America's Post-9/11 Torture Program*. New York/London: OR Books, 2011.

Chapter Two

....

What Is the Kingdom of God?

In 1896, George Stratton, a professor at the University of California, was considering the different theories in circulation at the time about how our brains process the things we see with our eyes. In order to test his ideas, Professor Stratton became his own lab rat. He created a device he could wear over his eyes that caused him to see everything upside-down. When he was awake, he wore this contraption and forced himself to function in a newly upside-down world. Whenever he went to sleep and took off the googles, he tied a dark blindfold over his face so that he would never see the world properly upright. For his longest experiment, he saw only an upside-down world for eight solid days.[1]

Throughout his experiments, Prof. Stratton kept a detailed record of his adjustment to this new experience of visual (mis)perception. He carefully described two developments unfolding simultaneously.

First, although his reversed visual perspective was initially very disorienting, he slowly adjusted to it, so that by the end of his experiments he had become thoroughly at home—at least functionally—in his new, upside-down world. His vision never corrected itself; that is, his brain never compensated by "righting" his view of the world while he wore the goggles. Everything continued to look upside-down to the professor, but he did eventually get used to it. He described how, over time, he was able to go for walks, write letters with pen and paper, reach out and grab distant objects, drink a cup coffee, and perform any number of routine activities as if upside-down were the only way he had ever seen the world. Other scientists have reproduced Stratton's experiment more recently and have reported similar results, with test subjects wearing their upside-down goggles as they went downhill skiing and rode a bicycle through busy city streets.[2]

The second development is especially interesting for our current purposes. Professor Stratton also detailed a parallel process that may best be described as a mental contest developing within his own mind. While his eyes always saw the world upside-down through his goggles, his memory stood ready as a mental guardian, resisting the change by continuing to insist that the visual image was false. His mind or memory—perhaps we could say his "mind's eye"—maintained and persistently reasserted the mental images of what it knew he *should* be seeing, that is, everything right-side up. These right-side up images drawn from memory were in constant conflict with the upside-down visual images that his mind now had to register because they were the images his eyes actually perceived. Stratton's descriptions of this mental contest sound like a perceptual tug-of-war coursing back and forth in his imagination as his mental processing tried to figure out what to do with the (seemingly) abnormal visual stimuli sent to his brain. The professor eventually describes a mental resting place that depended on whether his eyes were open or closed. As he continued to look through the goggles, Stratton became increasingly proficient at functioning in an upside-down world; his mind finally acquiesced and stopped contesting what his eyes saw. But whenever he took off the goggles and replaced them with the blindfold, so that the reversed visual images disappeared, his mind quickly relapsed into recalling the world right-side up. Now, with eyes closed, all imaginary activity occurred in the right-side-up world safely preserved within his mind. As he drifted off to sleep, Prof. Stratton was, once again, a right-side-up man living in a right-side-up world.

Prof. Stratton's description of the internal perceptual tug-of-war sparked by his goggles experiment is helpful, I believe, in illustrating the sense of ethical disorientation that is often experienced by Jesus's disciples, ancient and modern, as they begin to think through the practical, real-life implications of implementing Jesus's teaching. It has become a truism to acknowledge that Jesus's view of acceptable behavior among his followers is anything but intuitive.

> Blessed are you who are poor, for yours is the Kingdom of God; but woe to you who are rich. (Matt. 5:3; Luke 6:24; my paraphrase)[3]

> Blessed are those who go hungry, for you will be filled; but woe to you who are well fed now, for you will go hungry. (Matt. 5:6; Luke 6:25; my paraphrase)

> Love your enemies. Do good to those who hate you. Bless those who curse you. Pray for those who mistreat you. If someone strikes you on one cheek, turn to him the other also. If someone takes your cloak, do not stop him from taking your tunic. Give to everyone who asks you, and if anyone takes what

belongs to you, do not demand it back. Do to others as you would have them do to you. (Luke 6:27–31)

This short collection of Gospel sayings only scratches the surface of what several scholars have described as the upside-down, counterintuitive character of Jesus's ethical teaching.[4] Observing the upside-down nature of the teaching is one thing; figuring out what to do with it in real life is another matter altogether. Here is where Prof. Stratton's visual experiment offers a useful analogy for any disciple trying to implement Jesus's upside-down ethic in today's apparently right-side-up world.

Defining what is normal is often a matter of familiarity. If we have known only one way of doing things, then it is difficult, if not impossible, to imagine doing those things in any other way. That is, until someone with a broader range of experience than ours steps in and demonstrates a new, previously unthought-of alternative, an alternative that may be perfectly natural for the other person. Scientists call this a "paradigm shift."

Jesus introduced just such a paradigm shift for his listeners when he announced the arrival of God's kingdom and described the alternative, counterintuitive behaviors he expected of his disciples, who were new kingdom citizens. Let's face it. On the surface, a great deal of Jesus's ethical teaching sounds ridiculous by any sensible standard. We live in a world where, generally speaking, the rich and the well-fed are considered blessed, fortunate, safe, and secure, whereas the poor and the hungry deserve our sympathy—and maybe our donations—but certainly not our congratulations.

Refusing all claims to retribution (no matter how lawful), allowing others to take advantage of our generosity, offering unmeasured, unqualified benevolence that never expects repayment, not even a tax deductible receipt, is not only upside-down behavior, it is downright irresponsible in many people's minds. Yet, such upside-down actions are precisely what Jesus says *will* characterize genuine members of the kingdom of God.

By deciding to follow Jesus, his followers must put on the upside-down goggles of kingdom morality. Initially, Jesus's way of seeing the world will be disorienting, maybe even downright frightening. Living as kingdom citizens demands that Jesus's disciples take significant risks; at least, true discipleship will appear risky from the perspective of our natural and conventional way of viewing life's decisions. While we were studying the Sermon on the Mount together in a class, one of my students exclaimed that Jesus could not possibly have meant for us to take his teaching literally. Living out the Sermon on the Mount in any straightforward way, she said, would mean the extinction of the church. Christians would be massively exploited and oppressed out of existence! In lodging this protest, my student was vividly expressing the internal tug-of-war that begins immediately once a person considers Jesus's kingdom ethic seriously. It is a contest over our heart, mind, will, and obedience.

Will we take Jesus seriously?

To return to the analogy between Christian discipleship and Prof. Stratton's experiment, Jesus essentially says to us, "Anyone who wants to be my disciple must put on my kingdom goggles and live accordingly. Once you do this, much of what I tell you to do will seem upside-down, backwards, and inside-out. But trust me. I am modeling and teaching you the way that my heavenly Father has always wanted his children to live in this world."

The good news is that if we persist in wanting to see the world from Jesus's kingdom perspective and then do what he asks, we will eventually reach that tipping point of familiarity where viewing the world upside-down becomes more and more comfortable. It may never appear right-side up. Following Jesus always remains an exercise in counterintuitive decision-making, going against the grain, swimming upstream against the current, marching to the beat of a different drummer—or whatever topsy-turvy metaphor you prefer. But, with enough time and experience, living an upside-down life as citizens of the kingdom of God will slowly become more natural to anyone who follows Jesus consistently, for the Holy Spirit's work of sanctification will conform us more and more to the image of Christ himself. One day you may even go downhill skiing or ride a bicycle with your kingdom goggles on.

Long-term spiritual success is a matter of "fixing our eyes on Jesus" (Heb. 12:2). Taking our eyes off Jesus, turning away from him, is the equivalent of putting on Prof. Stratton's blindfold. With the upside-down images removed, the older, deep-seated instincts of how we were born and raised to live in a fallen world reassert themselves because they never completely leave us—at least, not in this life. The seemingly "normal," right-side-up perspective on life only appears to be normal because we are sinners who are most comfortable living out the status quo of our fallen, sinful world. Our own fallenness naturally aligns itself with the fallenness of the world we live in, so that our native preference for living right-side up rather than upside-down is always more than ready to reemerge as a serious contender for control over our ethical and spiritual lives. This internal debate between seemingly right-side-up and apparently upside-down responses to life's daily challenges will continue with frustrating predictability until the day we die or the moment Jesus returns on the clouds of heaven. Either way, only then will we finally be able to see clearly, without doubt, hesitation, or second thoughts, that Jesus's upside-down way of

self-denial, sacrificial service, peace, forgiveness, and unremitting, unconditional mercy is the only true way of living a meaningful life that is pleasing to
God. In the meantime, the disciple's only chance for long-term faithfulness is
to wear Jesus's kingdom goggles 24/7, knowing that eventually Jesus's kingdom
lifestyle will become every disciple's (super)natural preference.

Beginning with Jesus Rather Than Paul

In making this argument about kingdom living, I am implicitly affirming two
important points. First, Jesus's proclamation of the kingdom of God is a foun-
dational component to his ministry. That Jesus taught about the kingdom of
God is hardly controversial nowadays. The New Testament scholar Bruce Malina goes so far as to say, "Even the most skeptical historian would agree that if
Jesus spoke about anything, he spoke about the kingdom of heaven."[5] I will go
one step further. In my estimation, the actual *arrival* of God's kingdom in and
through Jesus's earthly ministry is *central* to his teaching, at least according to
the synoptic Gospels. In fact, we understand the significance of Jesus's ministry
only insofar as we understand his message about the kingdom.

My second affirmation is more controversial and, at least in the minds
of some, requires a bit of justification. I am also assuming that a proper view
of Christian ethics must begin with a correct understanding of Jesus and his
kingdom teaching. Although this may sound like a foregone conclusion to some
readers, others insist that any biblical study of Christian ethics must begin with
the apostle Paul, not with Jesus. An example of this preference appears in the
important work of Richard Hays, *The Moral Vision of the New Testament*, where
Hays offers three reasons for his insistence that a study of New Testament
ethics must begin with the Epistles of Paul rather than with the Gospels.[6]

First, Hays reminds his readers that Paul's letters are the earliest New Testament documents, written well before the earliest Gospel, and they do not
contain any explicit references to the earthly Jesus or his teaching. Therefore, to
begin with Jesus creates the false impression that Paul was formulating his own
ethics as he reflected on the things that he knew about Jesus's prior ministry.
But Paul's letters do not offer much evidence that this is what he was doing.[7]

Second, Paul's letters contain a great deal of didactic teaching and reflection, unlike the Gospels, which are primarily composed of narrative material.
Though the Gospels do preserve some instructional sayings, Paul's letters are
a much richer source of ethical instruction. Therefore, any analysis of New
Testament ethics must begin with them.

Third, Hays argues that any analysis of New Testament teaching must focus on the documents themselves rather than on the subjective, historical reconstructions required to grapple with the teachings of the historical Jesus. Before we can understand what Jesus may have said, as distingushed from what the Gospels—with their different theological tendencies and idiosyncratic uses of tradition—claim that Jesus said, we must first have a cogent theory of who Jesus actually was. But that is a problem for New Testament study because the focus of such study must be on the final canonical documents, not theoretical reconstructions attempting to peer behind those documents.[8] Since the Gospel accounts have all passed through a shaping process, first as oral tradition and then by way of the many compositional decisions of the individual authors, the Gospels writers' presentations of Jesus are further removed from their original setting than is Paul's teaching. Beginning with Paul is simple and straightforward; beginning with Jesus puts the need for historical conjecture over and above the work of interpreting the text.

In light of these arguments, I still insist that a proper understanding of Christian ethics must begin with Jesus. Why?

First, the priority of focusing on the biblical text, as important as it is, does not mean that those texts must be studied only in chronological order. That claim has the ring of something I am tempted to call the chronological fallacy: a chronological approach to interpretation may be required when investigating how a theme or topic developed over time, but the compositional date of a text (which is frequently subject to debate) should not be confused with the date of the traditions and the ideas contained within that text. The traditions about Jesus were not the invention of anonymous communities who felt themselves free to invent unhistorical Jesus stories out of nothing more than their own immediate felt needs (such as comfort during times of Roman persecution or exclusion from the synagogue) inflamed by pious, overactive imaginations. We must grant to the earliest Christians what I refer to as a positive presumption of ethical concern, which means that they well understood the difference between passing along complete fabrications as if they were true, on the one hand, and relating the traditions of eyewitnesses burnished with some editorial license, on the other. Even Hays admits that the Gospels, including John's unique story line, were not invented out of whole cloth.[9] They may not be the literary equivalents of exact, photographic reproductions of the historical Jesus, but they do make up masterful portraits in which each Gospel author captures Jesus's likeness by preserving and retelling in his own way the earlier traditions about Jesus's teachings and actions.

Second, as Hays also admits, there simply is no getting around the fact that

Jesus is "the definitive paradigm" for the obedient Christian life and what it means to be in right relationship with the Father.[10] The preferred metaphor in the synoptic Gospels depicting Christian discipleship is "following Jesus," with the Lord urging his followers to conform their lives to his. Obviously, following after Jesus is a particularly apt turn of phrase for the Gospel story line, but the evangelists did not invent it themselves. Paul urges the church in Corinth to "follow my example, as I follow the example of Christ" (1 Cor. 11:1). "Following after Christ Jesus" is also Paul's definition of what it means to live an obedient Christian life for the Roman church (Rom. 15:5; see also 1 Pet. 2:21; Rev. 14:4). Even though we can never know how much Paul knew about Jesus's earthly life and ministry, these references demonstrate that Paul was repeating a much wider Christian consensus. Christians were defined as Jesus followers. They were expected to be like Jesus and to conform their lives to his example, which means in effect that Christian ethics must begin with Jesus—not only his teaching but also his personal behavior. The things that Jesus did, and the Gospel narratives that describe his actions, can contain ethical lessons every bit as important as the sayings found in Jesus's ethical instruction. We are not limited to didactic, overtly instructional sayings alone. Jesus also teaches by example. Fortunately, in recent years there have been a number of substantial publications in the field of New Testament ethics from scholars like Richard A. Burridge, David P. Gushee, Glen H. Stassen, and Allen Verhey that all begin from this same starting point: Jesus.[11]

The New Testament insists on describing its ethics as a *Christian* ethic, the ethic required of every Jesus follower. As a distinctly Christian ethic, it is universally applicable to all believers everywhere. There are not different classes of believers, more ethical rigor being expected from some than from others. Because all Christian disciples by definition claim that they are following (or want to follow) Jesus, and since Jesus came to this world bringing the kingdom of God, Christian ethics necessarily begins by embracing Jesus and soaking in everything he has to say about living in his Father's kingdom. As he tells the disciples, "Your heavenly Father knows [what you need]. But seek first his Kingdom and his righteousness and all these [other] things will be added to you as well" (Matt. 6:32-33).

Mark, the Cross-Cultural Communicator

The Gospel according to Mark wastes no time in introducing the core of Jesus's message. The first sentence declares, "The beginning of the gospel/good news

[Greek: *tou euaggeliou*] about Jesus Christ/Anointed One [Greek: *Christou*], the Son of God." The political and religious significance of Mark's carefully selected words are lost on the average reader today, but to his original audience this sentence was a thunderous shot across the bow of human history. Mark crafts a brilliant act of cross-cultural communication that would have grabbed both Jewish and Greco-Roman readers by the shoulders, shaking them wide awake.

For Jesus's fellow Jews, he is declared to be their Anointed One, the Messiah, which is the meaning of the Greek title *Christos*. More specifically, Jesus is the royal Messiah, the descendant of King David who now takes the ancient royal designation "Son of God" as his own. The Davidic Covenant had promised that a never-ending dynasty would occupy Israel's throne, and that the king would be God's own son. Yahweh had declared: "I will be his father, and he will be my son" (2 Sam. 7:14). The royal psalmist remembered God's promise, "I will proclaim the decree of the LORD: He said to me, 'You are my Son; today I have become your Father'" (Ps. 2:7).

Furthermore, by referring to this straightforward declaration of Jesus's royal messiahship as "good news" Mark ties it together with the prophet Isaiah's vision of the Servant of the LORD found in Isaiah 61:1, "The Spirit of the Sovereign LORD is on me, because the LORD has anointed[12] me to preach good news to the poor."[13] In other words, Jesus is both the messianic king and the Spirit-filled servant in the Isaiah mold; he combines these two figures into one by proclaiming the gospel message in his own lifetime, and whose life and ministry continue to be the content of the gospel today. Jesus is the proclaimer and the proclaimed, the messenger and the message, the bringer of the good news and its subject matter. The Gospel of Luke conveys a similar perspective by describing how Jesus once read Isaiah 61:1 at a synagogue service in his home town of Nazareth and declared, by way of interpretation, that Isaiah's words were at that very moment being fulfilled in him (Luke 4:16–21). According to the synoptic Gospels, Jesus pursued his ministry with a definite messianic self-understanding, announcing the good news about both the coming of God's kingdom and his own role in its arrival.

Remember, though, that this is a cross-cultural sentence that would also grab the attention of a Greco-Roman (Gentile) reader who knew nothing at all about Jewish messianism, the prophet Isaiah, or the God of Israel. Mark's Gospel is written in Greek, and the word translated as gospel/good news had a long history in Greek society. The word *euaggelion* was commonly used to describe the divine messages delivered through dreams, visions, and oracles to the designated virgins lodged at shrines scattered across the Greek world, places such as Delphi and Korope. It could also be used for announcements of important political events, especially when those events involved news of military victory. In fact, *euaggelion* had become a technical term for delivering good news from a distant battlefield about the hometown's victorious army.[14] Proclaiming good news then passed into Roman usage, where it was closely associated with the elevation of a Caesar in the imperial cult. Announcements about the Caesar's birthday, his ascension to the throne, or a Roman victory on the battlefield all gave occasion for another proclamation of good news, the gospel.[15]

The title "Son of God" is as reminiscent of the Roman imperial cult as is the word "gospel." The Roman senate divinized Julius Caesar after his death, elevating him to the status of the "divine Julius" (*divus Iulius*). Consequently, Julius's adopted son and successor, Octavian, also known as Augustus, became "son of the divine Julius" (*divi Iuli filius*), setting a pattern for subsequent Caesars, who were consistently identified as a "son of the divine" (*divi filius*). Although the Romans understood that there was a difference between being deified (*divus*) and being God (*deus*), the Greek language was not as clear in maintaining the distinction. Even though no Caesar was ever officially designated "son of God" (*dei filius*), Greek inscriptions often translated the Latin title "son of the divine" (*divi filius*) with the Greek words "son of God" (*huios theou*), the title found in Mark 1:1.[16] Undoubtedly, in the minds of many, the distinction between the two designations was eventually lost.

The opening sentence of Mark's Gospel, then, was every bit as evocative for non-Jewish readers as it would have been for Jews, and in very similar ways. To summarize once again, Mark's Greco-Roman reader would have understood that a divine message concerning an imperial, divinized figure, which may have included word of a military victory, is presented in the story of a Jewish preacher named Jesus Christ who lived and died in the land of Palestine. Hearing that message as good news would have been as shockingly inconceivable for the average Roman citizen as it would have been teasingly momentous for the average Jew. Yet, despite these different evaluations of Mark's words, none of his readers would be surprised to learn that this would-be king, Jesus Christ, the Son of God, came announcing the arrival of a new kingdom.

The Kingdom Has Come

Jesus went into Galilee announcing the good news (*euaggelion*) of God saying, "The time has been fulfilled. The Kingdom of God is here. Repent and believe the good news." (Mark 1:14)

Understanding the full significance of Mark's opening sentence prepares the reader for his following description of Jesus's announcement about the imminent arrival of a kingdom. After all, kings have kingdoms; they rule over them. Curiously, however, King Jesus does not claim to inaugurate his own kingdom; instead, he announces the arrival of God's kingdom. But Jesus is clearly the agent of this kingdom, since it is the individual's response to him and his message that determines whether or not God's kingdom brings blessing or judgment to the listener. Heeding Jesus's call to first repent and then to believe that what he says about the kingdom is true, which requires a distinctive attitude toward Jesus himself, is a prerequisite for entering into this kingdom when it arrives.

What kind of kingdom, then, is this? We do not normally think of kingdoms as being portable, as "coming" or "arriving." Kingdoms are typically stationary, though their borders may expand or contract. Kings are the ones who move about, coming and going.

As the sovereign Creator who spoke the universe into existence, Israel's God was always understood to be the king of all creation. As the Creator, Yahweh never stopped ruling over all things, making the cosmos God's kingdom. The psalmists frequently remind us of this fact:

> The LORD reigns, he is robed in majesty;
>   the LORD is robed in majesty
>   and is armed with strength.
> The world is firmly established;
>   it cannot be moved.
> Your throne was established long ago;
>   you are from all eternity. (Ps. 93:1–2)

The LORD reigns over everything he has made. The Old Testament never uses the phrase "kingdom of God"; it prefers to describe the various ways in which "God reigns" as Creator-King over the universe. Wherever God reigns, there is God's kingdom. Since God reigns over everything and everyone, God's kingdom is everywhere, including everyone—even encompassing those who do not recognize him. The majority of God's subjects remain spiritually blind and persistently rebellious against his lordship, but human disobedience does not diminish the extent of the Creator's rule.

But our Creator-King is also the covenant-making God who forged a unique relationship with the people of Israel. Thus there are two different, yet related, dimensions of God's kingship operating simultaneously. While Yahweh reigns over all humanity, whether they recognize it or not, only Israel is blessed with the unique relationship that focuses God's kingship specifically on their guidance, blessing, and protection. Recall God's introduction to the Sinai Covenant:

> Now if you obey me fully and keep my covenant, then out of all nations you will be my treasured possession. Although the whole earth is mine, you will be for me a kingdom of priests and a holy nation. (Exod. 19:5-6)

While this is not the place to rehearse Israel's long, turbulent history of obedience and disobedience to the Sinai Covenant, we should know that they never fully succeeded in becoming the holy, priestly kingdom God had wanted on this earth. Eventually, a new expectation emerged in which God one day would finally accomplish for himself what Israel could never do. In the unspecified future, Israel would be restored to perfect covenant faithfulness, and through them God would rule over all the nations of the earth, finally unifying the two different dimensions of God's reign as Creator-King and as Covenant-Maker.

Daniel 7 expresses this future hope for God's kingdom on earth in Daniel's vision of the heavenly Son of man entering into God's presence:

> In my vision at night I looked, and there before me was one like a son of man, coming with the clouds of heaven. He approached the Ancient of Days and was led into his presence. He was given authority, glory and sovereign power; all peoples, nations and men of every language worshiped him. His dominion is an everlasting dominion that will not pass away, and his kingdom is one that will never be destroyed. (Dan. 7:13-14)

In Daniel's vision, God's kingdom is the last in a sequence of earthly empires that have been represented by four grotesque hybrids of savage beasts (Dan. 7:3-12). Significantly, this bestial pattern is broken by the final, divine kingdom, which is represented by a human being,[17] one who is interpreted as being the representative of all God's righteous people (Dan. 7:18, 22, 27). The message is clear. Human empires are constructed and maintained by savagery and violence. Only God can establish and then reign over a humane kingdom founded on the power of universal righteousness, justice, and mercy that will never end.

Similarly, the prophet Isaiah anticipated a restored Israel delivered from exile and beautifully reestablished on Mount Zion as a beacon of holiness and righteousness to the entire world.

> How beautiful on the mountains
> > are the feet of those who bring good news [*euaggelizomenou*],[18]
> who proclaim peace,
> > who bring good tidings [*euaggelizomenos*]
> > who proclaim salvation,
> who say to Zion,
> > "Your God reigns!" (Isa. 52:7)

Isaiah's gospel announcement that "your God reigns" is the Old Testament equivalent of Jesus's preaching the good news that the kingdom of God has come near. Such passages as these would be loudly and harmoniously resonating in the background (or even in the foreground) for any first-century Palestinian audience, stirring up a chorus of anticipation every time Jesus spoke about the imminent activity of God's reign on earth. No wonder Mark tells us that the "news about [Jesus] spread quickly" (Mark 1:28), and, at least initially, "the people came to him from everywhere" (Mark 1:45). Jesus was announcing the arrival of God's long-anticipated *redemptive reign*, the *saving sovereignty* of the LORD Almighty revealed here and now in living color as God actually showed up to rescue his people and to set the world straight:

- to free them from demonic oppression (Mark 1:21–28, 34);
- to heal them (Mark 1:29–34, 40–45; 2:1–12; 3:1–5);
- to forgive their sins (Mark 2:1–12);
- to form a new, inclusive community composed of all those who received God's forgiveness through trust in Jesus (Mark 2:15–20).

Jesus's earthly ministry is God the Father's invasion of history as the royal Liberator, the gracious, Spirit-empowered Savior intervening to rescue his people from the power of sin, oppression, and injustice, restoring them to a right covenantal relationship, as Yahweh establishes his universal, redemptive reign on earth.

But Jesus also embarked on a radical redefinition of this kingdom and what its establishment would look like, cutting it free from many traditional assumptions. Of course, the most prominent point of redefinition involved the necessity of a suffering, dying messiah who is enthroned on a cross, who reigns now through the community of followers who accept the necessity of their own suffering as an essential component of their commitment to follow Jesus. More immediately in Mark's unfolding drama, Jesus's initial collection of parables explores a variety of unexpected kingdom twists (Mark 4:1–34).

Most significantly, God's kingdom does not come with overwhelming, irresistible force, knocking people off their feet and sweeping them irretrievably into its iron net; nor is the kingdom's arrival self-evident—just the opposite. The kingdom's appearance easily goes unnoticed because God's reign begins within individual human hearts, where it seeks out the fertilizer of faith. This is why Jesus's kingdom parables focus on such traits as individual seeds with idiosyncratic growth rates, various types of soils making different contributions to the end product, differing responses to the kingdom message, the tininess of the gospel seeds, the kingdom's minuscule beginnings, and the fact that initial responses develop in fits and starts and sometimes fail to reach completion; all of these observations highlight the personal nature of God's redemptive reign over individual lives.

The redemptive reign of God does not grow in the abstract by gaining control over systems, organizations, collectives, cultures, political parties, or governments. The saving sovereignty of God's reign on earth expands as more and more individuals surrender themselves to the lordship of Jesus and trust in his proclamation of good news. These acts of personal surrender to Jesus and his message enlarge the membership—the citizenship of God's kingdom—which is the only means of kingdom growth described anywhere in the Gospels. The kingdom expands as individuals surrender themselves to God's saving sovereignty. Jesus's disciples become the new citizens of God's coming kingdom.

Jesus's diverse farming/husbandry metaphors also highlight how irrelevant human activity is to the growth of God's kingdom. Nowhere in the Gospels does human effort contribute anything whatsoever to the kingdom's advancement, development, or success. The kingdom of God is just that—God's. It is a matter of God's reign coming to God's people in God's way at the moment of God's choosing.[19] Jesus says: "Night and day, whether [the farmer] sleeps or gets up, the seed sprouts and grows, though he does not know how. All by itself the soil produces grain" (Mark 4:27-28). Jesus's point is clear: while the planter sleeps, the kingdom grows *all by itself*. God's saving sovereignty expands through the spiritual dynamic at work between the gospel of Jesus Christ (the seed) and the individual recipient (the soil). Each new confessing, repentant, forgiven, renewed, and trusting sinner whose life is redirected by following after Jesus is evidence of the kingdom's borders expanding step by individual step, one person at a time through the saving sovereignty of our redeemer God.

Eliminating Impostors

Christian theology has not always been attentive to Jesus's teaching and the evidence in the Gospels describing the kingdom of God. There has been a deep-seated tendency to connect the coming of the kingdom to human activity in ways that tie the kingdom's arrival and development to any number of social programs, political agendas, or the work of cultural engagement. For instance, a congregational hymn often included in the worship portion of my former college's annual graduation ceremony includes these chorus lines: "Lord, to you our hands and hearts we offer; keep us faithful to your call, we pray. Guide in us the work that brings your kingdom, as we rest in you." While it sounds appropriately pious to ask that God help us do "the work that brings the kingdom," as we have seen, there is no warrant in the Gospels for such prayers. Jesus does teach us to pray that God will cause his kingdom to come (Matt. 6:10), so perhaps we may consider prayer to be a secondary "work" for the kingdom. Otherwise, the closest we can come to laboring for the kingdom is by doing the work of evangelism, following the model left to us by Jesus himself: proclaiming the gospel, calling for repentance, and having conversations with the inquisitive as regular acts of very generous seed-sowing.

Unfortunately, the human inability to grow the kingdom seems difficult for God's people to accept. Whether it is due to our overly activist inclinations or from harboring too lofty an opinion of ourselves, the church regularly neglects Jesus's unequivocal voice in the Gospels in order to give itself an active role in causing the kingdom to come or to otherwise misconstrue the significance of God's redemptive reign on earth.

Different traditions have implemented this misunderstanding in different ways, though they all are born of similar mistakes. Going back at least as far as Albrecht Ritschl (1822–1889), the German theologian and guardian of Protestant liberalism, large swaths of the Protestant church have tended to identify the kingdom of God with moral and humanistic programs of social reformation, assuming that God's kingdom on earth is established by social and political activism to rectify society's ills and bring humanity under God's universal rule of love.[20] According to Ritschl, the church is "called to make the Kingdom of God its task . . . [seeking] the moral unification of the human race, through action prompted by universal love to our neighbor."[21] A similar perspective informed the influential theology of Walter Rauschenbusch (1861–1918), the father of the Social Gospel movement in America.[22]

Another version of such kingdom-activism appears in the increasingly influential theology of neo-Calvinism, as developed by Abraham Kuyper (1837–

1920), the Dutch clergyman, philosopher, theologian, and politician (prime minister of the Netherlands). I suspect that Kuyper remained deeply influenced by his early education in theological liberalism, despite his preference for emphasizing the Creator's "cultural mandate"—as opposed to universal love—for humanity and for charging disciples as redeemed humanity to work toward cultural transformation. While Kuyperian neo-Calvinism may not directly assert that God's kingdom arrives or grows through the creation of a Christian culture, at times the rhetoric comes precariously close to saying just that.

In his book *The Calvinistic Concept of Culture*, the late Henry Van Til (1906–1961), who was a professor at Calvin College, the school where I formerly taught, warns his readers that "the kingdom of God is not established by man's cultural striving," although it is unclear whose cultural striving he is referring to, Christian or non-Christian.[23] On the other hand, he counterbalances this single statement about God's kingdom with multiple warnings about the necessity of a thoroughly Christian society as the prerequisite for the Christian community's attempts to "lead wholly Christian lives." The life of society and the life of the church are so interwoven with each other, according to Van Til, as to become thoroughly interdependent. Elsewhere, Van Til highlights the urgency for Christians to build "a Christian culture in order that the Christian faith survive."[24] In effect, Van Til interprets Jesus's charge that the disciples "seek first the kingdom of God and his righteousness" (Matt. 6:33) as a call to "seek first the creation of a Christian culture so that you may be able to live righteously." One can only wonder how the earliest disciples ever managed to make a go of it, surrounded as they were by what could only be judged an utterly non-Christian culture.

I suspect that the trap into which neo-Calvinism falls is the desire to create a Christian culture in order to lead *comfortable* Christian lives, free from inconvenience, disadvantage, and the threat of suffering. Jesus and the apostles, however, were convinced that the hostility aimed at them by the surrounding culture, no matter how harsh, had no bearing whatsoever on their prospects of remaining faithful citizens of God's kingdom. As far as the New Testament is concerned, suffering accompanies obedient discipleship like ticks on a dog. We should not forget Jesus's words of congratulations: "Blessed are those who are persecuted because of righteousness, for theirs is the kingdom of heaven" (Matt. 5:10). Experiencing antagonism from those who stand outside the kingdom is an identifying characteristic of true kingdom citizenship. Examining the unhealthy effects of this natural human inclination to be comfortable followers of Jesus who invest themselves in maintaining the most comfortably convenient brand of discipleship possible will reappear throughout this study.

There is another problem with neo-Calvinism's understanding of the kingdom's relationship to culture. At its heart lies an all-too-common confusion between (a) building the kingdom, which only God can do, and (b) living as obedient kingdom citizens, which every disciple is required to do. Kingdom citizenship certainly has important social and political implications. Looking at some of those implications is, after all, the purpose of this book. Furthermore, living out those implications in the kingdom's upside-down Jesus lifestyle may even prove attractive to many observers in the watching world. Undoubtedly, this is what Jesus had in mind when he told the disciples: "You are the salt of the earth. . . . You are the light of the world. . . . Let your light shine before men, that they may see your good deeds and praise your Father in heaven" (Matt. 5:13-16). But imagining that living a faithful kingdom lifestyle is the equivalent of building the kingdom on earth is a bit like putting the cart before the horse. Confusing cause with effect in this way is a real mistake.

Others have confused the kingdom of God proclaimed by Jesus with the Creator's universal sovereignty over the universe. America was founded by adherents to this particular view of God's kingdom—especially the Puritans. H. Richard Niebuhr describes their perspective:

> This kingdom of God was not . . . something that came into the world from without; it was rather the rule which, having been established from eternity, needed to be obeyed despite the rebellion against it which flourished in the world. It may be likened to the rule of a universal Caesar against whom ignorant tribes had made vain rebellion.[25]

Buried within this brand of kingdom theology is the assumption that *all* of human history is unfolding exactly as the sovereign God has always intended. In my opinion, that is a debatable assumption. But if you hold this view of history, it is a short step from there to imagining that my own personal history, the history of my specific nation, my ethnic group, or my religious organization is the fulfillment of the Creator-King's purposes for my particular stream of human events. In other words, the history of *my* country, church, or people group is *the* realization of God's kingdom on earth. For some, the kingdom of God becomes a society dominated by the church (*my* church, of course, not anyone else's church, unless *your* church happens to be affiliated with my church), since the church is the expression of God's sovereign agency in history.

Many Puritan leaders came to the New World believing that they would establish the kingdom of God and build the new Zion in the new Promised Land through their establishment of a specific religious society. They had precedent for these convictions: their English forebears had long believed, as John Eliot, missionary to the Algonquins in colonial Massachusetts, had written, that "England [was] first in that blessed work of setting up the Kingdom of the Lord Jesus" in the New World.[26] Thus the early seeds were sown for the development of Manifest Destiny, American exceptionalism, and the misguided notion that the United States is God's chosen agent for bringing righteousness and the blessings of God's kingdom to the rest of the world.[27]

We cannot forget, of course, that the Old Testament does insist that the Creator is always king over all the earth, so that there is a sense in which God is, in fact, the "universal Caesar against whom ignorant tribes had made vain rebellion." However, we have also seen both Testaments affirm that God's rule eventually will be accepted universally—remember that all the nations of the earth will come streaming to Mount Zion—as the nations respond to the light emanating from God's chosen, covenant people (Isa. 2:2–5; 43:10; 49:6; 51:4–5; 55:1–5; 56:6–8; 60:1–22; Micah 4:1–5). Jesus picks up this theme and makes it more pointed. It is the kingdom of God as he proclaimed it, beginning as the tiniest mustard seed, that eventually "grows and becomes the largest of all garden plants, with such big branches that the birds of the air can perch in its shade" (Mark 4:32). The church cannot establish this kingdom by prevailing as the dominant force in society, by writing a nation's civil legislation, by creating competitive alternatives to secular labor unions or public schools, or even by eliminating poverty—as marvelous as that would be.

No particular stream of human history, activity, or ideology can egotistically claim the mantle of God's authorized, providential kingdom bringer. History's one and only kingdom bringer is Jesus Christ, the Son of God. And the kingdom brought by that kingdom bringer only grows as the heavenly Father opens the eyes of more and more lost sinners, who then surrender themselves to Jesus, their Savior, Lord, and King.

Discussion Questions

1. How does the material in this chapter either agree or disagree with your current understanding of the kingdom of God?

2. If you find that you need to make some adjustments in the ways you think about God's redemptive reign in your life and in this world, what will those changes involve?

3. How do you think those theological changes should affect the ways that you live out your Christian discipleship?

Additional Reading

Beasley-Murray, G. R. *Jesus and the Kingdom of God*. Grand Rapids: Eerdmans, 1986.

Chilton, Bruce. *Pure Kingdom: Jesus' Vision of God*. Grand Rapids: Eerdmans, 1996.

Chilton, Bruce, and J. I. H. McDonald. *Jesus and the Ethics of the Kingdom*. Grand Rapids: Eerdmans, 1987.

Green, Joel B. "Kingdom of God/Heaven." In *Dictionary of Jesus and the Gospels*, edited by Joel B. Green, Jeannine K. Brown, and Nicholas Perrin, 2nd ed. Downers Grove, IL: IVP Academic, 2013.

Wright, N. T. *Jesus and the Victory of God*. Minneapolis: Fortress, 1996.

Chapter Three

Seek First the Kingdom of God

We discovered in chapter 2 that nineteenth-century liberal theology imagined the kingdom of God to be, at least in large part, a human accomplishment. One of the most influential popularizers of this view was the German theologian Albrecht Ritschl, for whom the Christian church, understood broadly as a Christianized society under the influence of deeply entrenched state churches, built the kingdom of God on earth and enlarged its borders by humanizing society through works of charity and a broad social vision that strove for peace on earth and good will toward all. Social reform was the kingdom labor of God's people, smoothing and lubricating the rough edges of human relationships with the love and compassion ideally modeled by Jesus of Nazareth.

One of Ritschl's acolytes was a young New Testament scholar by the name of Johannes Weiss (1863–1914). Weiss was not only swept up by the rising tide of Ritschlian theology; he was also swept away by Ritschl's daughter, Auguste. It did not take long for Johannes and Auguste to become husband and wife, making Albrecht Ritschl Johannes's father-in-law.

In 1892, Weiss published a landmark study entitled *Jesus' Proclamation of the Kingdom of God*. The book's drab title offered no hint of the earthshaking effect it would have on Protestant theology; in fact, the translators of the first English edition confidently proclaimed that Weiss's little book "marks the turning point from nineteenth- to twentieth-century New Testament research."[1] And they were right.

By carefully studying Jesus's kingdom teaching in the synoptic Gospels, Weiss experienced the kind of unexpected "paradigm shift" that is rare in academic studies. He slowly began to see that the Ritschlian view of God's kingdom on earth had nothing whatsoever in common with Jesus's view of the kingdom. The two perspectives were as different as chalk and cheese. For Jesus, the coming kingdom was entirely a miraculous work of God. Human effort had little if anything to do with it. The kingdom's coming was an "apocalyptic" event, apocalyptic in the sense that it brought an end to the current flow of world history. The kingdom arrived and expanded by way of God's ripping open the heavens above and stepping down into the muddled morass that we humans have made of his world. As far as Jesus was concerned, the kingdom's arrival would bring the final judgment, and that judgment was just around the corner. The coming kingdom meant that God would immediately punish the wicked, right every wrong, reward the righteous, and universally establish his divine reign throughout a re-created universe—here and very soon.

Needless to say, Weiss concluded that his father-in-law and Jesus of Nazareth stood worlds apart when it came to their views of the kingdom. Yet, knowing full well the notoriety that publishing his study would bring—in that it challenged the most influential systematic theologian of his generation, his own father-in-law—Weiss chose instead to remain a loving and loyal son-in-law. He did not have *Jesus' Proclamation of the Kingdom of God* published until three years after Ritschl's death.

Perhaps Weiss used the intervening years to further ponder the one outstanding conundrum raised by his conclusions. How were Christians today expected to carry out Jesus's ethical teaching? In Weiss's view, Jesus's counterintuitive, upside-down requirements for his disciples were only an "interim ethic," a short-term, temporary code of extraordinary behavior that would prepare his disciples for the kingdom's imminent arrival. But, in the end, Jesus's hopes for the kingdom were mistaken. The kingdom did not come. The apocalyptic in-breaking Jesus had anticipated never happened, leaving his followers to grapple with a seemingly irreconcilable tension. With the kingdom's apparent failure to appear, nothing had changed about life's requirements in the here and now. What were Jesus's disciples to do with his upside-down ethical demands as they continued to live their day-to-day lives in a right-side-up world that showed no signs of miraculous transformation? Sadly, in wrestling to answer this question, Weiss saw his analytical tour de force ultimately collapse into a heap of blasé platitudes that were indistinguishable from the liberalism he had initially demolished. Weiss finally concluded that, since today's Christians can no longer share Jesus's cosmic expectations, disciples must dispense with talk of the kingdom altogether and focus instead on the transformative power of divine love among the family of God: "We no longer pray, 'May grace come and the world pass away,' but we pass our lives in the joyful confidence that this world will evermore become the showplace of the people of God."[2]

The suffocating power of social convention, of wanting to preserve the status quo, reasserted itself all too quickly as Weiss shifted his focus from proper interpretation to pastoral application. Having uncovered what Jesus originally intended to say, he quickly muffled and reburied his original kingdom message because it was too inconvenient. In making this unfortunate decision, Weiss faced the same problem that Christians have always faced; it was a problem for Jesus's immediate followers, and it has haunted every generation of disciples since: Did Jesus really expect people to take his upside-down teaching literally over the long term? Or is Jesus's ethical instruction the odd, dispensable remnant of failed Jewish expectations for the end of the world, like the concentrated residue at the bottom of an evaporated theological puddle?

In asking these questions, we come full circle and return to the challenge of Professor Stratton's goggles. Are we expected to keep Jesus's kingdom goggles fixed firmly to our eyes, considering the ongoing struggle to follow an upside-down vision in a right-side-up world as part and parcel of Christian discipleship? Or are we justified in setting aside Jesus's kingdom ethics as a naïve, unrealistic ideal that is impossible to implement in the real world? Perhaps we are free to pick and choose, deciding for ourselves when, where, and how Jesus's teachings may be applied, modified, or ignored—depending on the situation and its likely results?

A Theological Framework

At this point, sketching out a basic Christian theological framework will help explain the dilemma we face, including how Jesus's ethical teachings function and why they raise the kinds of questions they do in most people's minds. Although the synoptic Gospels do not make a large contribution to this particular framework, it is the historic theological orientation of orthodox Christianity (in the sense of universal and mainstream), drawn from the whole of the New Testament, that places Jesus's teaching in its larger context.

Jesus of Nazareth came to reveal God's unrealized intentions for this world. The kingdom arriving with Jesus will reshape humanity in conformity to the Father's original design. Obviously, both of the preceding sentences express important Christological presuppositions about the person and ministry of Jesus. On the one hand, Jesus was very much a man of his age, shaped by and interacting with the social, economic, religious, and cultural life of first-century Galilee and Judea. Jesus's contemporaries easily recognized him as one of their own. On the other hand, Jesus was sent into this world by God the Father as his one and only Son, the Savior-Messiah who had unique access to the mind of God and thus was uniquely able to exercise divine authority and to reveal God's intentions for this world. What Jesus said and did were exemplary, depicting and explaining God's will for the rest of us. In this regard, Jesus often mystified his contemporaries, and many of them, including his own disciples, could only conclude that he was seriously misguided, if not deranged.

What Jesus was sent by his Father to teach us was that God had originally intended human relationships to flourish as they were watered by a divine ethic of unconditional love, unending mercy, limitless charity, bottomless generosity, and perpetual peacefulness. To this end, all human beings, without exception, are distinguished from other living creatures by their possession of the image of God, the *imago Dei* (Gen. 1:26-27). Nowhere in Scripture are we ever told that humanity's possession of God's image has been lost, altered, or diminished in any way by the introduction of sin into God's universe. Genesis 3 tells that part of the tale of how God's good creation has "fallen" via the introduction of sin, abandoning the Creator's intentions, even as the image of God continues unchanged within us. Human beings now exist as divine image-bearers who are also burdened by the distorting corruption of sin. Human society actively cultivates the same sinful rebelliousness demonstrated by our first parents when they chose to ignore God's one and only command: "Everything in this world is for you, except this one tree; don't eat from it" (Gen. 2:16-17). Preferring to focus on the one thing they were forbidden to do, rather than the many things they were encouraged to do, the first human beings passed on their newly warped inclinations to everyone who came after. Deviating from God's design became forever preferable to following God's instructions. Simultaneously, God's image continues to shine within every human being, frequently revealing itself through a humanitarian conscience and tender acts of mercy in men and women who prove that God's creation is still a good place, where sin has not destroyed everything.[3]

Jesus's mission aimed to recast the Father's original vision for how the world was intended to be. For example, when he was pressed about the suitability of divorce, Jesus's answer turned back to the Creator's original plan for marriage in the Garden of Eden (Matt. 19:4-6; Mark 10:6-9). The first marriage, at which the Creator presided, becomes the paradigm for all marriages consummated among Jesus's kingdom citizens. Thus the apparent oddities of Jesus's ethical instruction are tied to this particular kingdom dynamic: recasting God's original vision in a world gone awry. Jesus's moral teachings are not made up of arbitrary, arduous, or counterintuitive rules designed to make the Christian life difficult, though obeying Jesus's teachings may indeed have that effect on a disciple's life. Jesus's objective is simply to explain the Creator's original design in a world run amok with rebelliousness, making a way for the image of God to be freed from the unrelenting burden of sin. Therefore, Jesus calls his listeners to "repent," to turn around 180 degrees. He tells us that we need to be "born again," to start over completely, ready to relearn from scratch everything we thought we already knew about life. Our problem is that trying to see the world from Jesus's perspective—by repenting, being reborn, and obeying Jesus's teaching—is like putting on Professor Stratton's goggles and then trying to ride a bicycle through the traffic jams of New York City.

It looks crazy!

Following the Reversal Theme

A great deal of Jesus's teaching is characterized by this kingdom-reversal theme, but as we will see, it is not limited to the Gospels alone.

The Gospel of Luke describes the whole of Jesus's impending ministry as typical of the way God "has brought down rulers from their thrones but has lifted up the humble. He has filled the hungry with good things but has sent the rich away empty" (Luke 1:52–53). Dethroning the rich and powerful while empowering the deprived and marginalized summarizes both God's way of judgment in the Old Testament and the prevailing ethos of Jesus's ministry. God's kingdom brings a clear reversal of values for all its citizens, thoroughly subverting the commonly accepted norms of polite society. In fact, Jesus makes adherence to this reversal axiomatic for his followers:[4]

> If anyone would come after me, he must deny himself and take up his cross and follow me. For whoever wants to save his life will lose it, but whoever loses his life for me and for the gospel will save it. (Mark 8:35 and par.)

> If anyone wants to be first, he must be the very last, and the servant of all. (Mark 9:35)

> Anyone who will not receive the kingdom of God like a little child will never enter it. (Mark 10:15 and par.)

> It is easier for a camel to go through the eye of a needle than for a rich man to enter the kingdom of God. (Mark 10:25 and par.)

> Many who are first will be last and the last first. (Matt. 20:16; Mark 10:31)

> Whoever wants to become great among you must be your servant, and whoever wants to be first must be slave of all. (Mark 10:44 and par.)

The greatest among you will be your servant. Whoever exalts himself will be humbled, and whoever humbles himself will be exalted. (Matt. 23:11-12; Luke 14:11; 18:14)

Whoever humbles himself like this child is the greatest in the kingdom of heaven. (Matt. 18:4)

The fullest expression of the kingdom-reversal theme appears in Luke's version of the Beatitudes, where the "blessings" familiarly known from Matthew's Sermon on the Mount (Matt. 5:3-11) are accompanied by a unique and parallel set of "woes":

> Blessed are you who are poor, for yours is the kingdom of God.
> Blessed are you who hunger now, for you will be satisfied.
> Blessed are you who weep now, for you will laugh.
> Blessed are you when people hate you, when they exclude you and insult you and reject your name as evil, because of the Son of man. . . .
> But woe to you who are rich, for you have already received your comfort.
> Woe to you who are well fed now, for you will go hungry.
> Woe to you who laugh now, for you will mourn and weep.
> Woe to you when everyone speaks well of you, for that is how their ancestors treated the false prophets. (Luke 6:20-22, 24-26)

Here the full effects of the kingdom's reversal of values are tied to the final judgment and the threat of divine punishment. Throughout the Old Testament, such announcements of woe appear principally in the prophetic literature, where they warn the wicked of God's impending condemnation (Isa. 3:9, 11; 5:8, 11, 18, 20-22; Jer. 48:1; 50:27; Hab. 2:6, 9, 12, 15, 19; Zech. 11:17). Against this Old Testament background, Jesus, too, explicitly connects his warnings for the rich, the powerful, and the self-satisfied with the coming judgment of God. In several of the following sayings, the point of connection is the typical absence of repentance, faith, and obedience that tends to go hand in hand with an enjoyment of the comforts and self-satisfaction of worldly success:

> Woe to you, Korazin! Woe to you, Bethsaida! If the miracles that were performed in you had been performed in Tyre and Sidon they would have repented long ago in sackcloth and ashes. But I tell you, it will be more bear-

able for Tyre and Sidon on the day of judgment than for you. (Matt. 11:21-22; Luke 10:13)

Things that cause people to sin are bound to come, but woe to that person through whom they come. It would be better for him to be thrown into the sea with a millstone tied around his neck than for him to cause one of these little ones to sin. (Luke 17:1-2)

The Son of Man will go just as it is written about him. But woe to that man who betrays the Son of Man. It would be better for him if he had not been born. (Matt. 26:24; Luke 22:22)

Jesus's words of woeful warning provide additional evidence of the apocalyptic nature of God's kingdom. Though the final judgment has not yet occurred, the outline of that judgment has already begun to be drawn into the fabric of this life, first in the individual's acceptance or rejection of Jesus, and second, in the consequent decision to abide by or to ignore the ethical reversal at the heart of Jesus's kingdom teaching. The final execution of that judgment may wait for the future, but the lines of division are already becoming evident. The separation is now under way. These woes forewarn all those who are rich, comfortable, highly esteemed, and self-satisfied—those who reject Jesus or put impediments in the way of others—of their eventual doom if they do not repent and reverse their lifestyles now. A graphic illustration of this connection between Jesus's warning not to ignore this kingdom reversal, on the one hand, and the final judgment, on the other, appears in his parable of the rich man and Lazarus. Here Jesus describes the complaints of a deceased rich man about his punishment in the afterlife. In answer to his complaints, God replies: "In your lifetime you received your good things, while Lazarus received bad things; but now he is comforted here and you are in agony" (Luke 16:25).

Obediently following Jesus and doing what he teaches is the only way to avoid these impending woes, and he clearly expects his followers to implement his ethics of reversal immediately, here and now. Disciples are to adopt the attitude of humble service modeled by Jesus himself, the suffering Messiah who "came not to be served but to serve, and to give his life as a ransom for many" (Mark 10:45). Disciples must renounce the quest for status and the titles that go with it (Matt. 23:8-10), no longer clamoring for public recognition or the most honorable seats at the table (Luke 14:7-11). Instead, disciples prefer extending their own hospitality, not to the rich and highly regarded, but to "the poor, the maimed, the lame and the blind" (Luke 14:13, 21), because they know that "it is more blessed to give than to receive" (Acts 20:35).

The Kingdom Reversal in Paul

Paul's letters reveal that the kingdom-reversal theme was effectively passed along by Jesus's disciples, becoming a part of the moral fabric of the early church. A thorough treatment of the reversal theme in Paul's writings would require more space than is available in this study, but the one passage that I examine here will be sufficient to make the point. Once the reader knows what to look for, it will not be difficult to see many similar examples throughout Paul's writings.

The testy Corinthian church was not only argumentative in its relationship with the apostle, but certain combative members were also suing each other in the local Roman court. Paul was shocked by this news and chided them for taking their disputes "before the ungodly for judgment" (1 Cor. 6:1, 6). Several important points emerge from Paul's discussion of this problem in 1 Corinthians 6:1–9, all of them expressing his commitment to making his churches' behavior conform to Jesus's teaching about the apocalyptic kingdom and its ethical reversal.

First, notice that Paul concludes his corrective instructions by reminding the Corinthians of who will and who will not be inheriting the kingdom of God (v. 9). The plain implication is that Paul's instructions have been shaped by his understanding of kingdom ethics. He is not merely offering his own considered advice as he does elsewhere in this letter (1 Cor. 7:8, 12, 25, 40), but he is drawing from a more traditional, widely held understanding of how disciples should behave as citizens of God's kingdom. The apostle is reproducing or elaborating on the kingdom ethic that has been handed down from Jesus to the church.

Second, by forgetting the eternal priority of their membership in God's kingdom, Paul says, the Corinthians are failing to live out Jesus's ethic of reversal, an ethic that he obviously sees as the standard for Christian behavior here and now. Paul exhorts them:

> The very fact that you have lawsuits among you means you have been completely defeated already. Why not rather be wronged? Why not rather be cheated? Instead, you yourselves cheat and do wrong, and you do this to your brothers. (1 Cor. 6:7–8)

Here Paul is paraphrasing a selection of Jesus's sayings as he reminds the Corinthians that it is better to be robbed and misused than to seek so-called justice in the secular court system. For example, Jesus teaches:

> Do not resist an evil person. If someone strikes you on the right cheek, turn to him the other also. And if someone wants to sue you and take your tunic, let him have your cloak as well. If someone forces you to go one mile, go with him two miles. Give to the one who asks you, and do not turn away from the one who wants to borrow from you. . . . Love your enemies and pray for those who persecute you. (Matt. 5:39–42, 44)

These admonitions from the Sermon on the Mount—neatly summarized in Paul's rhetorical questions "Why not rather be wronged?" and "Why not rather be cheated?"—are further evidence of the kingdom-reversal theme at work in the apostle's teaching several decades after Jesus. Paul is emphatically reminding the Corinthians that their citizenship in the kingdom of God demands that they not pursue "justice" or retribution in the courts against those who have injured them. They are told, instead, to follow the way of their Lord by allowing themselves to be cheated and wronged without pursuing legal satisfaction.

The final observation concerns the important role played by Paul's apocalyptic understanding of the final judgment. He explains the lofty role that disciples will have in that judgment, but he also points out that they do not need to wait to experience the significance of that role or exercise its authority. Their status at the final judgment is a result of who they are already, so they should be exercising those same prerogatives in this life.

> Do you not know that the saints will judge the world? And if you are to judge the world, are you not competent to judge trivial cases? Do you not know that we will judge angels? How much more the things of this life! Therefore, if you have disputes about such matters, appoint as judges even men of little account in the church. (1 Cor. 6:2–4)

Paul expects the realities of kingdom citizenship, no matter how extraordinary, to be working themselves out in the Corinthians' daily lives. Don't forget that in the kingdom of God the last will be first and the first will be last. Therefore, the status of earthly judges is meaningless as far as the kingdom is concerned. But disciples of Christ, including (perhaps *especially*) "those of seemingly little account," will one day be elevated to positions of honor and authority, becoming judges themselves. They will sit with their heavenly Father in the clouds of heaven and assist in judging the fallen angels who rebelled against their Creator at the dawn of time. But this is not only the Christian's destiny; it is also the disciple's current privilege. The importance of our future status projects itself back into this current state of affairs because Jesus's apocalyptic kingdom has already broken into the world. The future has invaded the present with Jesus, and his followers are now to live their lives, not according to the generally accepted social and cultural norms of the world around them, but according to the new values intrinsic to the kingdom brought by Jesus. Consequently, Paul insists that the disciples should be capable of judging their own disputes among themselves. After all, could their mundane problems really be more serious than adjudicating the indictments brought by God against the fallen angels?

The Future Is Now

The challenge faced by Johannes Weiss and so many New Testament interpreters who have followed after him is the apparent impossibility of actually living out Jesus's kingdom ethic in the modern world. To any rational person, the ethics of reversal looks like a recipe for failure, marginalization, missed opportunity, demotion, professional stagnation, victimhood, and passivity. It is not surprising, then, that Weiss and many others have described Jesus's teaching as a temporary interim ethic relevant for only a short period of time while Jesus and his followers waited for the imminent establishment of God's kingdom with the fast-approaching final judgment. But since Jesus's expectations about the end of this age were wrong, his kingdom ethic does not need to be taken literally. Of course, other interpreters have offered different kinds of analyses and solutions to this problem, but whether they think that Jesus was wrong in his expectations or that his hopes had failed, it is not uncommon to come across any number of inventive rationales explaining why Jesus's ethical teachings do not need to be taken literally today.

For example, the magisterial reformer John Calvin certainly did not believe that Jesus's hopes for the kingdom were mistaken or that Jesus taught only an interim ethic that could now be set aside. But his commentary on the Sermon on the Mount consistently blunts the prick of Jesus's words in a way that, for all intents and purposes, sets them aside. For example, in his analysis of Matthew 5:39-42, Calvin begins by endorsing Augustine's argument that Jesus's command in verse 39 should not be taken literally. He agrees with Augustine that Jesus's intention is "to train the minds of believers to moderation and justice." Augustine insists that "this [saying of Jesus] does not lay down a rule for outward actions."[5] Instead, Jesus is disciplining the disciple's heart but not pro-scribing behaviors. Concerning verse 40, Calvin appeals to common sense and insists that "none but a fool will stand upon the words, so as to maintain, that we must yield to our opponents what they demand, before coming into a court of law."[6] Yet we have already seen that the apostle Paul endorses exactly such a "foolish" interpretation of Jesus's words in 1 Corinthians 6. Furthermore, Cal-vin repeatedly tries to silence any critics who might accuse him of weakening Jesus's intentions by resorting to various ad hominem accusations throughout his exposition. Such critics are merely "seizing eagerly on syllables," "cavilling about words," or "quibbling about words"—as opposed to "attending to the design" of Jesus's obvious intention.[7] But how can any reader attend to Jesus's intentions without attending carefully to his words and their syllables?

When all is said and done, the problem with any reading of Jesus's ethi-cal teaching that tries to set aside or moderate its contemporary relevance is that it fails to grapple with a central component of Jesus's message about the kingdom: the "already/not yet" dimension of Jesus's apocalyptic worldview, which refers to the fact that Jesus had no problem switching back and forth between two different perspectives on the kingdom's presence in this world.[8] Sometimes Jesus said the kingdom was "coming" or was "near." It had *not yet* arrived but was approaching (Matt. 6:10; 10:7; Mark 1:15 and par.; 14:25; Luke 10:11; 11:2; 21:31). At other times, Jesus declared that the kingdom of God had *already* arrived with him. It was here, now, "in the midst of us," and Jesus's ministry was the principal evidence of its presence (Matt. 5:3; 12:28; 13:11; 21:31; Mark 4:11; Luke 11:20, 32; 17:21). So the question arises: Is the kingdom here or not? Did it arrive with Jesus, or did it only begin to make its approach? The answer, according to the already/not yet understanding of the kingdom, is that both aspects of the kingdom are true simultaneously because they both are clearly endorsed by Jesus.

The most generally accepted way to account for this already/not yet dual-ity is to think of God's kingdom as having a genuine presence in the world even though it is not yet fully consummated. In other words, the kingdom is truly here, but there is much more to come in the future. Insofar as the kingdom is here now, it coexists with the fallen order of creation, and it must weave its way through the world's brokenness due to human sin. Remember, it is this sin that makes Jesus's kingdom ethic appear unrealistic and impossible to the average person. But once the kingdom has fully arrived in the future, sin and brokenness will finally be swept away, and the apparent foolishness of Jesus's kingdom ethic will be embraced by everyone as the divine norm always in-tended by the Creator.

The "not yet" aspect of the kingdom reminds us that this world is not yet everything God intends it to become. Nevertheless, the "already" aspect of the kingdom insists that Jesus's disciples, as citizens of God's kingdom, are called to carry out his kingdom ethic despite the fact that they will often feel that they are living in hostile territory. The church is the vanguard of heaven on earth. Disciples are called to be living representatives of the way things ought to be, exemplars of righteousness in a world of rebellion, models of peace in places of violence, witnesses to forgiveness in the face of vengeance. The church must be God's colony of holiness in the foreign land of fallenness.

A clear example of this apocalyptic already/not yet tension appears in the advice that the apostle Paul gives to the Corinthian church about their legal disputes (as we have seen above). The preceding analysis of the 1 Corinthians 6 passage makes it clear that Paul did not view Jesus's ethical teaching as unrealistic, passé, or the disposable remnant of failed apocalyptic expectations. Just the opposite. He insists that members of the church must find creative ways to actualize their kingdom citizenship by publicly conforming their behavior to Jesus's ethic of reversal, even when this includes allowing others to take advantage of them.

Notice that Paul's advice is directed by two distinct but related aspects of Jesus's kingdom teaching. First, believers must be willing to embrace the *inevitability of suffering* as they live out their discipleship. Paul is convinced that disciples must take Jesus's ethical teachings literally. The one thing Christians can be sure of is that living by the ethic of reversal will eventually bring pain, loss, and sorrow to one's life. Therefore, obedient disciples must prepare themselves to be wronged and cheated, to accept their mistreatment without complaint or recourse, and steadfastly to reject the so-called "sensible" advice of well-meaning counselors who would accuse them of adhering to a foolish and ridiculous lifestyle.

Second, Paul well understands that the kingdom has not yet fully arrived. The final judgment is still off in the distance. Yet the substance of those future realities has projected itself into the present like a huge cosmic searchlight illuminating every Christian's life today. One of the reasons that the ethic of reversal appears absurd to us is that we are most familiar with a world where the future arises out of the past and the present. The normal sequence of cause and effect works forward from now to the future, not backward from the future to now. However, this is not the case with the kingdom of God. The kingdom's already/not yet nature means that the final realities of the kingdom's future realization (the "not yet") are already at work, as if the future were projecting itself back into the present. Don't forget that Paul tells the Corinthians to boycott the secular courts and to establish their own court system instead. Why? Because disciples will judge fallen angels at the last judgment! Obviously, the Corinthians have *already* been constituted as a people fully capable of making righteous judgments because they are members of the already/not yet kingdom of God. Their conduct here and now should be determined by what they know they will become when the kingdom finally arrives in completion. Such Christian living is observable evidence that God's kingdom is already here making a transformative difference in the world.

Where the Rubber Hits the Road

The connection between thought and action is rarely as direct as we might like. Drawing the line from agreement with an argument, on the one hand, to living out the practical effects of that argument, on the other hand, is often a long and circuitous process. Learning to obey Jesus's ethical teaching is no exception. Therefore, accepting the contemporary implications of living out Jesus's already/not yet kingdom ethic will undoubtedly raise practical questions and hesitations for even the most devoted disciple.

No two situations are exactly alike. All of Jesus's teaching must be translated and applied to a modern world that is very different from ancient Palestine. The kinds of real-life situations confronting disciples today will entail any number of complicating factors that Jesus did not specifically address. After all, he could hardly speak directly to every conceivable ethical situation for time immemorial. Jesus's teachings are neither encyclopedic (covering all eventualities) nor casuistic (dictating specific actions in every imaginable case).

It is essential, however, that we take the basic principles at the heart of Jesus's teaching seriously. For instance, we have seen that Jesus taught his disciples that they must, at times, be willing to allow themselves to be taken advantage of. Paul reiterates this principle but then expands on it by permitting the Corinthian church to appoint its own judges for settling disputes within the Christian community. Here is an interesting case in which Paul slightly tweaks Jesus's teaching in order to fit a new situation. Paul allows for a judge to adjudicate the competing claims provided that all of the parties involved are brothers and sisters in Christ working to heal and restore their broken relationships (cf. Matt. 18:15–20). We see that Jesus's original teaching about the disciples' adopting a servant attitude toward nondisciples is subject to some modification when all the parties involved are believers.

Jesus's call to self-consciously become "the least of all" can, at times, sound very much like a command to let oneself be victimized, and allowing oneself to be exploited is never easy. It is one thing to imagine how difficult it must have been for first-century disciples to willingly carry a Roman soldier's baggage for two miles instead of the one mile required; but our modern, reflexive concerns about personal rights immediately rise up and rebel as soon as people try to impose themselves on us in a similar fashion today. Maintaining the status of a willing victim invariably raises a host of questions. Is it right to allow ourselves to be treated like a doormat for others to misuse? Are we inadvertently hurting the person taking advantage of us by allowing her or him to "get away with it"? What about the next person that exploiter is going to try to exploit? Perhaps we should try to stop such unjust behavior in order to protect the next would-be victim? Are we being socially irresponsible?

These are all important issues. But answering them appropriately requires one to know the details of any given situation. The point of Jesus's teaching is cultivating self-sacrifice and service to others, not creating pious doormats. The challenge for every disciple is to cultivate such deeply rooted habits of faithfulness and obedience that any "adjustment" we may want to make to Jesus's teaching is a truly appropriate and necessary modification that adheres to the spirit of Jesus's original intent. Self-deception and rationalization are ever-present dangers at this point. Most of us are constitutionally averse to genuine acts of self-sacrifice, especially when it promises to exact a personal price of the kind that others could perceive as shameful and humiliating. In these kinds of situations, it is far too easy to lapse into Calvin's commonsense excuse that "none but a fool will stand upon the words [of Jesus], so as to maintain, that we must yield to our opponents what they demand." I am afraid that Calvin's flippant disclaimer says more about the human penchant for rationalization and excuse-making than it does about the feasibility of actually *doing* the foolish things that Jesus expects his followers to perform. Obviously, one person's fool is another person's faithful disciple. Wisdom is certainly required in appraising a situation and determining what kind of response is most servantlike, most Christ-like, and most conducive to the other person's best interests. Yet it is far too easy for us to confuse self-preservation for spiritual insight and then masquerade our natural aversion to suffering as the weighty fruit of age and experience.

Some time ago a friend of mine came into a sizable inheritance after the death of his father. Even though the father had invested considerable time and energy in advance planning by preparing a will and informing all of the children and stepchildren about how the estate would be divided, my friend anticipated that certain family members were likely to dispute the father's decisions and contest certain portions of his will. However, my friend informed me that he had already decided that, come what may, he was not going to be a party to any disputes over any parts of his inheritance: if a family member laid claim to some part of the inheritance that had been left to him, he was not going to argue, fight, or try to defend his "rights." He simply was going to hand over whatever the other person wanted. My friend was going to take Jesus's teachings about money and material goods seriously. His conscience was gripped especially by the story in Luke 12:13-15, where Jesus refuses to intervene in a family dispute over an inheritance. Money and material possessions are not worth the damage that would be done to the family by fighting over such easily abused and misapplied concepts as rights, justice, equity, and fairness. Indeed, when my friend did travel back to the family home that summer, such complaints did arise, and my friend followed through on his decision, refusing to argue and allowing the unhappy family members to have whatever they wanted to take from him. Some people would undoubtedly have called my friend a willing victim who foolishly allowed himself to be exploited. On the other hand, I see a man of God who obediently follows the Lord Jesus better than most.

Being a Contrary

Various Native American tribes had a special place in their societies for people called Contraries. Among the Dakota Sioux this person was called a *heyoka*. As the name suggests, the Contrary had taken a vow to do everything in life backwards. He sat on his horse backwards, and even rode into battle that way. He said goodbye when he meant hello, scrubbed himself with dirt to take a bath, went shirtless when it was cold and wore a robe when it was hot. He laughed when he was sad and cried when happy. There was especially powerful medicine attached to the Contrary-*heyoka* because of the extreme difficulty and tremendous act of willpower required to maintain such a strenuous lifestyle.

This Contrary way of life is beautifully described in *The Way of the Sacred Tree*, a novel by Edna Hong that tells the story of Christianity's introduction to the Dakota Sioux of Minnesota. Among all the struggles, injustices, and misunderstandings suffered by these people, there is one Native American believer named Kaduza, who is trying to work out what it means to be a Dakota who follows Jesus. Kaduza eventually comes to see the Contrary-heyoka as a perfect point of comparison for explaining the Christian life to his fellow tribesmen:

Jesus is like a *heyoka*. . . . Jesus loved when others hated. He was tender when others were hard. He was hard when others were soft. He was silent when others chattered. . . . This is the new way of being. It is to be a *heyoka* in the world. It is to be a contrary to the world, to do the opposite of what the world expects! . . . There is a new way of being human, the *heyoka* way, the way of the [C]ontrary who goes contrary to the way of the world. And the cross is its sign. The cross is the symbol of the *heyoka* way.[9]

Christians are called to walk through the world as contraries, just as Jesus was contrary. The kingdom of God is a contrary kingdom intent on propagating more contraries who will walk backwards with Jesus through life. Behaviors and attitudes that lessen this contrariness are immediately suspect. The pain and discomfort created by this contrariness are embraced for their encouragement because they indicate that we are living out the kingdom reversal. The goal of the Christian life is not acceptance by or approval from those in league with the status quo, no matter how attractive they may be. The goal is personal conformity to the upside-down life of our crucified contrary, Jesus of Nazareth.

Discussion Questions

1. How do you respond to the idea of taking Jesus's "upside-down" ethical teaching literally?

2. Why do you react this way? What are the major issues or concerns at stake for you?

3. Can you tell a story where you were trying to obey Jesus's upside-down ethic? How did that turn out for you? What lessons did you draw from the experience?

Additional Reading

Burridge, Richard A. *Imitating Jesus: An Inclusive Approach to New Testament Ethics*. Grand Rapids: Eerdmans, 2007.

Kraybill, Donald B. *The Upside-Down Kingdom*. Scottdale, PA: Herald Press, 1978.

Stassen, Glen H., and David P. Gushee. *Kingdom Ethics: Following Jesus in Con-*

temporary Context. Downers Grove: InterVarsity, 2003; 2nd ed., Grand Rapids: Eerdmans, 2016.

Verhey, Allen. *The Great Reversal: Ethics and the New Testament*. Grand Rapids: Eerdmans, 1984.

————. *Remembering Jesus: Christian Community, Scripture, and the Moral Life*. Grand Rapids: Eerdmans, 2002.

Chapter Four

Living with Dual Citizenship

I found myself sharing a long wooden bench with six other demonstrators, all young men in their early to mid-twenties. Each of us was handcuffed to an iron pole running horizontally, firmly fixed to the wall behind our backs. We were watching the police-station booking room, which reminded me of a hyperactive beehive—men and women rushing back and forth consulting with one another on what our "narratives" should be. I quickly figured out that a narrative was the official story describing why we had been arrested and the charges that would eventually be brought against us. The chaos unfolding before me was due, in part, to one major problem: nobody knew who the arresting officers were for most of us, so no one composing these narratives knew anything about our stories or how we came to be sitting on the wooden bench, handcuffed to the wall. The men completing the arrest reports on their office computers had no clue as to why we had been seized and put into the "paddy wagon," except that we all had been marching in the anti-NATO protest through downtown Chicago and had apparently done something the police did not approve of. I was being given an interesting glimpse into the inner workings of the Chicago police force, watching them collaborate on inventing our stories and the charges they imagined would be most appropriate. Eventually, I was charged with "failure to disperse," even though no one in the station could have explained exactly how or why I had failed as a disperser.

Sitting there among my fellow criminals, I stood out. I was the only grey-haired man, with enough creases in my face to prove that I had graduated from college decades before any of my fellow protesters had even been born. In the course of the night, several officers did a double take when they saw me and asked, "What are *you* doing here?" which was usually followed by, "What do you do?"

I gave everyone the same answer: "I am a college Bible teacher." Most of my questioners raised their eyebrows, shook their heads, and walked away. One officer pressed further.

"What?" he replied, with an expression registering somewhere between shock and disappointment. "You shouldn't be here, doing things like this, you of all people!"

"No," I replied. "I am exactly where I should be." But before I could elaborate, he also turned and walked away shaking his head.

I strongly suspected I knew why he said what he did. In his mind, any middle-aged man who taught the Bible at a Christian college was responsible for modeling good citizenship. Christian citizenship undoubtedly meant advocating for law and order, always supporting the local police and showing deference and respect for government authority figures by obediently complying with their orders. In his eyes, I had violated all of these expectations.

For most defenders of this particular understanding of Christian citizenship, the crucial supporting passage appears in Romans 13. There the apostle Paul says:

> Everyone must submit himself to the governing authorities. . . . The authorities that exist have been established by God. Consequently, he who rebels against the authority is rebelling against what God instituted. (vv. 1–2)

I cannot say whether the policeman who walked away from me shaking his head had Romans 13 in mind or not, but this passage has played a significant role in shaping the political thought of certain strains of nonconfrontational, law-and-order Christianity throughout history. Paul's exhortation to "submit to" (some translations say "obey") "the governing authorities" has been particularly useful for encouraging the church to support the political and social status quo, whatever that may be.

The most egregious and well-known example is, of course, the German Protestant Church's appeal to Romans 13 as justification for its endorsement of Adolf Hitler and for Christian participation in the Nazi movement.[1] The Dutch Reformed Church in South Africa leaned heavily on Romans 13 to justify its cooperative support and implementation of the government's apartheid policies against black South Africans.[2] Many white churches in the southeastern United States saw Romans 13 as God's explicit command to combat the civil rights movement and to fiercely maintain their traditions of racial segregation.[3] Additional examples of such state-sponsored wickedness receiving unquestioned support from the Christian church, typically on the basis of Romans 13, could be multiplied many times over. J. C. O'Neill has written: "These seven ... verses have caused more unhappiness and misery ... than any other seven verses in the New Testament by the license they have given to tyrants, and the support for tyrants the church has felt called on to offer."[4]

Few people today would fail to condemn those sectors of the church that supported such historic evils as Nazism, apartheid, and segregation. Problems continue to arise, however, when we try to apply a similar critical analysis to our own time and place. What unrecognized evils is the church blindly endorsing and defending today under the guise of good citizenship? How may future generations of the body of Christ analyze the contemporary church's behaviors as those of good, conformist Christian citizens of America (or Great Britain, or France, etc.) at the beginning of the twenty-first century?

We know that hindsight is 20/20, but there must be a way for the faithful believer to acquire some godly foresight, even if forecasting the future is never 20/20. How about some way to acquire clear, penetrating "current sight" that peers into the truth of our contemporary laws, policies, mores, and behaviors? It is one thing for Christians to criticize past governmental mistakes—and those who supported them—once it has become socially acceptable to express a more countercultural, moral perspective. It was another thing altogether to risk losing friends, to be shouted down, or to face public ostracism as a contemporary critic of the overt racism confronting African Americans in the Jim Crow South during the 1950s and 1960s—and I daresay that few of us would have dared to speak out publicly. It remains sadly ironic that many of the most vociferous guardians of that barbaric racial status quo were pastors, elders, and deacons in the local church, absolutely convinced that by defending white privilege they were doing God's work in upholding local and state law.

It certainly was not acceptable to stand and defend the civil rights movement in most Southern white congregations while the marches and demonstrations were still taking place. After all, the protesters were breaking the law. It remains true in many Christian congregations today that endorsing government policy, whatever it may be, is the default position for genuine piety. Christian citizenship means being law-abiding, cooperative persons, submissive to the power of the state. But that conventional paradigm of good citizenship is subverted anytime a Christian stands up and speaks out to challenge the way things are.

What room is allowed for protest against unexamined conventions and agitating for an alternative—and more biblical, we would hope—vision of the way things should be? How does one acquire the insight and the ability to offer that kind of critique? On what basis can we adjudicate between the conservative defenders of the status quo, on the one hand, and the protesters calling for moral transformation, on the other?[5]

For any disciple of Jesus Christ, the place to begin such deliberations is in remembering that we all have dual citizenship. We are not only citizens of a nation-state, the United States or Canada or Mexico, and so on; more important, we are citizens of the kingdom of God. As the previous two chapters have demonstrated, the Christian's kingdom citizenship takes priority over all other allegiances and responsibilities, so that any discussion of social, political, or civil responsibility must occur under the umbrella of the universal lordship of Jesus Christ, the King of Kings now reigning over God's kingdom and every single one of its citizens.

Knowing how to respond to the practical problems that arise when the separate demands of our dual citizenship come into conflict with each other is not always easy. Various solutions have been proposed for such challenges throughout church history. Since we do not have time or space to explore them all in this study, I will simply lay out my starting points for the discussion offered in this chapter, building on the groundwork already established in the preceding chapters. So far our look at the kingdom of God in Jesus's teaching has led us to two conclusions.

First, every Christian must begin by remembering that our citizenship in the kingdom of God takes priority over any other claim to our loyalty, obedience, deference, or consideration. The issue is not that the believer has two allegiances of equal significance, making simultaneous claims on the disciple's life. Living the Christian life is not like ordering from a Chinese menu, selecting a few decisions from column A (God's kingdom) and a few alternative actions from column B (the earthly domain)—all according to one's personal preferences.

Kingdom citizenship does not work that way. The apostle Paul reminded the church in the Roman city of Philippi: "Our citizenship is in heaven. And we eagerly await a Savior from there, the Lord Jesus Christ" (Phil. 3:20). Paul is rhetorically motivating his Philippian readers to think of themselves not as citizens of Rome but as citizens of God's kingdom. As far as the apostle was concerned, Christians have only one citizenship that matters. Citizenship "in heaven" was Paul's way of referring to membership in God's kingdom (see chapter 5, below), which will be fully and finally established once Christ returns from heaven for his people. The apostle emphasizes the priority of his heavenly citizenship as a man who was never shy about appealing to his Roman citizenship whenever it could advance his apostolic mission (Acts 16:37-38; 22:25-29; 23:27). But when it came down to the things that truly mattered in life, Roman citizenship—something that Paul's peers would have paid dearly to acquire—counted for nothing in his estimation. In fact, as far as Paul was concerned, it was not even worth mentioning.

Second, prioritizing God's kingdom in this way means that some degree of friction will inevitably develop between the competing demands of the disciple's dual citizenship. Whenever that conflict occurs, it must always be resolved in favor of God's kingdom, whatever the consequences may be, including punishment for breaking the law. The bloody heritage of ancient Christian martyrs offers dramatic evidence of how seriously the early church took this principle of obeying Christ in opposition to Caesar. It is worth noting that Augustine of Hippo (AD 353–430), the man who laid down some of the earliest foundation stones for the notion that the earthly government may act with divine sanction, was nevertheless keenly interested in protecting the priority of God's kingdom. In his magisterial work *The City of God*, Augustine writes:

> The Heavenly City knows only one God as the object of worship . . . and in defense of her religious laws she was bound to dissent from those who thought differently and to prove a burdensome nuisance to them. Thus she had to endure their anger and hatred, and the assaults of persecution. . . . The Heavenly City in her pilgrimage here on earth makes use of the earthly peace . . . [but only] so far as may be permitted without detriment to true religion and piety.[6]

Disobedience toward earthly authorities is sometimes an unavoidable component of faithful kingdom citizenship.

Two passages in the New Testament specifically address the problem of competing allegiances and how disciples are to negotiate the tensions between earthly and heavenly citizenship. The first text concerns Jesus's answer to a question about paying tribute to Caesar (Matt. 22:15–22//Mark 12:13–17//Luke 20:20–26).[7] The second is Paul's controversial discussion of the believer's relationship to the Roman government (Rom. 13:1–7).

Paying Tribute to Caesar

When reading the Bible, it is always important to remember that it is a collection of ancient books written in situations very different from our own. This makes understanding the historical context of each passage crucial to accurate interpretation. Jesus's encounter with a duplicitous delegation of Pharisees and

Herodians, who ply him with a question about paying taxes to Caesar, is an excellent example of how important the historical context can be (Mark 12:13-17). For example, this passage has often been read as Jesus's brief disquisition on political theology, explaining, as Wayne Grudem says, "that there are to be *two different spheres of influence*, one for the government and one for the religious life of the people of God."[8] Grudem then elaborates by asserting that neither of these spheres of influence—governmental authority and religious obligation—is to meddle in the responsibilities of the other, giving his interpretation a decidedly conservative Lutheran twist. Aside from the fact that both Jesus and Caesar would have been shocked to learn that civil government and an individual's religious life were not to intersect with one another, anachronistic theological interpretations such as this are not reading the Bible as much as they are importing foreign ideological concepts and imposing them on the text. Attentiveness to historical detail will demonstrate just how wrong such two-realm, dualistic—civil/religious, government/church, and so on—interpretations have always been. As we have already seen, it is the same method of interpretation that was applied by the German Christian Church in justifying its support for Adolf Hitler.

To begin with, Jesus was not asked about the propriety of government taxation per se. He was asked a specific question about whether or not the nation of Israel, God's covenant people living in the holy land, should pay tribute—also known as the poll tax[9]—to a pagan, idolatrous conqueror, Tiberius Caesar.[10] The Roman *tributum capitis* was a tax levied on the male population of all conquered territories.[11] Tribute was paid in silver denarii, a coin minted by Rome for that very purpose. This is why Jesus specifically asks his questioners to bring him, not just any coin, but a denarius.[12]

Quirinius ordered a new census to be taken of Syria and Judea in AD 6 in order to recalculate the tribute owed to Rome. This order triggered a popular revolt that was led by Judas of Galilee, a man claiming to be the messiah and insisting that payment of tribute to Caesar was the equivalent of blasphemy and thus utterly impermissible for God's covenant people.[13] Though Judas was eventually killed and his revolt suppressed, the fervent religious nationalism motivating his grassroots resistance movement was never fully eliminated. In fact, the Jewish historian Josephus attributes the devastating Jewish Revolt launched in AD 66 to the simmering influence of Judas's rebellion against paying tribute. The historical Jesus stood midway between these two uprisings.

Knowing the historical context surrounding this question helps us understand the implications embedded within the exchange Jesus had with the Pharisees and Herodians. Any public teacher who was gaining the kind of popular following that Jesus had was bound to raise specific questions in the public mind, especially if they knew that Jesus was from Galilee, as was the rebel leader Judas. What does Jesus think about paying tribute to Caesar? Does he share Judas's attitude of resistance? Is Jesus also claiming to be Israel's messiah, who would, according to all Jewish expectations, abolish Roman rule? What better question to ask this man from Galilee than what he believes about paying tribute to Rome?

Jesus Slips the Noose

But these leaders were asking more than a politically loaded question. It was a trick question intended to trap Jesus, for the two allied groups confronting him had different political and religious agendas. The Herodians collaborated with the oppressive Roman government by their cooperation with the descendants of Herod the Great, the client-ruler established by Rome. They naturally supported the payment of tribute and opposed any civil unrest. Think of the Vichy government that enforced Nazi policies in occupied France during World War II. The Pharisees, on the other hand, were more representative of the common people who were oppressed by excessive taxation, and they were sensitive to issues of piety and the proper obedience to the Torah in ways that the Herodians were not.

An awareness of the roles these groups played in first-century Palestine is crucial to understanding how they framed their question in such a way as to possibily skewer Jesus on the horns of a dilemma. On the one hand, if Jesus were to answer, "No, (pious) Jews should not pay tribute to (pagan) Caesar," he would immediately signal to the Herodians that he was someone advocating rebellion against Rome. It would not take long for soldiers to track Jesus down and arrest him as just another would-be messiah fomenting popular revolt. On the other hand, if Jesus were to say, "Yes, we (subjugated Jews) should pay tribute to (conquering) Caesar," he would indict himself before the Pharisees, who would love nothing more than to broadcast among the common people that Jesus approved of the Roman occupation now desecrating the Promised Land. How long would he remain popular among the common folks then?

Yet, as an attentive reader of the Gospels might expect, Jesus responded to a trick question with a few trick questions of his own. He first asked his questioners to bring him a denarius, confirming that he knew exactly what tax they were talking about. Jesus then asked whose image and inscription were on the coin. A denarius at that time bore the inscribed profile of Tiberius Caesar wearing a laurel wreath on his head as a sign of divinity. Around the edge of the coin was the inscription, "Tiberius Caesar Augustus, son of the divine Augustus." The inflammatory title "Augustus" meant "the one to be served with religious awe."[14] Unsurprisingly, for some Jews the mere possession of such a coin was an act of sacrilege, a violation of the law. God's people, at least if they obeyed the second commandment, could not have anything to do with graven images or expressions of idolatry (Exod. 20:4-6; Deut. 5:8). The Roman denarius, with its idolatrous image of Caesar pretending to be a deity, violated every element of the Old Testament prohibitions. The fact that Jesus did not seem to possess one of the coins, whereas his opponents had no trouble getting their hands on one, is an evocative element of the story. Who was the truly pious man here?

Perhaps Jesus was twisting the knife a bit by asking his opponents to identify the "graven image" stamped onto the coin they were holding in their hands (Mark 12:16). His two-part response left them all hanging in the air just a bit longer since it required them to search their consciences in order to find an answer: "Give back to Caesar the things that are Caesar's and to God the things that are God's" (Mark 12:17). Like any good lawyer, Jesus did not ask his opponents a question without first knowing the answer. He had already identified "the things" that belong to Caesar by asking the earlier question about the image on the coin. The denarius obviously belonged to Caesar since it bore his image. Therefore, by paying tribute, God's people were not so much acknowledging Caesar's authority over them as they were returning his wayward property, as a good neighbor should do. Thus the opening clause in Jesus's statement created the possibility of a new mental framework for tribute payment, taking some of the sting out of its demands. Returning Caesar's denarius to him need not be viewed simply as a tribute payment; it could be redefined as the restoration of personal property to its rightful owner. From this perspective, paying the tribute was not an act of subservience as much as it was an act of neighborliness; and, of course, showing kindness to one's enemies is an important element of Jesus's ethical teaching (Matt. 5:44; Luke 6:27, 35; Rom. 12:20). Furthermore, returning this particular piece of Roman property helped to rid the land of idolatrous images, another act of piety.

The second clause in Jesus's statement confirms that he was not going to give his questioners a simple yes-or-no answer, as they had hoped. Instead, he concluded by saying, "Give back to God the things that are God's." But what exactly are the things belonging to God? How are they identified? Notice that the two clauses in the sentence are parallel to each other. Jesus had just identified Caesar's belongings by asking whose image was inscribed on the denarius, thereby establishing the principle (at least for the purposes of this exchange) that the property's owner is identified by looking for his image. In other words, God's belongings are similarly marked by bearing his image.

Jesus's annoying elusiveness either attracted or repelled his listeners—like the two opposite poles of a magnet. Those who were genuinely interested in what Jesus was trying to teach them were seduced into following his lines of innuendo into introspection and thoughtful consideration. Those who remained hostile, on the other hand, had already begun to shut down in frustration. But for a sensitive listener, Jesus's allusion to Genesis 1:26-27 is hard to miss.[15] According to the creation account in Genesis 1, all human beings were created as bearers of the image of God. Just as the denarius obviously belonged to Caesar, so every member of Jesus's audience—in fact, every human being in all of creation—obviously belonged to God as bearers of the divine image.

The simple but crucial lesson is that everyone belongs—lock, stock, and barrel—to their Creator. All that we have, all that we are, all that we achieve, all of our time, gifts, strengths, abilities—all of it belongs ineluctably to the Lord, and so, by further implication, all of it should be "given back" in service as repayment. We could call it the spiritual tribute owed to our one true king. The juxtaposition between what is owed to Caesar and what is owed to God is stark. Though Jesus did not come out and say it directly—another example of his subtlety in evading traps set by opponents—the lesson was plain. God is owed everything. Caesar is owed almost nothing. In fact, once the disciple had offered up everything that was owed to the Lord, exactly what was left for the emperor, other than the small, blasphemous denarius?

That particular question was like the elephant in the room at the end of this exchange. Jesus did not provide a direct answer to the implied question. He left his listeners to calculate their own solution to this equation of moral and spiritual algebra. But the implied answer is: "Nothing. There is nothing left for Caesar after the denarius." Far from teaching a two-realms doctrine that distinguishes secular from sacred, Jesus was implying his ever-present, universal kingdom-of-God doctrine whereby the Father's sovereignty swallows up everything in life.

This observation on God's sovereignty may help to explain a unique feature of Luke's trial scene, when Jesus appeared before the Roman governor, Pontius Pilate. In Luke 23:2, Jesus's accusers produced witnesses who charged him with insurrection. They insisted: "We have found this man subverting our nation. He opposes payment of taxes to Caesar."[16] Yet we search in vain for any Gospel text where Jesus ever said any such thing. Are these accusers simply lying?

There may be another answer. Perhaps a few perceptive listeners to Jesus's instruction about paying tribute to Caesar caught the spiritual drift of what it means "to give back to God the things that are God's," while intentionally forgetting the material significance of "returning to Caesar the things that are Caesar's." Prejudice can easily edit memory; the false accusations made against Jesus in Luke 23:2 may confirm the implication Jesus left hovering over his audience: once we have diligently offered up everything we owe to God, little if anything remains for Caesar.

In any event, as is often the case in such encounters, Jesus did not press his argument home. He left it to the audience to draw their own conclusions, while remembering, he hoped, that one day they all must give an accounting to the one whose image they bore. How many will be surprised to discover that they have shortchanged their Creator?

More Problems with Taxes?

Judea was not the only place where Jews confronted Roman soldiers and people objected to imperial tax rates. When the apostle Paul wrote his letter to the church in Rome (probably sometime between AD 55 and 57), the Christian community had recently experienced tumultuous times in the capital city. The emperor, Claudius, had expelled the Jews in AD 49-50, though they undoubtedly began to trickle back into the capital by the early to mid-50s. The Roman historian Suetonius explains that Claudius was responding to Jews rioting "at the instigation of Chrestos," a charge that many historians believe is a description of the antagonism stirred up over Christians preaching about Christ.[17] Early Jewish believers would have been included in Claudius's expulsion since, to the average Roman, they were indistinguishable from their kinsmen in the synagogue (see Acts 18:1-2). Christian concern about public perception, good citizenship, and the avoidance of unnecessary attention from civil authorities would have been prominent issues for both Paul and other leaders in the Roman church.

Furthermore, Paul was writing at a time when serious complaints about pervasive corruption among Roman tax collectors (the *publicani*) were approaching a climax. Public outcry eventually became loud enough that, in AD 58, the young emperor, Nero, "contemplated a noble gift to the human race" and proposed eliminating all indirect taxation.[18] It is difficult to imagine that Christian merchants struggling to conduct business in Rome, hampered by onerous taxation, had no outspoken opinions about the oppressive inequities embedded in the Roman equivalent of the IRS; all the more reason for Paul to be concerned about Roman Christians attracting unnecessary attention as tax protesters. Draw public attention to yourself and threaten the status of the church by announcing the gospel of Jesus Christ? You bet! Stir government hostility because you're not paying your taxes? Hmmm. With this fractious historical context in mind—recent expulsion and a looming tax revolt—I believe that James D. G. Dunn is exactly right when he observes about Romans 13:6-7: "It is a striking fact that the discussion builds up to its climax on the subject of paying taxes. This is unlikely to be accidental. . . . Nowhere else does Paul include such instruction in any of his letters, and there must have been some reason for his doing so here."[19]

Paul had specific concerns in mind as he wrote his letter to the Roman church, and describing a comprehensive political theology of church-state relations was not one of them. Recalling the church's precarious standing with the local government in a time of tax revolt is far more illuminating of Paul's argument in this chapter. The early church lived within an authoritarian state. There was no expectation that the average person could exert any meaningful influence in bringing about broad-based, systemic social or political change. Neither Paul nor his readers had any conception of participatory democracy. Modern strategies for popular political and social transformation through civil disobedience and nonviolent resistance were inconceivable at the time. Naturally, this does not mean that Paul was devoid of political opinions or that he might not write something of universal political significance for the church, regardless of its particular location in time and space, but it does mean that properly understanding Romans 13:1-7 requires that we keep the actual historical situation foremost in our mind.[20]

Observing God's Order

Several details in Romans 13 need elaboration for Paul's ethical instruction to become clear for the modern reader. The chapter's opening sentences twice affirm that government authority is put in place by God (v. 1).[21] God has established a hierarchy of civil authority to regulate the otherwise strong tendency toward unruliness in human society. Anyone who rebels against this ordering of authority, therefore, is rebelling against God's design (v. 2). Two details of Paul's vocabulary clarify his point.

First, Paul describes civil authority as part of the way God "orders" the world.[22] This idea of God's ordering, organizing, appointing or arranging is central to the passage, with several derivatives of the verbal root "to order" appearing five times in three verses (vv. 1 [twice], 2 [twice], 5 [once]). It is clearly

Paul's key concept. God "establishes/orders/institutes governing authorities" (v. 1) not by bringing any particular leader to power—though he may at times also do that—but by providentially creating structures of governing authority that exercise responsibilities delegated by God. When Paul says that "there is no authority except that which God has established" (v. 1), he is not claiming that divine providence places all rulers in their specific positions of power. He is saying that the various stations of authority that make up civil government are put in place by God's providential ordering of human society.[23]

Understanding Paul's use of "ordering" vocabulary helps to answer long-standing questions about Christian obedience to tyrannical rulers. The problematic logic, based on Romans 13, usually goes like this: If every governing authority is put in place by God, so that disobeying the authority is the equivalent of disobeying God, then even a man like Adolf Hitler must have been put in place by God, and disobeying even Hitler becomes the equivalent of disobeying God. This was, in fact, the logic used by many German Christians who swore allegiance to Hitler, the "divinely appointed" Führer.

Though some additional arguments will be advanced below for addressing the question of obeying Hitler, Paul's emphasis on *ordering* rather than *personnel* makes it clear that God establishes positions of authority, positions that are occupied at different times by different leaders of greater or lesser ability, wisdom, and moral fiber. Paul does not make God responsible for ordaining every leader who ever fills an office. Christians are obligated to respect the role of government per se in their lives, but that is a far cry from being obligated to obey, much less enthusiastically endorse, every wretched leader braying for national allegiance to his every foolish decision.

Subordination vs. Obedience

A second—equally important—matter of vocabulary arises once we notice that Paul does not command believers always "to obey" the governing authorities (Rom. 13:1). Translations that render Romans 13:1 along the lines of "obey the government" (Living Bible, Contemporary English Version, Good News Translation, Worldwide English) seriously misrepresent Paul's words. Instead of commanding obedience, Paul tells the church "to be subject/to submit" to the way God has "ordered" governing authority. If Paul had intended for the church always to obey the government, he could have used the common word *hupokouō* (obey) to make his point. But he doesn't do that; instead, Paul stays with the "order" word group and directs believers to be "subordinate"

(vv. 1, 5) to the authorities that "have been ordered" by God. In effect, he is reiterating the need for believers to cooperate with God's design in ordering human society.

Following the logic of verse 3 is crucial for understanding the full significance of Paul's refusal to tell the church that they must always obey the government. Notice that Paul's description of civil authority is utterly idealistic, in so far as he assumes that the church can always count on the government to faithfully enforce God's expectations. "Rulers are not a terror to those who do what is right but to those who do wrong. If you don't want to be afraid of the one in authority, *do what is right* and the authority will praise you" (my translation). Had Paul intended to deliver a lesson on Christian obedience, he missed a perfect opportunity to do so. Notice that he does not say, "Shed your fear of authority by doing what you are told; be obedient." Instead, Paul counsels the church to free itself from any fear of authority by always "doing what is right."

At least two assumptions are at work in this statement. First, Paul's argument assumes that government authorities will never be corrupt. Their judgments will always faithfully reflect God's judgments concerning what is good and bad, right and wrong, just and unjust. But we all know better. The claim that "rulers are not a terror to those who do what is right but to those who do wrong" is not always true, and Paul knew it. The civil rights demonstrators who walked across the bridge in Selma, Alabama, with Dr. Martin Luther King in 1965 were excoriated by the state's governor, condemned by the local sheriff, and beaten with clubs by the local police. It is no secret to us or to Paul that rulers can easily reward those who do wrong and become a terror to those who do what is right, but Paul is describing the ideal, the way things are supposed to be, for the sake of his argument.

Paul's second assumption is that when government functions as it should, citizens never need to be afraid about doing what is right because "the right" is always what governing authorities will want from their citizens. Those who do what is right can be confident in their Christian obedience because they are simultaneously being submissive to authority, as God requires. In an ideal world, a believer's act of submission will be synonymous with obedience because the perfect, incorruptible government will never ask its citizens to disobey God.

Unpacking these assumptions at the root of Paul's idealization of earthly authority also exposes the prick hidden in his argument. Paul knows that the Roman government does not measure up to this ideal. He cannot possibly instruct the Roman church always to obey a government that made public sacrifice to the Roman pantheon a civic responsibility; but he can tell them always to do what is right. When Christians act on what they know is right and those actions coincide with the government's expectations, Paul's argument predicts the happy outcome—"do what is right and the authorities will praise you." But when doing what is right puts the believer on a collision course with government expectations, Paul's instructions take on even greater significance: "*Still* do what is right."

God's own perfect government awaits the coming age, when Christ is seated on his earthly throne. As long as Jesus's disciples live in this world, however, they must anticipate times when the governing authorities will not praise them for doing what they believe is right in the sight of God. So Paul diplomatically commends the Roman government as much as he is able to in his description of the ideal, but he also assiduously avoids giving the church advice that could eventually lead it to compromise with the ungodly designs of a government that is out of step with God's vision of truth and justice.

Christians are not commanded always to obey their government or its laws. The church is told to be submissive and always do what is right. Obedience is one way of showing submission to authority, but submission and obedience are not synonymous. In some circumstances the submission God requires will work itself out as disobedience to governing authority. When a government expects believers to do things that the latter believe are wrong, things that will compromise their relationship with Christ, things that will violate their kingdom citizenship, then godly adherence to what is right demands conscientious disobedience against the government. At that point, faithful disciples remain submissive to misguided governmental authority, not by compromising their Christian conscience, but by freely submitting themselves to whatever punishment the authorities threaten to impose for disobedience.[24] Living out the values of the kingdom of God always comes first for the followers of Jesus.

Civil Disobedience

We are now at a point where we can recognize three components of Paul's instructions that offer a solid foundation for the legitimacy of Christian civil disobedience.

First, by explaining God's role in ordering the place of government in human relations, Paul subordinates all civil authorities under God, and not just any god, but Paul's God, the Father of Jesus Christ. In effect, Paul has desacralized the Roman state and its emperor, both of which regularly received sacrifices from its citizens.[25] Caesar is being told (were he ever to read the book of Romans) that he serves at the pleasure of the Christian God, a revolutionary claim. Rather than propping up the arrogant authoritarianism of Roman rule—or anyone else's rule, for that matter—Paul is actually taking his theological ax to its woody trunk and chopping it down to proper size. It is difficult for us today to fully grasp the provocative and subversive nature of Paul's words.[26] He twice describes civil authorities, including the emperor, as "God's servant" (Rom. 13:4), not because they predictably execute God's desires as a good servant should, nor because God promises to back up their every decision, whatever it may be, but because they function in a capacity that was "ordered" for them by the God who brings world redemption through the Son, Jesus Christ. Paul is dramatically leveling the playing field between rulers and the ruled. More than that, he has switched the parameters of the Roman playing field for another one entirely. Roman officials thought they stood on political grounds that were established by the gods Mars and Jupiter. To that fantasy Paul's says, "Not on your life!" Actually, though they do not know it, Roman officials stood on a playing field created and marked out by the Christian God. On that playing field everyone is equal, and all people, no matter their station in this life, will eventually be judged in the same way, by the same standard, by this same God.

Second, there is a subtle turn to Paul's teaching strategy that is quite profound. Overtly, he is instructing believers to remain cooperative, submissive members of society. Yet, even as he offers this highly conventional message, he is implicitly underscoring the church's supreme allegiance to the King of Kings above and beyond all other authority figures. The force of this reminder is to enable every Christian citizen to ask a crucial question: Are government authorities behaving like God's obedient servants in asking me to perform this action? And if I do what the government asks, will I be doing something that I believe is right and acceptable before God? Paul is implicitly reminding the church that obedience to Christ supersedes all other responsibilities. We obey the government when such obedience coincides with obedience to God; otherwise, we submit to governing authority by virtue of our disobedience, accepting the negative consequences, including suffering, of our higher obedience to the King of Kings.[27] Standing alongside the apostle Peter as he defied a direct order from the Sanhedrin, Christians testify with their lives that they "must obey God rather than men" (Acts 5:29; also 4:19).

Third, the thoughtful disciple is now left to deal with questions of personal conscience, a matter that Paul raises himself in verse 5: "It is necessary to submit to the authorities, not only because of possible punishment but also because of conscience." Paul's argument is that government officials (ideally) ask citizens to do what is right and then (only) punish those who do what is wrong—not wrong as defined by an arbitrary authority, but wrong as defined by God and our God-given conscience. Paul obviously does not believe that paying taxes, even to unscrupulous tax collectors, is either disobedient to God or a violation of Christian conscience, so he emphatically concludes, "This is why you pay taxes" (v. 6). But that conclusion hardly constitutes a blank check for necessarily prioritizing every government policy over Christian conscience per se. "Because of conscience" is a crucial declaration in its own right, especially when we remember that the real world does not operate in the way Paul describes governing authorities throughout this passage. "Because of conscience" becomes the church's inevitable explanation for its civil disobedience whenever the governing authorities come to believe their own mythology about extraordinary powers, providential selection, and divine right. The long and bloody history of Christian martyrs who died for their faith while defying local government should remind every disciple of the nonnegotiable priority of Paul's warning—"because of conscience."

Several issues of conscience arise when we take chapters 12 and 13 together, as they should be. Paul, in Romans 12:14, 17, and 19, insists that believers must never retaliate, seek vengeance, or resort to violence, but must always leave judgment to God's wrath. Paul then goes on (in Rom. 13:4) to grant the governing authorities responsibility for exercising the very functions that Christians are commanded to leave with God.[28] Consequently, there are certain government activities that must forever remain alien to the followers of Jesus. Whatever "bearing the sword"[29] may mean, whether it is the power of law enforcement, imposing capital punishment, or sending men to war, it involves some degree of violence and some acts of punishment, all of which must be foreign territory to the Christian.

Early Christian leaders understood this to mean, at the very least, that Christians could not join the military (see chapter 10, below) or serve as judges. Aside from the fact that men in these positions were required to participate in any number of idolatrous Roman rituals, soldiers had to be ready to use force in law enforcement; more important, they could be ordered to kill at any time.[30] Similarly, judges were responsible to punish, imprison, and impose the death penalty; but Christians were forbidden to involve themselves in any of these things. A typical discussion appears in *On Idolatry* (17.2-3) by Tertullian (AD 160-ca. 225). When answering the suggestion that Christians should seek positions of official authority—such as becoming a judge—in order to influence government positively, Tertullian points out that a man would have to find some way "to avoid the functions of his office . . . without passing judgment on a man's life [i.e., imposing capital punishment] or honor . . . without condemning or forejudging, without putting anybody in chains or prison or torturing."[31]

In other words, a Christian could only take the job after first deciding never actually to do the job, an obviously impossible scenario.

In a similar vein, one version of the *Apostolic Constitutions* 16.10 (ca. AD 375–380) makes an allusion to Romans 13:4 while insisting that "anyone who has the power of the sword, or who is a civil magistrate wearing the purple, either let him cease (i.e., resign his post in government) or be cast out (i.e., excommunicated from the church)."[32] The only way a Christian could honestly serve in the Roman government (and a post-Constantine government, at that!) was by deliberately avoiding all of his major responsibilities. It is apparent that early Christian leaders were not interpreting Romans 13 in light of a two-kingdoms theology, in which a temporal realm and a spiritual realm make parallel claims on the Christian's attention. Instead, the disciple was a citizen of only one kingdom, the kingdom of God, which is now invading a fallen world. John Howard Yoder explains that "these two aspects of God's work are not distinguished by God's having created two realms but by the actual rebelliousness of men."[33]

Martin Luther's two-kingdoms theology allowed him to recommend that Christians volunteer for the civic roles of hangman and executioner because "it is not man, but God, who hangs, tortures, beheads, kills and fights" when the state punishes criminals and goes to war.[34] Unfortunately, Luther merely demonstrates how blind he was to both the role of conscience and the priority of God's kingdom for every believer. God may well be the ultimate executioner standing behind a judge's guilty verdict, but that does not change the fact that the Father forbids his children from having anything to do with a process that kills, demeans, tortures, or seeks vengeance against another human being. Government authority is God's remedial measure to preserve some semblance of order among sinful human beings. Luther was correct to say that God is the one who punishes when a just, properly functioning judiciary renders a guilty verdict; but he was sorely mistaken in assuming that the divine Judge invites members of the church to share in his work of punishment.

Demonstrating in Chicago

In asserting the importance of conscience to Christian decision-making, Paul allows that some ethical questions may remain open for debate, as long as the debaters attend to the boundaries Paul has already marked out for Christian behavior. The necessarily cursory look at the two New Testament passages I have examined in this chapter hardly touches on every conceivable dimension of the Christian's relationship with government. Some additional study, for example, would remind us that Paul never hesitated to demand his rights as a Roman citizen and to hold government officials accountable when it served the purposes of his apostolic mission (Acts 16:35-40; 22:23-29; 25:10-12, 21; 26:30-32). Remaining submissive to authority can include demanding that authorities carry out their responsibilities properly, respecting the rights and privileges due to those they govern. Such submission occupies the midpoint on a continuum where unquestioning, dutiful obedience, on the one hand, and anarchy or violent revolution, on the other, take up opposite ends of the spectrum. Today Christian nationalism and the more revolutionary strains of liberation theology are prominent examples of these opposite polarities. Ironically, they both suffer from the same error of effacing the witness of the kingdom of God by conforming to the ways of a sinful world. As we have seen, Paul rejects both of these expressions of compromise.

We also recall that living in a modern democratic society gives the Western church political privileges and opportunities that the Roman church could never have imagined. Freedom of speech, freedom of assembly, the right to vote, the right to due process, the rule of law and other liberal democratic principles require modern readers of Romans 13 to squarely face the hermeneutical challenges involved in bridging the historical gap separating Paul's instruction to a church living under authoritarian rule from the situations of modern American Christians living under a republican form of government in a postmodern world. We should not be surprised if contemporary applications of the principles laid out in Romans 13:1-7 point us in directions that Paul did not directly address. Christians may disagree over the proper scope of civil disobedience and what kinds of government rulings or actions demand resistance from the Christian community, but Paul's failure to describe the scope of legitimate protest and resistance against government does not justify the prohibition of such resistance by supporters of the status quo. Just the opposite is true. As we have seen, Paul not only tacitly approves of nonviolent civil disobedience but he makes principled resistance against government overreach a Christian requirement when the circumstances demand it. Neither can we forget the numerous references to the blood of the martyrs in the book of Revelation (6:10; 12:11; 13:7; 16:3-6; 17:6; 18:24; 19:2) or John's descriptions of God's judgment against corrupt (and corrupting) government in Revelation 13 and 18. Søren Kierkegaard, one of the most acute thinkers in Christian history, reflects this New Testament perspective on conscience and government authority in his own inimitable fashion when he insists that the faithful disciple "does not care a fig whether there are laws or regulations or not; to him it is only so much cobweb. . . . If it is really conscience, conscience alone, then your regulations be blowed—I should only laugh at them. . . . Ultimately no force can compel the spiritual, at the most it can oblige them [Christians] to buy freedom at a higher price."[35]

Believe it or not, these were a few of the thoughts going through my mind as I decided to stand my ground against the wall of armored police, both on horseback and on foot, which was trying to forcibly remove anti-NATO demonstrators from the streets of downtown Chicago in May 2012. Tens of thousands of antiwar demonstrators had converged on the city as it hosted the leaders of NATO (the North Atlantic Treaty Organization). I was there at the direction of my conscience. My ethical values disapprove of the way the United States uses NATO to legitimate its military adventurism around the world. A large contingent of antiwar organizations protested in the march. Members of groups such as Iraq Veterans Against the War gave speeches about their experiences in Afghanistan and Iraq. Some of them intentionally imitated members of Vietnam Veterans Against the War who "returned" their combat medals in a 1971 anti-Vietnam protest in Washington, DC, by publicly throwing them away.

As the day's events started to wind down in Chicago, and people began to slowly disperse, I noticed rows of police on horseback encircling the crowd. A voice announced over a loudspeaker that we had to leave immediately by walking through a police corridor formed by two long rows of officers holding billy clubs. A solid line of horsemen started to move against the outer edges of the crowd, while row upon row of officers outfitted like storm troopers in a science-fiction movie—wearing body armor, helmets, visors, and holding tall Plexiglas shields and very heavy clubs—marched against the crowd. This turned a calm, peaceful gathering into an unnecessary showdown. Like ancient Greek infantry lined up in a phalanx formation, the wall of armored police pressed their overlapping shields against us, pressuring us to move where they wanted us to go. A woman standing next to me was shoved to the ground and would have been trampled underfoot had I not grabbed her arm and helped her to her feet. Another had her head bloodied when she was struck by a policeman's shield.

Eventually, I would be arrested and carried away with dozens of others, charged with failure to disperse. But why should any of us have immediately dispersed except to save ourselves from being pushed to the pavement by unruly policemen flexing their authoritarian muscles? We were American citizens exercising our constitutional rights. What good are those rights if they exist only on paper and we never use them?

I kept busy for the several hours I was in jail that night talking with my cellmate, a young man who grew up in one of Chicago's most violent neighborhoods. He was working for the Ron Paul presidential campaign and running for a seat on his local community council. He had been raised in the Roman Catholic Church but was now totally disaffected with what he saw as the uselessness of religion. Disillusionment with American politics was leading him to flirt with Marxism and violence as the only effective means of social change. I tried my best to explain Jesus's commitment to nonviolence, the radical alternative to society's ills offered by the kingdom of God, and Jesus's example of servant leadership through his suffering on the cross.

Fellow demonstrators occupying adjacent cells shouted out their own questions as we talked, and I tried to field them all as best I could. I kept asking myself: Is it wrong of me to wonder why I am the only Christian here to talk with these young men? How many other followers of Jesus were marching through downtown Chicago that day protesting American militarism around the globe? The United States is the greatest purveyor of death, violence, and destruction in the world today, demonstrating that American foreign policy has nothing whatsoever to do with the kingdom of God. How well does the American church discern that distinction?

Discussion Questions

1. Does this chapter introduce you to any new ideas? If so, what are they, and how might they change your current understanding of a Christian's relationship to government?

2. Can you think of some ways in which the church has confused Paul's instructions to "submit to governing authorities" with the supposed need "to obey governing authorities"? How would proper "submission" differ from "obedience" in these situations?

3. The apostle Paul did not hesitate to demand that his rights as a Roman citizen be respected when it served the purposes of his Christian mission. Can you think of areas in public life today where kingdom citizens may need to speak out and demand that their (and others') civil rights as American citizens must be respected?

4. How might this best be accomplished?

Additional Reading

Barth, Karl. *Community, State, and Church*. Eugene, OR: Wipf and Stock, 2004.

Cavanaugh, William T. *Migrations of the Holy: God, State, and the Political Meaning of the Church*. Grand Rapids: Eerdmans, 2011.

Joireman, Sandra F., ed. *Church, State, and Citizen: Christian Approaches to Political Engagement*. Oxford: Oxford University Press, 2009.

Storkey, Alan. *Jesus and Politics: Confronting the Powers*. Grand Rapids: Baker, 2005.

Yoder, John Howard. *The Christian Witness to the State*. Scottdale, PA: Herald Press, 2002.

———. *Discipleship as Political Responsibility*. Scottdale, PA: Herald Press, 2003.

———. *The Politics of Jesus: Vicit Agnus Noster*. Grand Rapids: Eerdmans, 1972.

Chapter Five

Aliens in a World of Politics

I had not seen my old friend Vance in many years. As young college graduates, far too many years ago, we had worked together for InterVarsity Christian Fellowship on various college campuses in Utah. Now we were old and
wizened—not quite senior citizens, but no longer young and spry either—with
more than enough gray hair between us to prove our elder status. We had both
pastored churches and been involved in some form of Christian ministry for
over thirty-five years, and we talked about the changes we had seen develop
within the church during that time. I asked Vance what he thought was the
most profound change. Without missing a beat he said, "Politics has replaced
theology in the church."

I couldn't have agreed more.

Theological conversation at the old-fashioned dinner table may never
have been as common as some folks insist, but in my former denomination,
the Christian Reformed Church, I was regularly told that there was a time
when most Sunday afternoon dinner conversations revolved around the biblical references and the theological issues raised by the morning sermon. Roast
preacher was often served up as well, probably very well done, but the main
item on the menu was theology and proper biblical interpretation. A person's
Christian identity was shaped through the corporate worship life of the local
church, the preaching of God's word, and collective reflection among God's
people as to how that Word applied to their day-to-day lives.

Nowadays, if you stick around for "fellowship time" after the typical
church service, you are more likely to hear debates about the upcoming election campaigns than you are to hear serious reflections on Christian theology.
The church lobby more often buzzes with partisan political debate than it does
with reflection, confession, joy, or even mild interest roused by the morning
sermon and Bible reading. Adding fuel to the fire, many television ministries

apparently believe that the best brand of Christian preaching always consists of political diatribe. Maybe I have the bad luck of tuning in only on the wrong days, but whenever I check up on certain programs featuring well-known preachers, all I hear are sermons containing accolades about American greatness, the virtues of conservatism, the evils of the Democratic Party, and the importance of supporting the state of Israel. Christian identity in this country has become securely linked to political allegiances, party platforms, making sure that people vote for the "right" candidate, passing "Christian" legislation, or defending the religious origins of the good ol' U. S. of A. Voting guides distributed in church lobbies receive more attention and are digested more seriously than the Bible, or so it seems.

To make matters worse, the church in America gives considerable attention to leaders and organizations that deliberately nurture this kind of misplaced identity. Such groups as the Moral Majority, Christian Coalition of America, American Family Association, Focus on the Family, Eagle Forum, Family Research Council, American Christian Lobbyists Association, Alliance Defense Fund, Traditional Values Coalition, Faith and Freedom Coalition, Wallbuilders, and others wager their continued existence on perpetuating the misperception that the "fruit of the Spirit" described by the apostle Paul (Gal. 5:22-23) consists of patriotism, love of the flag, support for the military, prayer in public schools, "traditional family values" (whatever those values may be), and strict adherence to Republican Party politics.

I once taught a continuing education course in Calvin College's adult-learning program, in which I offered a five-week survey of the Gospels of Matthew, Mark, Luke, and John, to about sixty attentive senior citizens. When we came to the Gospel of Luke, I explained that this book was distinguished by the special attention given to Jesus's teachings on the subjects of wealth, poverty, and generosity. After covering a representative selection of Jesus's instructions, I concluded the class with a few comments on the possible relevance of those teachings to modern life, and I returned to my office. On the way there, I ran into one of my students, and she let me know in no uncertain terms that she was very upset with me.

"I didn't expect to hear a speech about politics in a Bible study class," she said rather grumpily. I was surprised, to say the least. I honestly felt that I had done nothing more than walk through Jesus's teachings as I tried my best to explain what he was intending to say about money, wealth, poverty, and generosity within his ancient context. All of these topics are unavoidable when you read Luke's treatment of Jesus's life. You can hardly turn a page in that Gospel without being confronted with this cluster of issues in one way or another. Any practical suggestions I offered about the contemporary significance of the Lord's words were strictly nonpartisan. The real problem was the way in which this woman now ironically illustrated my friend Vance's complaint about the modern church. I talked to her about Scripture, and she took it to be only politics; but if I had spoken about her brand of politics, she would have taken it as Scripture.

At least two issues were on display in our conversation. First, this woman had no familiarity whatsoever with the particular content of Luke's Gospel beyond vaguely knowing that it described Jesus's life. I suspect that she had never before systematically studied the Gospel of Luke in her entire life, whether on her own or in a church Bible study. So reading about the ways in which Jesus repeatedly addressed economic concerns was a shock to her system. Jesus's strange, even alien perspective about generosity, his critique of wealth, and his embrace of the benefits of poverty were grating against her partisan predispositions like long gospel fingernails scratching against a hard political blackboard.

Which brings me to the second problem. She had become so deeply entrenched in viewing her Christian identity through a specific partisan-political lens that she had rendered herself incapable of listening to the New Testament without filtering it through that very partisan value system. Because she was more deeply vested in her politics than in the message of God's word, the voice of Scripture had been silenced. She did not allow the Bible to evaluate her politics because her politics were too busy evaluating the Bible and finding it lacking. Such priorities will lead inevitably to the creation of a "canon within the canon"—if there, indeed, remains any canon at all. In other words, we automatically ignore anything that does not properly cohere with our prior political commitments—or, worse yet, we reject it. On the other hand, whatever pieces of Scripture prove serviceable, rightly or wrongly, to the advancement of our preferred political goals we study, memorize, and put on bumper stickers for mass consumption. Pagans are not the only ones who practice idolatry.

Institutionally sanctioned mishandling of Scripture can be found in abundance only a few clicks away on the internet. Take a look, for example, at the *American Patriot's Bible* and its systematic confusion of God's work with ancient Israel in the Old Testament with the divinely ordained role of America, as God's chosen nation, in the world today.[1] Greg Boyd's damning review of it in the magazine *Christianity Today* says it all: "The text of the Bible is used merely as an excuse to further the patriotic agenda of the commentators."[2]

An even more blatant example appears in the *Conservative Bible Project*, the goal of which is the retranslation of the entire Bible in order to eradicate all traces of "liberal" bias, replacing it with the thoroughgoing conservative, "free-market capitalist" perspective we all know is the only view approved by God.[3] Naturally, the problem at issue is not theological liberalism but social and political "liberalism," as it is defined by the so-called translators' Republican politics. The online sponsors of the *Conservative Bible* explain, without any sense of shame or embarrassment, that "the rules guiding this translation are to use and be informed by conservative insights and terminology." Tough luck for God if he ever wanted to communicate something even remotely out of step with the current American conservatism.

Ralph Reed, the political wunderkind who once led Pat Robertson's organization The Christian Coalition, reflected in his book *Active Faith* on the changes that his conversion to Christ had made in his political commitments. His answer? None at all. "My religious beliefs never changed my views on the [political] issues to any degree because my political philosophy was already well developed."[4] In other words, Mr. Reed did not need divine instruction in formulating his political views. He already knew by way of his own innate, fallen, unredeemed political instincts what God should think about human community and the social interactions that describe the horizons of political action, so there was no need for Mr. Reed to give any attention to the possibility of alternative values or divine perspectives that he might discover in the Bible.

The numerous insidious problems extending like an invasive cancer throughout all of this idolatrous muddle-headedness should be obvious. As subjects of the kingdom of God, Christians are called to submit themselves to the Lord's instruction, remembering that Scripture is "useful for teaching, rebuking, correcting and training in righteousness" (2 Tim. 3:16). Once we no longer allow ourselves to be taught, rebuked, or corrected by Scripture, we have stopped reading the Bible as disciples who are residents of God's kingdom. To be fair, this is not only a conservative problem, though conservatives do represent a larger portion of the political partisanship taking up residence in today's church. Christian Democrats, liberals, and progressives may be a smaller contingent, but they can be just as prejudiced in their confusion of politics with discipleship. I once attended a public lecture offered by a leading Christian, a Democratic activist. His presentation was dismally predictable. During the question-and-answer period one of my colleagues stood up to note that the lecture could have been given by any representative of the Democratic Party. What was particularly Christian about his politics? Could he please explain how his Christian faith distinguished his political views from the standard Democratic Party platform? Unfortunately, the speaker could not answer the question, at least not with any conviction.

Of course, one can always sincerely believe, as many do, that God's immutable political convictions just happen to coincide precisely with one's own. But if that were the case, it becomes difficult to explain how so many culturally diverse believers scattered around the globe, all campaigning for different sorts of political systems with opposing convictions, can all be sharing in the same direct pipeline as heaven's one and only political perspective. Nothing characterizes the human species more consistently than personal hubris; but only sociopaths refuse to consider the possibility that their pipeline to God may not be as direct or as reliable as they imagine it to be. I believe that the Holy Spirit continues to speak through God's word, meaning that time spent studying the Bible can still teach, rebuke, correct, and train us in righteousness, just as it was always meant to do, provided that we approach the text with humility and a desire to learn.

Living as Strangers in a Foreign Land

So far I have argued that a proper grasp of Christian ethics must begin by understanding the person, ministry, and teaching of Jesus as described in the New Testament. Only by following him, after all, can anyone claim to be a Christian. The central theme of Jesus's teaching is the absolute priority of seeking the kingdom of God. The kingdom comes with Jesus, and he is its premier and model citizen. Christian discipleship is another way of describing kingdom citizenship, a citizenship that requires replicating the kingdom ethic taught and illustrated by Jesus's own life. Because of the already/not yet nature of the kingdom's presence in this world, Christian existence is defined by inhabiting two different overlapping ages—simultaneously. Disciples are not removed from the narcissistic whims and flagrant injustices of this current evil age (as the New Testament calls it), nor are they immune to its many hardships; but in the midst of this fallen world, disciples are called to be a living, breathing testimony to the present reality of God's future—and coming—kingdom. The principal evidence of the kingdom's arrival in this present age is the distinctive, identifiable behavior of its citizens. We have seen that, insofar as disciples continue to live and work in this world, they are to behave as cooperative members of civil society; but insofar as they are kingdom citizens first and foremost, allegiance to Jesus Christ will always trump any other authority making claims on their lives. As Stanley Hauerwas and William Willimon have rightly explained, Jesus's followers constitute a colony of foreigners, a beachhead of resident aliens in this world.[5] The church is composed of *heyoka*-Contraries

71

walking backwards through life, men and women whose peculiar lifestyles and alternative attitudes, whose upside-down ways of living out the requirements and disciplines of God's kingdom, make them odd bedfellows with the rest of society—a society that has not yet experienced God's redemptive reign. Once again, the apostle Paul reflects this already/not yet, upside-down perspective of Christ's resident aliens when he advises the Corinthian church:

> From now on those who have wives should live as if they had none; those who mourn, as if they did not; those who are happy, as if they were not; those who buy something, as if it were not theirs to keep; those who use the things of the world, as if not engrossed in them. For this world in its present form is passing away. (1 Cor. 7:29–31)

Paul is not instructing disciples to get married only so they can turn around and neglect their spouses; nor is he telling them that, if they buy a home, they should neglect it and watch it fall apart. But wise decision-makers consider the time and energy investment demanded by each new ingredient added to their lives, remembering that they marry, work, buy, and sell as kingdom citizens before all else. In light of these priorities, is this action worth the cost? How is that worth determined? Will it enhance or hinder my life as Christ's servant? Are the benefits ephemeral or eternal? Am I willing and able to pay the necessary price?

The entrances to medieval churches were often adorned with images of skeletons and graveyards to remind the members of the congregation as they entered for worship that life is short and unpredictable. Everything we have today may be swept away at a moment's notice like dust flying before heaven's broom. The only things remaining will be products of the obedient and righteous decisions directed by the parameters of God's kingdom. The key to living successfully within the already/not yet tension is found in learning how to hold on to the things of this life with a very light grip. While living in the world, kingdom citizens remain detached from it. Embracing the world, they never hold on to it. Caring for the world, they are never devoted to it. Invested in the world, they are never determined by it. Each circumstance is considered in terms of Jesus's promised kingdom-reversal: it will one day transform rich men into paupers and poor men into kings.

Several books in the New Testament develop this already/not yet tension in terms of church members existing as "strangers" and "aliens" in this world, waiting to enter their true, heavenly home. The existential tension inherent in being a resident alien is another way of describing the personal implications of citizenship in an already/not yet kingdom, as these New Testament verses show (all from the NIV version):

Philippians 3:19-20: "Their mind [i.e. those who are enemies of the cross] is on earthly things. But our citizenship is *in heaven*. And we eagerly await a Savior from there, the Lord Jesus Christ."

Hebrews 11:13-16: "They admitted [i.e., the Old Testament saints living by faith] that they were *aliens and strangers* on earth. People who say such things show that they are looking for a country of their own . . . they are longing for a better country—a heavenly one."

1 Peter 1:1: "Peter, an apostle of Jesus Christ, to God's elect, *strangers* in the world, scattered throughout Pontus, Galatia, Cappadocia, Asia and Bithynia."

1 Peter 1:17: "Since you call on a Father who judges each person's work impartially, live your lives as *strangers* here in reverent fear."

1 Peter 2:11-12: "Dear friends, I urge you, as *aliens and strangers* in the world, to abstain from sinful desires, which war against your soul. Live such good lives among the pagans that, though they accuse you of doing wrong, they may see your good deeds and glorify God on the day he visits us."

These verses highlight two important points. First, all followers of Jesus are aliens in this present age. It does not provide them with their true home, nor is it their final destination. The word translated as "alien" in these texts typically refers to those who are "strangers," "foreigners," or generally thought of as "other." They are people "who are not at home, or who lack native roots, in the language, customs, culture, or political, social, and religious allegiances of the people among whom they dwell."[6] The Old Testament precedent for this alien-stranger metaphor comes from the book of Exodus, where the alien nation, Israel, is liberated by God from Egyptian slavery and led out toward the Promised Land of Canaan. Identifying God's people as aliens and strangers in Hebrews and 1 Peter implies that the other features of Israel's story are also in play. These blessed aliens (followers of Jesus) must be moving out of an inhospitable land of servitude (this present age) and traveling toward a Promised Land of blessing and salvation (the new heaven and the new earth).

This biblical imagery of God's alien people has often been misused by the

Christian church. For example, when the first wave of Puritan settlers left the English shore and sailed toward the New World, they promptly adopted the story of Israel's Exodus from Egypt as their own.[7] Under the leadership of John Winthrop, the Puritans turned themselves into God's new chosen people. What would eventually become America was now the new Promised Land, God's newly chosen real estate given to his newly chosen people.

Unfortunately, the Puritan appropriation of the Exodus story was not only a serious misuse of Scripture, it planted the seductive seed for a destructive development in the American consciousness: a belief that the United States is God's special historical tool for combating evil, establishing righteousness, and executing his will for the rest of the world. Whether Americans were required to fight the British, Spanish, Native Americans, Mexicans, Germans, communists, or the threat of "terrorism," according to this view, the United States has always been God's servant nation, doing the Lord's bidding throughout history. This jingoistic mindset, which has come to be called "American exceptionalism" in its various permutations, has exercised a disturbing influence all throughout the history of this country. As a result of this history and the faulty biblical interpretation on which it is based, the American church needs to develop sufficient self-discipline to exercise an extra degree of humility and self-control when reading biblical texts that describe God's intentions for his people, especially if they are designated as strangers, foreigners, or aliens (see chapter 8 below).

Christians are made "alien" not via nationality—and certainly not because they are Americans—but by virtue of their relationship to Jesus Christ, as they wait to inherit the new heaven and new earth that will be re-created after the Father's final judgment. The point of this alien status, together with the earth/heaven dichotomy, is not to promote a cosmic or a philosophical us/them dualism but to highlight the Christian belief that God's saving sovereignty, which emanates from his absolute rule in heaven, is not yet fully established in this mortal life. To the extent that it has been established, God's saving sovereignty appears in the lives of those who have surrendered to Jesus Christ. Though none of these passages mentions the kingdom explicitly, when we examine the apostle Paul's references to the kingdom of God below, it will become clear that the earth/heaven duality mentioned in Philippians, Hebrews, and 1 Peter is only a different way of expressing the already/not yet tension inherent in the kingdom.

Second, the crucial piece of evidence demonstrating a disciple's kingdom citizenship is a noticeably different lifestyle, a lifestyle that sometimes will prove offensive to the powers that be. The principal demonstration of the kingdom's real presence is not miracles, signs, and wonders (though these may happen as well), success in electoral politics, or shaping the terms of public debate, but the transformation of repentant sinners who are now living godly lives, women and men who implement the ethics of reversal because they want to be like Jesus. By following the upside-down direction of Jesus's kingdom ethics, disciples are expressing the *already* presence of God's heavenly kingdom in this fallen world that is *not yet* fully conquered by God's redemptive reign. This is why Christians will (or, at least, should) appear out of place in society. Kingdom citizens are not only designated as strangers and aliens in the here and now; they will live a quality of life that makes them very strange strangers, sometimes becoming as alienating as they are alien, pilgrims with no place to lay their heads, social and cultural oddballs who simply will not play by the generally accepted rules in this world's game of life.

A significant extrabiblical witness to the transformational power of Jesus's kingdom ethics appears in a document known as the Letter to Diognetus.[8] Throughout the letter this writer explains that the church's faithful, gracious ways of living were a major factor in his own decision to follow Jesus:[9]

> While dwelling in both Greek and barbarian cities, as each one's lot is cast, and adhering to the local customs in both dress and diet and the rest of life, they show forth the remarkable and confessedly paradoxical character of their own citizenship. They live in their own homelands, but as resident aliens; they participate in all things as citizens, but endure all things as strangers. Every foreign country is their homeland but every homeland is a foreign country. . . . They spend time on earth, but they have their citizenship in heaven. . . . They love everyone, but are persecuted by everyone. . . . They are extremely poor, but they make many rich. . . . They are reviled, but they bless. They are insulted, but they show honor. . . . When they are punished they rejoice as those who are made alive. (5.4-16)

The author is a Christian who firmly grasps the believer's existential paradox of being a resident alien poised between heaven and earth, living as a citizen of God's already/not yet kingdom. This makes the church a "third race," as Christians were sometimes called in the ancient world. They are neither Greek nor barbarian, although they live among both of these groups. While a cynic might suggest that this idealistic description of the early Christian church was nothing more than the overwrought exaggerations of a fan cheering for his home team, multiple pieces of evidence from the ancient world tell us that such a church—such collections of faithful, loving, self-sacrificial people—actually existed. There may be a slight tint of rose-colored glasses here; yet the Letter to Diognetus is not describing a mythical community but flesh-and-blood people willing to live, suffer, and die (if necessary) according to Jesus's upside-down ethical teaching.

The exemplary description of practical Christianity found in the Letter to Diognetus is fleshed out by the allusions he makes to a number of New Testament texts drawn from both the synoptic Gospels, with their references to showing mercy while suffering for the kingdom ("they are reviled, but they bless," Matt. 5:10-11, 44; Luke 6:22, 28), and various New Testament Epistles, with their references to the next life ("their citizenship is in heaven," Phil. 3:20). This association provides substantiating evidence for the thematic connection I am suggesting between (a) Jesus's kingdom teaching and (b) the description of God's people as aliens, strangers, sojourners, and citizens of heaven. The kingdom is serving as a determinative concept without being mentioned explicitly. And even though it may happen in fits and starts, Jesus's followers make heavenly, eschatological life an earthly, temporal reality as they reproduce the exemplary kingdom lifestyle modeled for them by their crucified and resurrected Lord and Savior.

Paul's View of the Kingdom

Apart from his reference to the Christian's citizenship residing in heaven (Phil. 3:20), the apostle Paul does not explicitly describe believers as aliens, strangers, or exiled pilgrims in this world.[10] Neither is the kingdom of God a major theme in his writings. But the occasional references he does make to the kingdom create a vital bridge associating Jesus's teachings about kingdom ethics with the lifestyle instructions given elsewhere to disciples, who understand themselves as strangers and aliens in this life:

Romans 14:17-18: "For the *kingdom of God* is not a matter of eating and drinking, but of righteousness, peace and joy in the Holy Spirit, because anyone who serves Christ in this way is pleasing to God and approved by men."

Galatians 5:19-21: "The acts of the sinful nature are obvious: sexual immorality, impurity and debauchery; idolatry and witchcraft; hatred, discord, jealousy, fits of rage, selfish ambition, dissensions, factions and envy; drunkenness, orgies, and the like. I warn, as I did before, that those who live like this will not inherit the *kingdom of God*."

Ephesians 5:5: "For of this you can be sure: No immoral, impure or greedy person—such a person is an idolater—has any inheritance in the *kingdom of Christ and of God*. Let no one deceive you with empty words, for because of such things God's wrath comes on those who are disobedient."

Colossians 1:12–13: ". . . giving thanks to the Father, who has qualified you to share in the inheritance of the saints in the *kingdom of light*. For he has rescued us from the dominion of darkness and brought us into the *kingdom of the Son he loves*, in whom we have redemption, the forgiveness of sins."

1 Thessalonians 2:12: ". . . encouraging, comforting and urging you to live lives worthy of God, who calls you into his *kingdom and glory*."

2 Timothy 4:1, 18: "In the presence of God and of Christ Jesus, who will judge the living and the dead, and in view of his appearing and *his kingdom*, I give you this charge: Preach the Word; be prepared in season and out of season: correct, rebuke and encourage—with great patience and careful instruction. . . . The Lord will rescue me from every evil attack and will bring me safely to his *heavenly kingdom*."

All throughout the New Testament, Christians are told to prepare for the final judgment at the end of time, not by straining to read "the signs of the times" but by practicing the disciplines of godly living. Paul ties this common theme to the coming of God's kingdom, urging his churches to anticipate the kingdom's arrival in the same way that they prepare for God's judgment, by living a holy life. The difficulties inherent in such kingdom living will be compensated by an eternal reward, just as Jesus had promised. The community's lifestyle of holy obedience may not have been appreciated by all their contemporaries, but the Father has promised to reward his people for their faithfulness. The eschatological reversal (discussed in chapter 3, above) will be revealed at the final judgment, when God pronounces and executes his woes upon the rich, the gleeful and self-satisfied who benefited from all the comforts of this world. He will also bless and reward true disciples who embrace their status as aliens, those living as righteous (not self-righteous) strangers in an unrighteous world. Such an end-time view of ethics is the common touchstone connecting Jesus, Paul, and every other New Testament witness we have examined here. Whoever does not live a kingdom lifestyle "will not inherit the kingdom of God" (Gal. 5:21), just as all trees that do not produce good fruit will be chopped down and thrown into the fire (Matt. 3:10; 7:19; Luke 3:9).

Neither Paul, nor Peter, nor the author of Hebrews sees the kingdom as a heavenly, otherworldly entity existing apart from this world, despite their use of heavenly language. References to the "heavenly kingdom" simply recall the disciples' anticipation of the kingdom's "not yet" aspect waiting to be implemented when the enthroned, glorified Jesus "comes on the clouds from heaven" (Matt. 26:64; Mark 14:62). Thus the early church prayed, "Maranatha! Come, O Lord" (1 Cor. 16:22), knowing full well that they were asking for *the finalization* of the kingdom coming from heaven to earth. As for the worldly here and now, the social and moral strangeness of the Christian community provides temporal and immediate evidence that the kingdom of God has come—already, but not yet.

Kingdom citizens are anticipating the future establishment of an earthly theocracy, that is, God's direct, immediate rule over this earth when Christ returns. The church is called to wait, worship, pray, and obey while anticipating their coming king. Just as the ministry of evangelism is the closest any disciple can come to building the kingdom on earth, living out a kingdom lifestyle is the most the church can do for hastening Christ's return and translating the "not yet" into the "right here, right now" kingdom of God.

Engaging as Aliens

This survey of New Testament passages gives rise to two important lessons regarding the church's view of political activity. As we close this chapter, these two lessons will serve as an introduction to the further reflections on the church, politics, and social reform developed in chapter 6.

First and foremost, it bears repeating that there is no natural connection between the order of this temporal, material world and the coming kingdom of God. The kingdom's final establishment will not be the product of human social evolution; it will not arise naturally from world history; it will not be the fruit of humanitarian seeds conscientiously planted by social reformers; it is not empowered by "Christianizing" the social, political, or cultural landscape. God's kingdom is established only once God himself barges through the sheer fabric of world history, descending from heaven to burn away all evil from this fallen world now filled to overflowing with sin's dry tinder. Insofar as the kingdom is already here to cleanse, heal, and make people whole, it comes as the result of knowing Jesus Christ, not through political activism or social reform. Insofar as the kingdom is not yet here but continues to keep us in suspense, making us hold our breath while we wait, it is not because the wrong candidates won the election, not because the church's favorite issues were voted down, not because our preferred party was voted out of office. It is because Jesus, our Savior, has not yet returned

Second, even though this life is only temporary, living in God's creation carries important responsibilities for God's people. We dare not take a cavalier approach to the opportunities made available to us here and now. If the Holy Spirit leads sectors of the church to engage in politics, the church must act "with all its heart, as working for the Lord, not for men" (Col. 3:23). But as they engage society, kingdom citizens dare not forget that they act as aliens, foreigners, and outsiders who are ministering God's grace to a world that is not their home and is often inhospitable to what they have to offer. When the church forgets its place as an alien colony and invests in the things of this age, as if they were of ultimate value, God's people have lost their bearings. By all means, kingdom citizens should vote their conscience and become as politically active as they wish (if they happen to live in a country that allows such freedoms), but in doing so, they should think and behave as informed and faithful activists who understand how the upside-down priorities of kingdom citizenship should determine their politics. They cannot serve the Lord of the kingdom as naïve, calculating opportunists who only know how to dance the same routine as everyone else in the world's corrupted chorus line.

Discussion Questions

1. How should the idea of being an "alien" and a "foreigner" in this world shape the way Christians think and behave as they go through life?

2. Reread 1 Corinthians 7:29–31. Think of something/someone you hold dear. How do you hold it without holding on to it, knowing that this world will one day pass away?

3. Could the excerpt from the Letter to Diognetus be read as an accurate description of your church community? If not, why not? What can you as an individual contribute to bringing your church home closer to the model of the ancient church?

Additional Reading

Dunning, Benjamin H. *Aliens and Sojourners: Self as Other in Early Christianity.* Philadelphia: University of Pennsylvania Press, 2009.

Elliott, John H. *A Home for the Homeless: A Sociological Exegesis of 1 Peter, Its Situation and Strategy.* Philadelphia: Fortress, 1981.

Hauerwas, Stanley, and William H. Willimon. *Resident Aliens: Life in the Christian Colony.* Nashville: Abingdon, 1989.

Käsemann, Ernst. *The Wandering People of God: An Investigation of the Letter to the Hebrews.* Translated by Roy A. Harrisville and Irving L. Sandberg. Minneapolis: Augsburg, 1984.

Wilken, Robert L. *The Christians as the Romans Saw Them.* New Haven: Yale University Press, 1984.

Chapter Six

How Is the Kingdom Political?

I am a child of American fundamentalism. Though I suspect some would call me a wayward child, until I was seventeen years old my family rarely attended any church other than an IFCA congregation (which stands for Independent Fundamental Churches of America, an organization of nondenominational churches that pride themselves in not participating in denominational organizations). I remember well the "spiritual lifeboat" mentality that prevailed throughout this church environment when I was a young person. Christian people did not participate in the sinful activities characteristic of this world; in fact, that was how Christian people distinguished themselves as Christian—by remaining separate. There certainly was no room for such things as political engagement in that sectarian view of spirituality. The world was expected to go to hell in a handbasket. There was little point in working to make it a better place. Believe it or not, this isolationist brand of fundamentalism is a substantial branch in the ecclesiastical heritage of the modern Christian Right movement. The transformation from isolationism to political activism is due largely to the efforts of one man.

Whether you agreed with him or not, the Rev. Jerry Falwell will forever be remembered as the man who almost singlehandedly hauled American fundamentalism into the battleground of political activism. Since he created the Moral Majority in 1979, it has become commonplace to hear conservative church members associate their spiritual visions for national renewal and moral revival, not with the traditional mission of preaching the gospel or growing the local church, but with the strategies necessary for gaining dominance in electoral politics and setting public policy.[1] One Christian activist organization says that "engag[ing] our culture and claim[ing] it for Christ, begins with your vote. Remember, only you can elect your future. . . . The only way to continue with the freedom we possess is to see a national moral revival. We've got to mobilize millions of new voters."[2]

Voting for revival, what an unusual concept.

A more recently formed organization, called Reclaiming the Seven Mountains of Influence, announces in one of its promotional videos: "When we lose our influence [over society] we lose the culture and when we lose the culture we fail to advance the kingdom of God. And now a generation stands in desperate need. It's time to fight for them and take back the mountains of influence."[3]

As these quotations illustrate, the modern conservative church is repeating the same mistakes highlighted in our earlier discussion of both the Protestant liberalism of the nineteenth century and the neo-Calvinist Kuyperians of the twentieth century. The first mistake arises from the belief that the best thing the church can do for itself and the world is to climb into the driver's seat of history. Acquire worldly power. With power comes influence, and with influence comes renewal. The more power and influence, the more cultural reclamation. According to this view, only when the church possesses enough power to influence the terms of public debate, "to pull the levers of government and turn the wheels of the larger society for the good of the nation"—only then can the church say that it is accomplishing its mission on earth by growing the kingdom.[4] Temporal politics becomes the principal means of society's spiritual transformation.

The second, closely related, mistake is the assumption that kingdom citizenship requires God's people to foster moral and religious cohabitation between the church and society, such that disciples can feel comfortable and at home in the world, while the world allows itself to be tutored and reconstructed by the church. Though few may admit to it, there is a nascent nostalgia for the Roman emperor Constantine in this overt Christian imperialism. Just as Constantine endorsed Christianity as the preferred religion of his fourth-century empire, so would the Religious Right love to see its particular view of Christianity imposed on the rest of America (see note 9 below).

However, none of this popular theology has anything to do with the New Testament, its explanation of God's kingdom, or the status of Jesus's disciples in this world. We should recognize by now that these popular attitudes face major obstacles as soon as we engage the New Testament passages presented in the previous chapters. Wherever the church labors for social acceptance and/ or political power, genuine kingdom citizens will do better to remember "that friendship with the world is hatred toward God" (James 4:4). It is impossible to love both at the same time. Nothing indicates a more intense love affair with the world than an uncritical adoption of its strategies and methods for gaining power and exerting influence. "When in Rome, do as the Romans do" may have been a philosophy that tickled the ears of Caesar, but it is abhorrent for kingdom citizens. How can a gathering of aliens and strangers ever become the dominant, most influential voice in the society from which they are estranged? How can a collection of foreigners on pilgrimage through this earthly vale of tears ever exercise the kind of residential power required to "pull the levers" and "turn the wheels" of a culture?

They can't. It will never happen, at least not until pigs fly. Disciples must stop thinking and behaving as if they thus can transform society themselves; pursuing such goals is evidence of a colossal failure of Christian conscience. If the church does not give up this delusion, the inevitable evolutionary trajectory leads to shedding the qualities that mark disciples as resident aliens in exchange for the "respectability" required of anyone who wants to get his or her hands on the levers of power. The inevitable turn of the screw comes in realizing that worldly respectability frequently shows itself to be utterly disreputable in the kingdom of God. Jesus instructs his followers in a thoroughly contrary model of leadership:

> Jesus called them together and said, "You know that those who are regarded as rulers of the Gentiles lord it over them, and their high officials exercise authority over them. Not so with you. Instead, whoever wants to become great among you must be your servant, and whoever wants to be first must be slave of all. For even the Son of Man did not come to be served, but to serve, and to give his life as a ransom for many." (Mark 10:42-45)

Jesus's intention to live an exemplary life, which his disciples are deliberately to emulate, could not be stated more clearly. And the model Jesus gives is completely upside-down. Though there may be rare exceptions, the options life gives us tend to be: (a) faithfulness to Jesus, which keeps disciples among the powerless, or (b) gaining worldly power and influence, which is best accumulated at the expense of not being like Jesus. This is not to say that kingdom citizens should deliberately pursue irrelevance, although many in the church make themselves irrelevant by pursuing social and political agendas contrary to the kingdom. Jesus's disciples ought to know that they possess the most relevant message anyone can ever hear: the gospel message and its many related implications. But God's people cannot buy effectiveness at the cost of faithfulness, at least not if God's measure of effectiveness is what most concerns them.

As we keep these things in mind, let me offer a few suggestions on how Christians may live as salt and light in this world (Matt. 5:13-16), while they are making peace with the fact that, rather than being comfortable and successful power brokers on the world stage, faithful disciples are more likely to remain a disadvantaged minority who are typically consigned to the margins.[5] Jesus warned that his pathway is unusually narrow, and only a few will find the small passage that leads to true discipleship (Matt. 7:13-14). Therefore, as John Howard Yoder suggests, instead of asking, "What can the church do to tip the scales to its advantage?" the church should be asking itself, "In a situation where I know that I cannot tip the scales, on what other grounds can I decide what to do?"[6]

The Politics of the Kingdom

Living out the kingdom lifestyle of resident aliens who follow Jesus in a world not considered home requires a continual, self-conscious reorientation of thinking and acting. Spending one's life swimming against the current does not happen cheaply or automatically. It demands frequent introspection, self-awareness, an ability to recognize and acknowledge one's mistakes, a willingness to make adjustments, immersing oneself in God's word, grasping a clear vision of the crucified and resurrected Jesus, and an ability to deconstruct the anti-kingdom propaganda that bombards us day in and day out from both religious and secular media. Three principles are particularly crucial to this process.

First, since only the church can be the church, *kingdom behavior can be expected only of kingdom citizens.* Though kingdom ethics may have universal value, it is not directly translatable into public policy because the public does not inhabit the kingdom. Even with the indwelling power of the Holy Spirit, following Jesus and living concretely like a true citizen of God's kingdom is not easy. How can those without the Spirit be expected to do it? Jesus warns his disciples that they may well suffer for the kingdom, which is not something to ask willy-nilly of the public at large. The church is not society, and society is not the church. Therefore, Jesus's followers have no business expecting anyone else to adhere to the kingdom's standards of behavior. By the same token, society and the government (or the nation-state) have no business instructing God's people in what they may and may not do in obedience to their Lord. Of course, Christian citizens should take advantage of every opportunity to speak up in public-policy debates, lobbying for mercy and justice throughout society, and advocating for kingdom values *insofar as they are translatable* to the world at large; but the church cannot afford to forget that there is a great difference between public advocacy and a description of Christian discipleship.

As I write this chapter, the US Supreme Court has just issued its verdict allowing for gay marriage in all fifty states. Naturally, religious conservatives are up in arms, protesting the court's decision as an assault on their faith. But by what logic is that the case? How does allowing others to do something that you believe to be wrong necessarily challenge either your belief or your freedom to abstain from such behavior yourself?

It doesn't.

Personally, I believe that the New Testament prohibits homosexual behavior among God's people and identifies it as evidence of humanity's fall into sin. This is how I (and the Christian tradition) understand Paul's message in Romans 1:18-32.[7] But, unlike my conservative brothers and sisters, I must observe that Paul does not proceed to use his criticism of homosexual behavior as a platform for launching a political campaign to transform Greco-Roman society according to the standards of God's kingdom. Paul is instructing the church about the world and why it is the way it is. He is not urging the church to change the world by draping it with a veneer of kingdom ethics. He certainly showed no fear that sin in society posed any threat to God's kingdom. Paul's attitude was to let the world be the world while the church strives to exhibit its life in the kingdom.

Of course, disciples living in a modern democracy have options for shaping their society that were never available to Paul. But the church must remain cognizant of the difference between explaining (a) the kingdom behavior required of disciples and (b) the public values derived from kingdom expectations that disciples may hope to implement throughout society for its own benefit, expectations that society is always free to reject. For instance, God's people are commanded never to seek revenge. This is a kingdom value. Kingdom citizens are commanded to love their enemies and to turn the other cheek. Yet God does not expect that all people everywhere will live lives of nonretaliation. In fact, one of the divinely ordained functions of civil government is to punish criminals, to seek justice, and to exact vengeance (Rom. 13:4-5), activities that Christians are explicitly prohibited from doing (Rom. 12:2, 14-21). We saw in chapter 3 how Paul identified this particular contradiction as the reason disciples had no business bringing civil suits into a Roman court (1 Cor. 6:1-11). In Paul's mind, kingdom values prohibit Christians from pursuing secular lawsuits, but it is not the church's place to expect everyone else in society, that is, those who are not members of God's kingdom, to surrender their expectations of justice here and now. What the church can and should do is advocate for a fair court system, the judicial exercise of mercy and forgiveness, the humane treatment of prisoners, the abolition of the death penalty, and prioritizing rehabilitation over mere incarceration. Insofar as kingdom living is God's ultimate estate for redeemed humanity, the final expression of human fulfillment, disciples should find creative ways to encourage people outside the kingdom willingly to approximate God's kingdom values. But the church has no business expecting people who are not disciples to live as if they were. Beginning that process first requires conversion, surrendering to Christ's Lordship.[8]

In the gay marriage debate, for example, the church should have been in the vanguard of protecting and defending members of the LGBT community against discrimination and hate crimes; the church should have helped to advance their equality before the law and to offer an accepting community where all repentant sinners are equally welcome to worship the resurrected Savior, who died for all people, both gay and straight. But acceptance is not the same as approval. Scripture also makes it clear that within the kingdom of God the only approved form of sexual activity occurs between a man and a woman who are married to each other. So the question should be: How does the church live as an accepting community for all repentant sinners, whether they are guilty of greed, alcoholism, adultery, theft, anger, bank fraud, illicit business dealings, covetousness, or homosexual activity (*not* orientation), while simultaneously supporting them as they renounce their sins and accept Christ's forgiveness?

Haunted by the Ghosts of Christendom

The American church has a long and conflicted history of comfortable coexistence with a civil society that just happened (for important historical reasons) to share a great many of its social values, even if the similarities were often only skin deep. In fact, for many claiming the title Christian, the coexistence of church and society became such a harmonious union that whenever an unhappy society thought to ask for a separation or a divorce from its religious "partner," the church responded in desperation, like a panicked spouse afraid to live alone. Some sectors of the church have gone running after society like a jilted lover chasing her faithless Romeo, promising to change, to do better, to try harder, if only society won't walk away . . . please, come back! A rather sorry state of affairs. In my view, those "liberal" sectors of the church that have embraced gay marriage illustrate this first reaction: the church willingly conforms to changing social norms in order to remain "contemporary" and maintain its influence, however illusory that influence may be.

Other sectors of the church, however, take a different approach. These folks clamor to strengthen their grip on society, unwilling to let it go, hoping to maintain some vestige of social influence, fearing that society's departure from the church's traditional religious values will somehow diminish the church or threaten its existence. This is the strategy of religious conservatives who describe gay marriage as an imminent threat to traditional families and turn to the courts as their favorite arena for social combat, a place where the church fights to maintain its influence by forcing society to conform to its religious expectations. But is the outcome influence, or is it tyranny?

Neither of these strategies for maintaining the church's place in society has any foundation in the New Testament. The church is warned against conforming to the world (option 1) and is certainly never told to control it (option 2). Oddly enough, both of these misguided urges arise from the same problematic root: nostalgia for an overly familiar relationship between the church and the world that assumes that society must provide a safe and comfortable place in which the church can stretch its legs.[9] My mind goes bonkers at the thought that anyone could read the New Testament and arrive at such a conclusion. The church is supposed to be made up of the visible citizens of the kingdom of God, who comprise a third option, an alien race of humanity: resident aliens on pilgrimage to heaven; members of a society in which they are never truly at home; advocates for social justice and renovation who are never naïve enough to confuse even the most idealized social experiments with their Lord's demands for holy, kingdom living. Typically, in Western history, the church has been able to secure as much comfort in secular society as it has been willing to compromise in order to gain a seat at the social table. Given the repeated warnings found in the New Testament about the inevitability of Christians suffering for the gospel, I can't help but wonder whether the protests coming from the Religious Right about the moral decline of America have more to do with self-interest than a genuine love of neighbor. In other words, the more society behaves like the church, however superficially, and the more the church can dictate the terms of society's functioning, the more comfortably convenient life becomes for the church as it maintains its cultural privilege. Also, the less likely the church is to suffer. Keep in mind, of course, that the American definition of Christian suffering is not martyrdom but inconvenience.

Let me offer one more example. I believe that every member of God's kingdom should be committed to living a life of nonviolence. In my view, Jesus's teaching in the Sermon on the Mount and his consistent behavior throughout his life, including his arrest, trial, and execution, all make this conclusion fairly straightforward. By implication, every follower of Jesus is called to be a pacifist, refusing to have anything to do with attacking, harming, or killing others, which means that Christians should also refuse military service (see chapter 9, below).[10] Whenever I state my views on this matter, I typically hear two different but related responses to my position. First of all, some fellow pacifists believe that their nonviolent lifestyle is the way to eliminate all conflict from this world. Pacifism becomes a global strategy for the pursuit of world peace if only believers would advocate strenuously enough to attain it.[11] The second kind of response from more skeptical "realists" amounts to a warning that adopting an ethic of nonviolence will leave the world a playground for criminals and tyrants. Who will stop the world's barbarians if all of society becomes pacifist? The conversation typically and inevitably turns to Hitler and World War II. I am asked, "Do you really think that we should have ignored Hitler, stayed out of World War II, and allowed the Nazis to take over Europe?" Historically, in times of war, this latter realist response easily joins forces with patriotic nationalism and makes pacifists the target of persecution and violence, as happened to many Mennonites who chose not to buy war bonds during World War I.[12]

Many things could be said in answer to these two reactions, but for our purposes it is enough to note briefly one erroneous assumption that they have in common. Once again, church and society are presumed to be linked together as comfortable bedfellows; society can make the church appear more sophisticated, while the church makes society appear acceptably religious. In this comfortable cohabitation, it is easily assumed that a claim about Christian ethics automatically includes a declaration about public morality. But why should anyone make that assumption? We shouldn't. The things that disciples of Jesus are called to do or not to do as citizens of God's kingdom are a far cry from the decision-making processes of secular government and public policy. But this fundamental insight is totally obscured when the church, in its insecurity, is unwilling to stand alone, to think independently of surrounding social norms, and succumbs to the temptation of believing that its moral values require social approval in order to be legitimate.

Of course, kingdom ethics will have an important role in determining the way individual kingdom citizens behave in the light of government policy, but kingdom citizens are not surprised or disappointed when government decision-making follows its own course without first consulting with them. So, whether or not God intended the United States to enter into World War II is a very different question from whether or not Christians had any business taking up arms to kill each other in Europe and North Africa. Only God knows the answer to the first question. I believe that the New Testament answers the second question very clearly. Recall, again, the lessons found at the heart of Romans 12 and 13: disciples are specifically forbidden from participating in some of the God-given responsibilities delegated to secular government (see chapter 4, above). Kingdom ethics and worldly ethics are two different kettles of fish, whatever one may think of the universality of natural law.[13] Kingdom ethics will become the global concern of all humanity only when the Son of man returns on the clouds of heaven in preparation for the final judgment. Until then, world peace is a pipe dream. In the meantime, Christians are called to live peaceably as Christ's already/not yet witnesses to the presence of heaven on earth, lobbying (even vehemently) for creative policies more likely to produce peace than war, but never confusing their witness to the world with their status in the kingdom.[14]

Retiring the Cultural Mandate

The second principle is that *disciples are called to live countercultural lives because they follow Jesus, not because it is a strategy for transforming society.* The only true hope for this world is found in following Jesus Christ. The kingdom of God expands as more and more repentant sinners answer that call, surrender to Christ's lordship, enter into the Father's redemptive reign, and live out the ethics of the kingdom. As Stanley Hauerwas has often said, it is not the church's job to turn the world into the kingdom of God, but to be the kind of people who witness to the world about their king, Jesus, and his living presence among them.[15] There are a variety of ways in which Christians fall prey to this common confusion, but a sizable portion of the misunderstanding occurs under the neo-Calvinist rubric of the "cultural mandate," or the more recent moniker "Dominionism."[16] This mandate is ostensibly the divine charge for God's people to go out into all the world as culture-makers—transforming, redeeming, and renewing all aspects of human society wherever they go. The key passages used as biblical grounds for this mandate are Genesis 1:26–30 (the creation of Adam and Eve) and Genesis 9:1–17 (God's charge to Noah after the flood). Unfortunately, the way neo-Calvinists and Dominionists handle these texts provides better examples of *eisegesis* (reading the interpreter's preconceptions into the text) than they do of exegesis (discovering whatever the text has to say for itself), since they make the texts carry an unnatural load of social, cultural, and political relevance. Even Richard Mouw, a leading Kuyperian philosopher and neo-Calvinist advocate, confesses that "Calvinists seem to have an unusual facility for finding detailed cultural guidance in the biblical record."[17] Indeed, they do.

As I have argued above, disciples must remember that Christian ethics begins with Jesus and his kingdom, not with creation, whether before or after the Fall, and not with creation's jump-start after the Flood. Certainly, the basic constitution of human beings as the image of God is central to any discussion of human responsibility in this world; but the more fundamental question for a disciple is not what it means for me to be God's image—or to exercise dominion—but rather how I should, as the fallen image of God, live my life today in obedience to Jesus, God's perfect image, who now has dominion over me. Abraham Kuyper is famous for correctly declaring that "every square inch" of this world belongs to Jesus Christ. That truth, together with the Creator's charge for humans to have "dominion" (according to the King James Version) over creation, is at the heart of the Kuyperian, neo-Calvinist "cultural mandate." Unfortunately, too many people have taken this to mean that the Lord Jesus, having conquered all worldly territories, now gives his people permission to enter into any field of endeavor (it does, after all, belong to him), making themselves successful on the same terms as anyone else in the field, exercising God-given dominion as they do so. According to this interpretation of the cultural mandate, the hallmark of Christian witness becomes success in one's chosen profession. Worldly success is the presumed sign of divine blessing. With God's blessed success under your belt, you will eventually become the kind of Christian leader a university gladly invites as a commencement speaker. Why else was Donald Trump—known to TV watchers by the two-word phrase "You're fired!"—asked to deliver the 2012 convocation address at Liberty University, even though he never attended the school?

Tragically, pursuing this kind of cultural mandate all too easily becomes a recipe for turning the church into an irrelevant carbon copy of all the worst qualities the world has to offer. For instance, Christian political activists tend to use their political power in the same way other manipulative power brokers do, an observation that leads James Davison Hunter to charge that "contemporary Christian understandings of power and politics are a very large part of what has made contemporary Christianity in America appalling, irrelevant, and ineffective—part and parcel of the worst elements of our late-modern culture today, rather than a healthy alternative to it."[18] What the lordship of Jesus Christ ought to mean for kingdom citizens is that, whatever line of work disciples are called to pursue, they will always live and work as kingdom citizens, whether or not kingdom ethics are advantageous to their success. Members of God's kingdom must reconcile themselves to the fact that, in all probability, unless they work in a very unusual environment, obeying Jesus will make them less competitive and less likely to rise to the top than are their worldly counterparts. In fact, kingdom living can easily cause disciples to sink to the bottom of the pool, descending the economic ladder of downward mobility. As baseball manager Leo Durocher put it, "Nice guys finish last."

What is the likelihood that a politician who never lies but only tells the truth, never badmouths or misrepresents an opponent, keeps every campaign promise, answers every reporter's question honestly and straightforwardly, is forthright about what she will do once in office, and obeys all campaign finance laws—what are the chances that this candidate will ever win an election? It may be possible, but it does not seem likely, not in today's political environment. On the other hand, how many sad stories appear about Christian politicians who are accused, caught, convicted, and booted from office because they broke the law or were discovered in some indiscretion? Far too often, the siren song of political influence becomes more appealing than living as a faithful kingdom citizen.

I once read a particularly sad example of this mistake published by Dr. James Dobson and his organization, Focus on the Family. After the 2012 reelection victory of President Barack Obama, Dobson sent out a national newsletter lamenting the Democratic success. The three-and-a-half-page letter dealt almost exclusively with party politics, extolling the superiority of the Republican Party over the Democrats. This is standard fare. For many Americans, God is a Republican. The truly disturbing portion came when Dobson finally admitted: "I'm sure you are discouraged in the aftermath of the National Elections. . . . *Nearly everything I have stood for these past 35 years went down to defeat.*"[19]

When I first read that quote, I was shocked. Here was a Christian leader with a national reputation admitting that for the past thirty-five years he has been investing his life in matters so ephemeral, so transitory, so utterly subject to the shifting sands of public whimsy that it all could be undone and swept away by a single political campaign. If that is true, then Dobson was also confessing (whether he recognized it or not) that he has not been laboring for the kingdom of God. All these years he has simply been another political activist, not a minister of the gospel. His late nights and early mornings of glad-handing, lobbying, arm-twisting, cajoling, and fundraising were as misdirected as a bird dog on a false point. He has little to show for all that time and energy, because politics will never usher in the kingdom, and only God's kingdom will never go down to defeat.

Of course, as outlined above, none of this is to say that disciples can't or won't make a difference in the world. This is not an argument for social inactivity.[20] Rather, it is a reminder that whatever influence God's people may have in this world develops as a byproduct of living as obedient kingdom citizens first and foremost. Sometimes the effects may be far-reaching, but most of the time the consequences will probably not be felt beyond the immediate witnesses. Strategic thinking is always a smart thing to do. Spirituality does not demand stupidity. But asking whether or not a given action will prove to be "effective" or "successful" is not the first question for kingdom citizens to ask themselves. The more pressing question is: What does Jesus require of me in this situation? How do I act as a member of God's kingdom here and now, come what may, remembering that "whoever wants to save his life will lose it, but whoever loses his life for me [Jesus] and the gospel will save it" (Mark 8:35; cf. Matt. 10:39; 16:25; Luke 9:24; 17:33; John 12:25)?[21]

I once knew a Christian businessman who was an excellent example of such kingdom citizenship. He rightly understood that the primary purpose of owning a business was not to make money but to serve people. So he made a practice of hiring the kinds of people who were considered unemployable by the average business owner. The majority of his workers were mentally and physically handicapped, recovering drug addicts, convicted felons, and other kinds of people generally considered liabilities to a productive workplace. Though my friend's businesses were successful, he certainly never achieved the level of profitability that was possible had he hired a "better"-quality employee. But he was following a Lord and Savior who called him to love the marginalized, to help the helpless, to esteem those whom society despised, and to give to those who had nothing of their own.

Faith Is Risky Business

The third principle calls us to remember that *risk-taking is normative for anyone who follows Jesus*. If we never venture outside our comfort zone, then we are not following Jesus; we are only walking the dog. The kingdom's already/not yet duality ensures both continuity and discontinuity between this current age and the final establishment of God's reign. Insofar as the kingdom has not yet fully arrived, Jesus's followers remain subject to the temporal realities of this world. The limitations of human frailty afflict us all, without exception. Even the holiest saint eventually dies, decays, and becomes food for worms. But to the extent that God's heavenly reign has already arrived, kingdom citizens are called to look beyond the temporal into the eternal and to be directed by that heavenly reality hovering in the distance just above the horizon, flickering enticingly at the edges of our peripheral vision.

One of the practical results of acting in harmony with that flickering perception of God's "not-yet" kingdom is the never-ending possibility of miracles, of experiencing the improbable made actual, the unlikely become certain. The "already" declares that the impossible may actually be possible, just as the "not yet" insists that faith, sometimes feeling its way through the darkness, is the only way forward. Thus faith becomes the gateway to seeing new horizons, for faith is always a venture. Faith always involves risk. Without risk there can be no miracles.

Politics has been defined as "the art of the possible"; in that case, following Jesus is profoundly antipolitical, for living as a disciple frequently looks impossible, offensive, indiscreet, awkward, uncomfortable, hazardous, rude, irrational, and sometimes even dangerous.[22] Living by faith becomes a watershed issue. All who are unwilling to be tarred by faith's social indiscretions show themselves to be more concerned with social niceties than with conformity to a crucified Savior. Such people cannot be kingdom citizens, for according to the New Testament, their love of this world, with its comforts and considerations, constitutes hatred of God (James 4:4; 1 John 2:15-17). On the other hand, anyone who is willing to take risks, responding to God's call to venture out in faith despite the warnings and catcalls of this world's realists, may well find themselves producing social, cultural, and political benefits extending well beyond anything a sane, discreet, reasonable society is capable of doing on its own.[23]

There are no simple formulae for how a socially conscious disciple should proceed. It goes without saying that a strong devotional life, including Bible study and prayer, with the support of a good Christian community, are all components of an essential foundation for personal action. From this foundation there often arises a sense of calling, a calling to serve others, to make a contribution to some area of need—locally or globally. Since the focus is on helping others rather than maintaining ideological purity, there will always be room for collaborating with others—whether or not they follow Jesus—and the inevitable disagreements about the most appropriate, workable, and effective methods. For instance, some activists are committed to the importance of private agencies, while others will want to take advantage of public resources for addressing social problems. A third group will see some combination of public and private approaches as the most effective way to address the community's social, economic, and moral ills. One thing is certain: systemic problems such as poverty, unemployment, public education, and discrimination are so vast that they will never be solved through the work of private agencies alone, whether they be individual or church-based community programs.

Christian activism demands Spirit-led creativity from kingdom citizens who are both willing and able to think outside the box, refusing to remain confined to the preexisting compartments carved out for us by the status quo. Neither Republicans nor Democrats have all the answers. In fact, neither party is even asking all the right questions, and not enough Christians stand up to push back against their leaders because far too many excel at following the party line—particularly the members of megachurches (see chapter 7, below). It is no surprise that, behind closed doors, certain leaders of the Republican Party refer to members of the Religious Right as their "useful idiots," worker bees providing the raw labor needed to carry out the party's bidding.[24] When the church falls into lockstep behind worldly leadership—which is the only kind of leadership offered by any political party or campaign—reading from the approved transcript, saying what everyone else is saying, doing what everyone else is doing, thinking only what they are told to think, it comes as no surprise when the church eventually looks more like campaign headquarters or a dues-collecting social club than it does a community of risk-taking disciples living contrarian lives for a crucified Savior, behaving as though up were really down and down were really up.

Discussion Questions

1. How does making citizenship in the kingdom of God central to Christian identity influence the way Christians should think and act in their society?

2. Does this "kingdom perspective" cause you to change or to reevaluate the way you approach political or social issues? If so, how and why?

3. Does abandoning the idea of a cultural mandate mean that the church should give up any hope of influencing society? Explain how this chapter helps you answer this question.

Additional Reading

Cavanaugh, William T. *Migrations of the Holy: God, State, and the Political Meaning of the Church*. Grand Rapids: Eerdmans, 2011.

Ellul, Jacques. *The Politics of God and the Politics of Man*. Edited and translated by Geoffrey W. Bromiley. Grand Rapids: Eerdmans, 1972.

Hauerwas, Stanley. *After Christendom? How the Church Is to Behave If Freedom, Justice, and a Christian Nation Are Bad Ideas*. Nashville: Abingdon, 1991.

Joireman, Sandra F., ed. *Church, State, and Citizen: Christian Approaches to Political Engagement*. Oxford: Oxford University Press, 2009.

Sider, Ronald J. *Just Politics: A Guide for Christian Engagement*. Grand Rapids: Brazos, 2012.

Yoder, John Howard. *The Christian Witness to the State*. Scottdale, PA: Herald Press, 2002.

————. *Discipleship as Political Responsibility*. Translated by Timothy J. Geddert. Scottdale, PA: Herald Press, 2003.

————. *The Politics of Jesus*. Grand Rapids: Eerdmans, 1972.

Chapter Seven

When Disobedience Is a Virtue

My wife and I had recently moved into a new community and were in the early stages of visiting local congregations, searching for a church home. On this particular Sunday morning, the pastor of the church was telling his congregation about a recent dream. I had no idea how often a dream served as the basis for his Sunday sermon, but I was curious to hear about it. In this dream the pastor was leading a team of people through the African savannah when he noticed that the group was being stalked by a large mass of hungry lions. The group's only means of defense was a gun held by another person at the opposite end of the crowd. The pastor frantically began to shout instructions for the gunner to shoot his rifle at the lions in order to scare them away and halt their attack. But rather than shoot immediately, as he was told, the man paused to consider whether or not shooting at the lions was the right thing to do. Was the pastor's order correct, or was there a better, more effective course of action he could take? The pastor mockingly mimicked the man's hesitations, making it very clear that solid citizens do what they are told immediately without hesitation, whereas people who pause to think for themselves and consider the rightness or wrongness of a command have fallen victim to the "sin of personal autonomy," which is ruining modern society. (I winced at the hearty "amen" that erupted from the man seated behind me.) The pastor drove his point home: faithful Christians obey the authorities without hesitation, that is, without thinking for themselves. In secular society, that means we all must obey the government. For Christians, it means that church members always obey their pastor.

My wife and I left the service early knowing that this was not going to be our new church home. I had a strong urge to tell the usher, who nodded politely as we walked out the door, that Adolf Hitler would have loved his pastor. I am certain that neither of them had ever heard of Pastor Kurt Scharf, a solitary shepherd who courageously raised his voice to condemn the Nazi Party from his pulpit when all the ecclesiastical and secular authorities above him were busy enforcing Nazi policies. Pastor Scharf was disciplined by his denominational leaders and then convicted in the local civil court for audaciously believing "that he doesn't need to obey legal decisions." He was convicted of the crime of "'individualism' in refusing to acknowledge official church orders."[1] Rather than march in lockstep with those around him, Pastor Scharf took the time to prayerfully think for himself, and his conscience compelled him to defy the authorities. Had Pastor Scharf committed the sin of personal autonomy or was he faithfully following Jesus?

Scharf's story is compelling because he was so unusual, the irritating needle in the haystack pricking at tender Nazi toes. Tragically, most of the German haystack, most Christian church members, were not following Scharf's lead, though he and others like him implored them to follow. Most citizens were performing exactly as they were instructed by Nazi authorities, many of them doing what they were told without question, much less protest. Very few shared in Scharf's brand of "individualism" as he was evicted from his parish for preaching the truth.

Most human beings seem hardwired to obey authority, which is why a figure like Pastor Scharf grabs our attention. He is the exception to the rule, and that is unfortunate because the human penchant to obey authority figures blindly, regardless of the authorities' moral standing or the propriety of their commands, has been one of the open, festering sores of human history. This tendency provides the seedbed for suicide bombers; it constructs a hothouse for discrimination and apartheid; it becomes the playground of genocide and ethnic cleansing, where Hutu kill Tutsi, Turks gun down Armenians, and Serbs slaughter Croatians—simply because they are following orders and doing what everyone else is doing around them. C. P. Snow observed, "When you think of the long and gloomy history of man, you will find more hideous crimes have been committed in the name of obedience than have ever been committed in the name of rebellion."[2]

Whether this tendency toward obedience to authority and social conformity is an evolutionary adaptation enhancing group survival or a trait designed by the Creator to facilitate obedience to God's direction, there is no doubt that in this fallen world such servility becomes a double-edged sword, inflicting harm as well as nurturing the good.[3] Not all authority is just or legitimate, and some commands should never be obeyed, no matter what their source is. Consider another example, not of defiance but of compliance. In 2004, a man claiming to be "Officer Scott" called more than seventy fast-food restaurants across America and instructed the manager on duty to isolate a female employee who had ostensibly been accused of stealing from a customer. The agreeable managers were given increasingly perverse instructions on how to interrogate, undress, strip-search, and sexually abuse their coworkers. The vast majority of the managers followed "Officer Scott's" instructions. They may have hesitated, asked questions, or stalled, but when all was said and done, they did as they were told: the managers followed directions and performed sexual assault on their co-workers, while the employees submitted to their managers and surrendered themselves to abuse.[4] All of them will spend the rest of their lives wondering how they possibly could have performed (or surrendered to) such repugnant acts simply because an unknown voice told them to do so over the phone.

When must we do as we are told, and when must we resist? As citizens of God's kingdom, Christian disciples find the meaning of their lives in a relationship with a Savior who asks for their complete obedience. Jesus is Lord. We are the Lord's servants, and failure to carry out his instructions is sin. Jesus warned his followers: "Not everyone who says to me, 'Lord, Lord,' will enter the kingdom of heaven, but only the one *who does the will* of my Father" (Matt. 7:21). He goes on to commend the "wise builder" because "he hears these words of mine and *puts them into practice*" (Matt. 7:24), unlike the foolish builder, who hears what Jesus says but does nothing about it.

Responding obediently to divine authority is an essential ingredient for kingdom citizenship. But this is easier said than done in a world where discerning God's voice presumes spiritual attentiveness and sensitivity to someone called the Holy Spirit. Let's face it, God is invisible, and it has been a good two thousand years since anyone slapped Jesus on the back after telling a good joke. Heeding the voices we hear coming from the people we can actually see is remarkably simple when compared to obeying the upside-down instructions of an invisible God, who sometimes asks us to walk alone in the opposite direction from everyone else. This is especially true when the human authorities hold positions that we have been taught to respect and trust, or that claim to speak with divine authority. Is that voice in my head and the churning in my gut really God's prompting, or is it only my imagination?

Though I have used two dramatic examples to introduce the concerns of this chapter, we all regularly face the challenge of knowing when to submit and when to disobey authority. Often the authority is as seemingly benign as public opinion, the status quo, cultural expectations, tradition, or peer pressure. Yet, for a people who believe they have been called out of darkness into the light, who understand that living by the standards of God's kingdom will frequently put them at odds with the practices and expectations of a fallen world, defying authority in some way should be common practice. Perhaps it means befriending the outcast shunned by everyone else at school. Or calling friends to account for laughing at a racist remark. Paul's admonition in Romans 13:5—to act "because of conscience"—is one of the implications he draws from Romans 12:2: "Do not conform any longer to the pattern of this world, but be transformed by the renewing of your mind" (see chapter 4, above). Learning to defy the patterns of this world by renewing our minds after the model of Jesus and cultivating a genuinely Christian conscience requires learning when, where, and how to disobey any authority, no matter how familiar, issuing wrongful directives, regardless of the consequences. From this perspective, every Christian is called to be a dissident. Discipleship is the life of dissent from this world in the affirmation of Jesus and his kingdom.

How can the example of Pastor Scharf be replicated more widely throughout the church? Assuming that we can all agree that he did the right thing in defying Nazi authorities, and that he defied those authorities, not out of sheer cussedness, but in obedience to Jesus Christ, how might we learn to cultivate the kind of dissident individualism that got him defrocked, that has led Christian martyrs to their doom, and that pointed Jesus to his cross? Not every disciple is asked to suffer such dramatic consequences, but all are called to march to the beat of a different drummer, wherever that drummer may take them.

Teaching Disciples to Say No

First Peter 2:13–20 offers a discussion of Christian citizenship in language similar to Paul's advice in Romans 13:1–7. Of particular importance is Peter's emphasis on "submitting to," as opposed to obeying, governing authorities while following one's individual conscience (vv. 13, 19).[5] A great deal could be said in exploring this passage, but I will focus on only two points. First, I note how Peter's lesson on submission is set within the framework of the disciple's dual citizenship and two different sets of relational priorities (v. 17). Second, Peter goes on to describe a dramatic example of Christian faithfulness when the relational priorities of these two kingdoms collide (vv. 18–20).

In verse 17, Peter reminds his readers that followers of Jesus live in two different realms simultaneously. Each realm has its own populations and rulers, and God's people distinguish between them. We can see these distinctions clearly when we analyze the verse's structure. Verse 17 is a four-part sentence with a chiastic structure: this means that the first half of the sentence is mirrored by the second half. Line one (A) is mirrored in line four (A′): the two phrases are linked by (1) the repetition of the word "honor" and (2) a focus on the church's external relations with society at large (everyone and the king). Similarly, lines two (B) and three (B′) mirror each other: both lines address the believer's internal relationships with the church community and with God. By setting up the structure this way, Peter draws a distinction between the Christian's obligations to civil society and its rulers, on the one hand, and the believer's loving devotion to the body of Christ and its Savior God, on the other hand.

> A: honor everyone (external, secular)
>   B: love the brotherhood (internal, spiritual)
>   B′: fear God (internal, spiritual)
> A′: honor the king (external, secular)

Believers must show respect to everyone they meet, regardless of who they are, whether commoner or king. The average laborer is as worthy of honor as those on the loftiest tier of royalty, and the emperor is no more deserving of deference than is the lowliest peasant.[6] Peter is hinting at a revolutionary egalitarianism that sticks out like a sore thumb within the context of first-century Greco-Roman culture, where the poor were often maligned, slaves composed the bulk of the empire's labor force, and slaveowners could legally beat, maim, rape, and execute their human property any time they wished.[7]

Disciples were also to be unique in the way they dealt with one another. Verse 17 contrasts the Christian's relationship to those outside of the community of faith with the loving relationships created among brothers and sisters inside the church. Jesus followers all become members of a new family, God's family, a community deserving love and devotion that goes far beyond mere honor and respect.

The second point for our purposes arises in verses 18–20. Here Peter depicts a situation so foreign to our modern sensibilities that contemporary readers, including some commentators, can easily overlook it altogether.[8] Peter recognizes that there may be times when Christian slaves must disobey their pagan masters—a terrifying prospect for any slave who valued her life. After reminding slaves that submitting to "everyone" (v. 13) includes submitting to their masters "with all respect" (v. 18), Peter adds a curious twist to his argument. Verse 19 applauds anyone who "bears up under the pain of unjust suffering because of a conscious commitment to God," in which case "you suffer for doing good and endure it—this is commendable before God" (vv. 19, 20b, my translation).

Notice two things. First, the Christian slave described in verse 19 is suffering unjustly. She has not done anything wrong (at least as far as God and Peter are concerned), but she is being punished nonetheless. Second, the slave's disobedience was motivated by her "conscious commitment to God," and God commended her actions even as she suffered the master's displeasure. The Christian slave has faced a serious dilemma: the master commanded her to do something that violated her Christian conscience (v. 19). She considered her options, undoubtedly prayed for divine guidance, and then made the choice that no sensible slave should ever make: she deliberately disobeyed the owner who held her life in his hands, thereby submitting to the consequences.

First Peter 2:18-20 describes one of the most dramatic examples of civil disobedience in the New Testament. A slave, typically considered a nonentity, a nonperson with no right to a personal opinion, certainly with no right to an opinion at variance with her master's, has found salvation in Jesus Christ. Now, with instruction and encouragement from her Christian brothers and sisters, she has self-consciously begun to live her life in order to please the Lord Jesus; she is now God's slave first and foremost. The cultural status quo no longer defines her place in the world. Earthly barriers, limitations, demands, and power structures cannot be the final arbiters of what she can hope, dream, think, say, or do. She has become a citizen in the kingdom of God, which means that she will honor her human master, but he cannot control her life completely. Her highest obligation now is to follow Jesus, the Lord who teaches her to live an upside-down existence in accordance with God's upside-down values. Thus, when the master's command is questionable to her, which is itself a shockingly rebellious admission—for a slave actively to cultivate independent thinking—a godly conscience becomes more compelling than the whip. Her submission to unjust suffering is the final proof that the kingdom of God has arrived, that this world is not the slave's true home, that reality has been redefined, that worldly authorities cannot control us unless we let them, and that no personal possession is as precious as the purity of an undefiled, godly conscience.

Justice has also been redefined by the gospel, though society does not know it. What Roman law defined as a just punishment—for no slave has the right to disobey a master—the kingdom of God declares unjust, for obedience to Jesus is always the higher calling no matter whose human interests are contradicted. Stanley Hauerwas aptly captures the issues as stake in this human drama when he says, "Rightly witnessed to, the gospel so transforms the social vision of those who receive it that the result appears . . . *to be a form of craziness.*"[9] So we return to our question: What personal qualities are required in order to become such a crazy, obedient slave, and how may they be cultivated so as to become normative throughout the church? I believe that someone named Milgram can help us find an answer.

Shocking People to Death

Dr. Stanley Milgram was a young psychology professor at Yale University in 1960 when he began his now famous experiments regarding obedience to authority. As a young Jewish academic, reflecting on the extermination of six million European Jews by Nazi Germany, he wondered whether such horrors were possible in his own country, the United States. While popular opinion insisted that such crimes could never happen in America, Professor Milgram was more cynical—and realistic. He suspected that, given the right (or wrong) circumstances, the basic goodness of a people (whether German or American) had little relationship to their ability to cause harm when following orders. So Milgram created an ingenious experiment to test his hypothesis, an experiment he reproduced in nineteen different variations with one thousand participants, ages twenty to fifty, seeking to isolate and understand the importance of different factors in the behavioral equation of obedience to authority.[10]

Participants responded to an advertisement looking for volunteers to participate in an education experiment. The premise of the experiment was to learn about the effect that punishment has on memory and learning. Three people were involved: the researcher, who posted the advertisement, a teacher, and a student. The student was strapped into a chair, typically in a separate room where she could not be seen, with an electrode attached to her arm. She was told that she would have to learn a series of word pairs, and she would receive an electric shock of increasing intensity every time she made a mistake. While listening to these instructions the student, who actually was not a volunteer but an actor secretly in league with the researcher, mentioned that she had a heart condition and wondered aloud about the danger of receiving electric shocks. With the unwitting teacher (the only one of the three who was actually a volunteer) standing beside her, the researcher assured the student that the shocks would not be harmful.

The teacher was then seated before an impressive-looking "shock generator" with a row of thirty switches ranging from 15 to 450 volts. The teacher was to ask the student a series of questions about the matching word pairs. When the student gave a correct answer, the teacher moved on to the next question. When the student gave an incorrect answer, the teacher was told to pull a switch giving the student an electric shock, moving sequentially up the row of switches administering a higher level shock with each incorrect answer until the maximum level of electricity, 450 volts, was reached.

What the volunteer teacher did not know was that the impressive-looking generator did not actually produce any electricity. The person answering the questions was never really shocked. She was an actor scripted to begin complaining and protesting when the shocks reached 75 volts. Following her script, the complaints gradually increased; eventually, the complaints became screams. At 150 volts the panicked student demanded to be released. If the teacher hesitated or suggested that the student should be relieved and the experiment stopped, the researcher calmly insisted that the teacher must continue until every shock level had been completed. The screams and protests persisted until the unseen student fell silent at 330 volts, apparently due to her heart condition. Even then, the researcher insisted that the questions and the shocks must go on, so that, as far as the teachers knew, they were administering electric shocks to an inert, perhaps even dead, body.[11]

Before publicizing the results of his research, Milgram surveyed an assortment of people, including psychiatrists, college professors, undergraduate and graduate students, and middle-class adults. After explaining the nature of his experiment, he asked them to predict both how they would behave in this situation and how the actual participants behaved.[12] One hundred percent of those surveyed insisted that they would disobey the researcher at some point and stop administering the shocks, typically when the student began protesting. They also gave their fellow human beings the benefit of the doubt, predicting that only a tiny fringe of sociopathic personalities would have proceeded beyond the student's first complaints of pain.

Unfortunately, most of us believe that we are better than we are, and few of us come to grips with how bad we can be. The shocking truth (no pun intended) is that 65 percent of Milgram's subjects continued to shock their victim to the maximum level possible, long after the screams and pleading had given way to ominous silence. Some volunteers did eventually refuse to cooperate, but they were a definite minority. Milgram's results are no less disturbing today than they were almost sixty years ago, especially in light of a 2010 French television program that reproduced Milgram's experiment. On live television, 80 percent of the contestants continued shocking the students long after they cried out in pain and begged to be released.[13] Undoubtedly, the fevered chants of the studio audience, stomping their feet and urging the contestants to continue with higher and higher levels of pain, were a factor in the 15 percent increase of French sociopathy over Milgram's Americans.

Dissecting Authority

What Dr. Milgram's experiment demonstrates is that the decisions we make and the actions we take are rarely if ever determined by personal values alone. We mistakenly assume that individuals are the primary source of their own behavior, acting according to their own personal code of ethics. In fact, nothing could be further from the truth. Nobody makes moral decisions in splendid isolation. We are all rather like a lump of clay sitting at the center of a lifelong collective art project, continually being shaped by our peers, molded by our place in the social hierarchy, refashioned by group expectations, and influenced by the demands of authority figures and our own sense of self-preservation.[14] Given the right circumstances, these group dynamics can override individual values, leading normal people to do monstrous things. Many of Milgram's subjects surprised themselves at the intense levels of pain they were able to inflict on another human being, violating their own deeply held moral code of not hurting another person. One man confessed, "What appalled me was that I could possess this capacity for obedience and compliance."[15] Milgram concluded that, for most people, the power of an authority figure to shape human behavior is overwhelming. He warns: "Relatively few people have the resources needed to resist authority. . . . It is not the substance of the command but its source in authority that is of decisive importance."[16] In the end, Milgram laments the "capacity for man to abandon his humanity, indeed, the inevitability that he does so, as he merges his unique personality into larger institutional structures. This is a fatal flaw nature has designed into us."[17]

Milgram performed his experiment in numerous variations in order to identify the different elements that bind authority figures to their followers. Making changes to these relational components can affect the authority figure's influence. We will focus on only two of these traits, although I highly recommend that the reader take a look at Milgram's published results to learn about the other factors involved. We will look at these two aspects of authority to better understand the role they can play in teaching Christians how (1) to distinguish legitimate from illegitimate authority and (2) to cultivate a Christian conscience that will stand firmly with Christ even if it means standing alone against earthly authority.

Justifying Authority

First, Milgram explains that *authority ties itself to a message that explains and legitimates the authority and its decisions.* For instance, the researcher explains the design of her experiment, how it will work, what the results will be, and how it will eventually benefit society. A convincing explanation legitimates whatever actions are called for by the experiment, even if it includes giving electric shocks to a screaming volunteer.

Or consider the televised speech of the president of the United States explaining why he believes the nation must go to war. He sits in the Oval Office, the presidential seal on his desk, marshaling what he insists is the crucial evidence from his military advisors, applauding the constitutional distinctives of the United States of America, explaining how another war is supposedly unavoidable if we hope to maintain world peace. Nine times out of ten the public stands to applaud.

Persuasive messaging is vital to authority. Whether that message comes in the guise of politics, philosophy, theology, ideology, theory, or propaganda, an authority figure creates legitimacy through the power of a convincing explanation. Effective messaging allows listeners to believe that their obedience is serving a desirable end, no matter how distasteful their obedience to those demands may be. The ends justify the means, at least when the authority's words are convincing. "Control the manner in which a man interprets his world, and you have gone a long way toward controlling his behavior."[18]

If the message is repeated often enough, and the listener becomes convinced enough, the authority's explanation is eventually assimilated into the person's understanding of the world. It is no longer questioned; it is assumed and becomes the believer's default position, so that any new evidence challenging or contradicting the accepted message is automatically dismissed or ignored.[19] Do you remember your last political debate with someone who only watches the news from one particular television network? How open was that person to new evidence or counterarguments offered from a different perspective? Once the content of repetitious messaging has been excused from answering questions posed by critical thinking, then it has become indoctrination: that is, a strongly held belief having its own internal logic, self-evident only to believers, hovering above the messy world of counterevidence and public demonstration.

But politicians, demagogues, and advertising agencies are not the only ones who use the power of messaging. The Christian church also has a message that requires communication. We first hear this message through the gospel of Jesus Christ. It is then elaborated through regular Bible study into a comprehensive way of living, where obeying the Lord Jesus is life's guiding directive. Christians discover what God asks of them by becoming familiar with the sound of his voice. Recognizing God's voice is a gift to faithful, long-time students of his word who put the Lord's directions into practice. This is how a depraved human mind is slowly transformed into the redeemed mind of Christ (Rom. 12:2). It is a process called sanctification, and it is neither easy nor automatic. Our human tendency is to cling to as much of the old, unredeemed mindset as possible, minimizing the amount of Christ-like upside-down transformation occurring and protectively maximizing the old-time, business-as-usual worldview preserved from our pre-Christian attitudes on life. It is a lifelong contest for supremacy.

In this respect, every disciple resembles the character Gollum in Tolkien's *The Lord of the Rings* trilogy. Gollum is a slobbering, pathetic subterranean creature, clawing and clutching feverishly at his "precious" ring, unwilling to let it go. For Christians, our own "precious" thing is the carnal mindset and consequent immorality that we spent a lifetime inhaling from the materialistic atmosphere swirling around us before we first met Jesus. Allowing these precious, unredeemed preconceptions to be challenged, torn down, and re-placed by the new, regenerate mind of Jesus is so difficult that it sometimes never happens.[20] Occasionally, a dramatic historical event will pull back the ecclesiastical curtain to reveal the truth about God's people and about whose mind is truly precious to them.

Professor David Gushee has written an important book about one such moment in church history, entitled *The Righteous Gentiles of the Holocaust: A Christian Interpretation*. Gushee's work describes the personal characteristics of those Christians who risked their lives, by disobeying civil and military authorities, in order to rescue Jews from the extermination camps of Nazi Germany.[21] We will focus on only two of Gushee's many important observations.

Of primary significance, Gushee observes that Bible reading and prayer were regular disciplines among the few Christians who helped to rescue Jews. Many of them could describe a deeply personal religious experience that motivated their activities. Their character had been shaped by the diverse scriptural teachings (especially in the four Gospels) on grace, compassion, empathy for those who suffer, obedience to God, Christian duty, and the importance of sound theological thinking over and above political allegiance.[22] Repetitious exposure to the biblical priority of following Jesus, no matter how difficult the journey, had become the default position for their lives.[23] Jesus must be followed and obeyed even at the risk of breaking human laws, for his message was the word of the kingdom of God that superseded everything else in life, whereas the Nazi message pertained only to the kingdom of this world, the realm from which Christians had been redeemed.

Strength in Numbers

Although the decision to break the law by rescuing Jews may seem an obvious choice to us today, we should not forget that only a few in Germany actually made that difficult decision. The majority of German Christians offered no outward objections to Nazi policies. For instance, not a single public protest was ever launched by a Protestant church leader against Germany's euthanasia laws when they were implemented.[24] When push came to shove, bad theology, fear, rationalizing, and self-preservation all trumped actualizing the gospel message, which leads us to Gushee's second, tragic observation.

Christian rescuers were few and far between.[25] Rescuers, in general, were the exception to the rule in World War II; but rescuers claiming to be motivated by their Christian faith were rare even among this small group of heroes. This lamentable fact (at least lamentable for me as a Christian) requires a deeper analysis than we can give to it here, but it certainly illustrates just how difficult and unusual it is for self-professed Christians to give themselves over *completely* to the thoroughgoing, inside-out transformation desired by Christ.[26] The widespread nature of this spiritual challenge is illustrated time and again by the historians who study the Christian church in Nazi Germany. For example, Richard Steigmann-Gall's research on Nazi views of Christianity concludes: "Christianity, in the final analysis, did not constitute a barrier to Nazism. Quite the opposite: For many . . . the battles waged against Germany's enemies constituted a war in the name of Christianity. . . . Nearly all the Nazis surveyed here believed they were defending good by waging war against evil, fighting for God against the Devil, for German against Jew."[27]

This is a chilling conclusion for anyone who loves Jesus.

My point in turning our attention to Nazi Germany is not to single out the German church or to suggest that the Third Reich was the only disastrous political movement that has co-opted Christianity and bastardized the gospel.[28] I have chosen these examples from the history of Nazi Germany because this is one of the few episodes in modern history that is relatively free of partisan wrangling. Almost everyone, regardless of nationality, political persuasion, or religion, will agree that Adolf Hitler and his Nazi doctrine were a consummate evil. I am confident that the majority of my readers will agree—whether their politics are Republican, Democratic, independent, socialist, Green Party, libertarian, or anarchist—that the bulk of the German church, both Protestant and Catholic, allowed the rules of this-worldly citizenship to smother their responsibilities as citizens of God's kingdom.[29] No one in a church composed of true pilgrims, strangers, and aliens in this world could ever uniformly adhere to the policies of the Nazi Party.

From this shared starting point, let me go on to say something that is perhaps more provocative: There is a close analogy to be made between the behavior of the American church today and that of the German church in 1933. No, America may not face the reincarnation of Adolf Hitler or National Socialism (whatever the current administration's political opponents may say). But, like the people of Germany, we all live within a shared moral universe that defines both good and evil and then brings various forces to bear in pressuring us to conform. The Nazis managed to create a moral universe where racism and brutality were approved, even encouraged. The German people behaved accordingly. Anti-Semitism and eugenics were morally good, while racial integration and opposition to the state were morally evil. Peter Haas rightly insists that "the Holocaust was not the incarnation of evil but instead reflected the human power to reconceive good and evil and then to shape society in the light of the new conception."[30]

Haas offers a crucial insight. Whether we recognize it or not, we all live within analogous ethical systems, where we blithely accept cultural definitions of good and evil without exercising any critical thinking. The issue is not the particular guise adopted by evil—whether it wears the face of Nazism, communism, consumerism, capitalism, imperialism, racism, or the class system—but the fact that evil always exists without always being self-evident to us. The moral universe created by twenty-first-century America is not identical with the moral universe envisioned by the gospel of Jesus Christ. But that will be shocking news to many members of the church in America. This confusion makes the American church typical. The bulk of the German church did not fail because it was German but because it was human. The burdensome millstone hanging from the neck of world history is sinful human nature, a human nature that would rather create its own moral universe than live obediently in God's. When given a choice, human nature always prefers to cling to its own precious, self-serving ideologies (no matter how idiotic, uninformed, xenophobic, or grotesque) over the self-renunciation, self-sacrifice, and servanthood demanded by the gospel of Jesus Christ. Therefore, all Christians of every nation must ask themselves in a spirit of repentance, humility, and self-examination: What kind of moral universe is the church inhabiting today? What redefinitions of good and evil have we accepted for our own cultural convenience? What kinds of immorality are we ignoring, or even heartily endorsing, because we are more heavily invested in partisan politics, nationalism, capitalism, consumerism, discrimination, and the many other idolatrous ephemera born of the kingdom of this world than we are in following Jesus Christ?

The Benefits and Dangers of Community

The second factor highlighted by Milgram in his examination of the different ingredients empowering authority was *peer influence*. The company we keep is more determinative of personal behavior than many of us suspect, for both good and bad. Most actions become easier with the support of others, especially when those actions are subversive. And when the action means compliance with the status quo, it becomes mindless repetition. Milgram discovered that if a hesitant teacher was able to watch other teachers successfully refusing to shock their pleading students, then levels of disobedience rose dramatically. In fact, 90 percent of Milgram's teachers defied the researcher and refused to shock their students any further after watching several of their peers (who were also in league with the researcher) successfully disobey instructions.[31] Milgram's conclusion is vital: "When an individual wishes to stand in opposition to authority, he does best to find support for his position from others in his group. The mutual support provided . . . for each other is the strongest bulwark we have against the excesses of authority."[32]

It comes as no surprise, then, to learn that the majority of Christian rescuers during World War II were bolstered by a support network of like-minded people, whether in the local church or elsewhere, who all shared in the dangers, encouraging one another along the way.[33] That ancient slave who finally screwed up enough courage to say "No" to her master knew that she was not acting by herself. Although no one else could suffer the master's beating for her, she was sustained by a family of brothers and sisters in Christ who also believed that her act of civil disobedience was a necessary step in following Jesus. She knew they were praying for her; they loved her and would be there to tend her wounds, take her into their homes, clothe her, and feed her if need be. She could rest in the knowledge that she would not face her owner's wrath alone.

Unfortunately, the dark side of human nature means that there is also a dark side to community, including Christian community. The same group dynamics that support positive transformation can also blind a person to his own gradual corruption if the group is corrupt. Sebastian Haffner's autobiography, *Defying Hitler: A Memoir*, is a fascinating testimony to the infectious, corrupting power of a community bound together for evil purposes.[34] Haffner was staunchly opposed to Hitler, National Socialism, and everything the Third

Reich was doing to his country. Yet, as he finished his university law degree, the government imposed a new requirement forcing all graduates to attend a Nazi indoctrination camp before they could take the bar exam. Refusing to attend this camp meant losing the chance to practice law.

Haffner was certain that his hatred for Hitler was unshakable. It would serve him well as a protective shield against the Nazis' ideological bombardment, insulating his true self against any unwanted changes. He would enter the camp an anti-Nazi, and he would exit it the same way. What Haffner had underestimated, however, were the sly and subtle ways in which members of a group conform themselves to one another, whether they intend to or not, whether the group behavior is admirable or not. To his utter horror, Haffner confesses that, by the time the camp had concluded, he was talking, behaving, and thinking like a Nazi. The man who began by hating Hitler was now clicking his boots, shouting "Sieg Heil," and meaning it. Inch by miserable inch, he had surrendered his scruples to the camaraderie—to the fellowship—of his enforced Nazi community. Toward the close of his memoir, Haffner agonizes: "I realized that I was well and truly in a trap. I should never have come to the camp. Now I was in the *trap of comradeship.* . . . 'We' had become a collective entity and with all the intellectual cowardice and dishonesty of a collective being we instinctively ignored or belittled anything that could disturb our collective self-satisfaction. . . . It was remarkable how *comradeship actively decomposed all the elements of individualism.*"[35]

The ethos of fellowship and group support can either elevate the individual to stand apart, to think independently, and to act heroically, or it can destroy the individual by pulling her down into the quagmire of conformity, where mindlessly repeating the group's scripted mantras can pass for brilliance and even earn a PhD.[36]

Navigating Uncertainty

The church father Augustine of Hippo wrote in his *Confessions*: "You have made us for yourself, O Lord, and our heart is restless until it rests in you."[37] Augustine was reflecting on humanity's need to walk in obedient fellowship with the Creator. I cannot help but wonder if the innate human desire to submit to authority is a twisted remnant of that particular restlessness, originally placed within us for our own good: an urge to hear, follow, and obey the sovereign Lord who wants to lead us in the ways of blessing, goodness, and worship. I imagine that a collection of such obedient individuals, all responding instinctively to the same desire to obey God, would quickly form a beautiful human community, where serving one another's best interests would not be the exception but the rule.

Yet, having lost touch with the Creator and deliberately disconnected our need for authority from the supreme authority, our quest for new authority figures has become one of humanity's greatest failings. We run from God's direction, wanting our independence, only to wander into the waiting arms of a thousand lesser demigods who are happy to exploit us for their own purposes. The ability to torture another human being, pull the switch on the gas chambers, and gun down innocent women and children is not an unusually repulsive ability possessed by only a few bad apples. As Milgram has shown, this "is normal human behavior" when following orders.[38] And the crimes do not need to be this dramatic. Despising and neglecting the poor simply because they are poor; clutching at our wealth while bypassing the needy all around us; labeling or discriminating against others because they are not like us—all these behaviors, and a million more like them, are evil acts thoughtlessly committed in the normal course of daily life because we have surrendered our minds and wills to another deceitful, corrupting authority speaking from an ungodly moral universe. Such authorities surround us. They take the form of talk-show hosts, pastors, politicians, teachers, radio personalities, authors, financial advisors, even friends and family. They also pressure us in the more diffuse forms of peer pressure, cultural expectations, tradition, corporate climates, office memos, performance standards, and classroom lectures.

Disciples need to keep their eyes riveted on Jesus Christ while exercising the habits of critical discernment. As I have mentioned above, two essential factors in protecting ourselves against fraudulent, misguided authority figures are (1) remaining faithful students of the Bible who not only study God's word but implement the lessons we learn, and (2) finding support for our biblically informed lifestyle among like-minded disciples who will fortify the courage necessary to protest and disobey whatever authorities are competing against the ethics of Jesus.

By way of conclusion, then, let me briefly offer a few practical suggestions for implementing these practices.

First, remember that we all will one day stand before God's throne to give an account of our lives (1 Cor. 3:12-15; 2 Cor. 5:10). I will be responsible for what I have done or not done, in obedience or disobedience to Jesus. No one else can stand in my place. And I cannot stand up for anyone else. Christian discipleship concerns the believing individual's taking the risk of launching out into the midst of uncertainty to follow Jesus wherever he leads.[39] Thus the primary question for all my Bible study becomes: Have I heard his voice directing me in this passage, and how will I respond? Naturally, posing the question in this way leaves plenty of room for the misinformed and the unhinged to make a mess out of Bible reading.

But what else is new?

There will never be a sufficient consensus on anything in this life—including biblical interpretation and social activism—to eliminate all of life's uncertainties. If we act only in the absence of uncertainty, then we will never do anything but wait and invent new excuses for our inactivity. Living a biblically directed life is the only way to deconstruct the false moral universes erected by this world and replace them with the moral universe created by the kingdom of God. Of course, as long as we remain in this world, we are partially blinded and crippled by the misshapen universe we are working to leave behind, so our interpretations and conclusions must be held lightly. *But they must be held*. Uncertainty never justifies apathy.

Second, there comes a time when the individual must act and act alone if necessary, while being prepared to accept the consequences of those actions, whatever they may be. It is no accident that Peter Haas introduces his discussion of Germany's Christian rescuers by saying: "A common feature of any principled dissent . . . [is] that the rescuers are *deviants*, people who are *misfits* in their society. . . . [Their actions] grew out of the rescuers' experience as social and political *outcasts*."[40] Principled individualism, what the status quo will always condemn as the deviant behavior of misfits and outcasts, is the distinguishing characteristic of Christian faithfulness in this fallen world.

Unfortunately, there are many pious voices that want to sedate this brand of individualism by wrapping it up tightly in the maudlin, anesthetic gauze of "community life." Christian gatherings easily become the most repressive, stultifying crowds that squash the last vestige of creative individualism from their members: Never act alone. Never step out of line. Never speak when others are quiet. Never question authority. Never doubt what everyone else believes. Never question the way it has always been done. Never try to think outside the box. These are the conformist platitudes repeated by the crowd in its self-serving attempts to constrain passionate individuals, preventing them from acting for the sake of conscience.[41] At times the Christian church has become the most oppressive, do-nothing herd of them all.

So we must learn to discern the difference between a fellowship that participates in God's kingdom and a collective that exists only to replicate carbon copies of the citizens of this world. I can recall two epic decisions in my life where I became convinced that God was calling my wife and me to make a radical, risky change in the course of our lives. In both instances, the leaders of our local church told us that we were making a terrible mistake, that God would never lead us in the directions we were considering. However, I took these warnings with a very large grain of salt because I knew that they were the natural outgrowth of an upbringing in a particular denominational tradition. My friends were reflecting the prejudices of a moral universe that I did not share.

I also knew what the Spirit was urging me to do. And in both instances there was a small circle of friends who prayed with my wife and me and studied God's word with us, and who also encouraged us to trust in the Lord, to move forward in faith despite the uncertainties, and to do what we needed to do in following Jesus. In retrospect, I can say unequivocally that in both cases the pastor and elders were wrong in discouraging us from acting. My wife and I would have missed out on some of the most transformational and miraculous experiences of our young lives had we not taken the risk of breaking from the crowd and acting independently in obedience to what we believed was God's call.

I began this chapter by telling the heroic story of Pastor Scharf and wondering how the church could reproduce his example more widely. Annemarie Grosch was asking herself the same question as she reflected on her life in the German church after the war. Ms. Grosch had been a staunch member of the Confessing Church, which had resisted Hitler's attempts to control the church in Germany. In explaining why the resistance was so small, she mused, "You can't demand that an entire people be full of heroes."[42]

Is that true? I wonder.

Even if it is unreasonable to expect an entire nation to be full of heroes, an altogether different standard must be applied to citizens of God's kingdom. This is not just any nation. If heroism is defined as exemplifying the character of Jesus when society insists that you cannot live that way; if it means loving your neighbor when your compassion invites harassment and danger to your door; if it means acting alone after everyone else has abandoned you; if it means ostracism, suffering, or even death because you are convinced it is the only way to follow your Lord faithfully—then Ms. Grosch is mistaken. Every citizen of God's kingdom is commanded to be a dissident hero. According to Christ's standards, what we call heroism, the New Testament calls discipleship.

Discussion Questions

1. Have you ever found yourself in a situation where your Christian principles brought you into conflict with someone else's expectations? How did you handle the situation?

2. Can you think of some authority figures (legitimate or illegitimate) who have had too much control over your life? What adjustments can you make in order for the lordship of Jesus to have more prominence over these other figures?

3. What contemporary issues need to be critiqued and/or corrected by the Christian church today? Explain the biblical basis for your answer. What might be a strategy that could make progress on this issue?

Additional Reading

Bonhoeffer, Dietrich. *The Cost of Discipleship*. New York: Macmillan, 1963.

Chaleff, Ira. *Intelligent Disobedience: Doing Right When What You're Told to Do Is Wrong*. Oakland, CA: Berrett-Koehler, 2015.

Gushee, David P. *The Righteous Gentiles of the Holocaust: A Christian Interpretation*. Minneapolis: Fortress, 1994.

Kierkegaard, Søren. *Practice in Christianity*. Princeton: Princeton University Press, 1991.

Milgram, Stanley. *Obedience to Authority*. New York: Harper Perennial, 2009.

Press, Eyal. *Beautiful Souls: Saying No, Breaking Ranks, and Heeding the Voice of Conscience in Dark Times*. New York: Farrar, Straus and Giroux, 2012.

Stassen, Glen Harold. *A Thicker Jesus: Incarnational Discipleship in a Secular Age*. Louisville: Westminster John Knox, 2012.

Chapter Eight

Taking Exception to Exceptionalism

It was a Fourth of July weekend in the rural western state where my wife and I often spent our vacations and currently reside. We typically visited different local churches during our stay, and this Sunday we decided to try out a new Baptist church that we had never seen before. As we stepped inside the small wooden sanctuary, we were warmly welcomed by everyone we met. Up front, where I would normally have expected to see the pulpit or a lectern, was the impressively constructed bow of an old sailing ship, with a sizable mast extending to the ceiling. I eventually guessed that the boat was supposed to represent a pilgrim ship landing at Plymouth Rock.

The opening hymn was announced, and everyone stood to sing a rousing rendition of "America the Beautiful." Successive "Scripture readings" consisted of excerpts from the Declaration of Independence and the US Constitution, especially the Bill of Rights, all recited at the appropriate liturgical moments by a rugged gentleman in cowboy boots who spoke in a deep baritone voice and sported a beautiful handlebar mustache. The remaining worship hymns consisted of "The Battle Hymn of the Republic" and "God Bless America." Eventually, we were offered a sermon on the blessings of American freedom—vaguely rooted in halfhearted connections to Romans 8:1-4—and the freedom now available to us through the Holy Spirit.

Though I did not doubt the Christian faith of the men, women, and children attending this very American worship service on that Independence Day morning, I wish I could have talked with them about their blatant idolatry. The so-called worship service was a consummate example of a brand of civil religion known as "Christian nationalism," the misguided and destructive confusion of love of country—and the ill-defined "God" who blesses that country—with service to Jesus Christ.

The full-frontal display of Christian nationalism described here is not limited to church sanctuaries. I recently saw a Christian fish symbol attached to the back of a black Hummer cruising down the road. This particular fish looked like it had swallowed an entire American flag, its interior emblazoned with red, white, and blue. Or consider the walls of a local restaurant decorated with six-inch crucifixes embroidered in the colors of the stars and stripes. The intended message is straightforward while remaining sufficiently vague to allow room for personal interpretation: America is a Christian nation, God loves America, Christian America performs God's work on earth, or maybe Christian values are synonymous with American values. Who knows? The message is somewhere in that ballpark.

But such ambiguity is no problem for American civil religion. In fact, religious (but definitely not political) ambiguity is essential to its success and longevity, for religious imprecision is required if civil religion hopes to remain civil. "Civil religion . . . permits all beliefs to exist provided none make exclusive claims."[1] This explains why we often hear public officials confess their faith in God, but seldom hear similar statements of surrendering to Jesus Christ. There is a conundrum at the heart of American Christianity's infatuation with civil religion, a conundrum that also defines the oxymoron known as "Christian nationalism."

What's So Civil about Civil Religion?

Civil religion is as old as humankind. Once the earliest cavemen organized themselves into social groups, believing that the health and well-being of their community depended on giving proper attention to the spirits, civil religion was born. The first known Christian discussion of civil religion appears in St. Augustine's treatise *The City of God* (books 6 and 7), which he wrote in order to defend the Christian church against accusations that Rome had fallen to the Visigoths because the church refused to participate in the civic ceremonies of Roman religion.[2] Here the essential ingredients of civil religion are laid bare, whether in Rome or the United States: religious language ("one nation under God"), symbols (the flag, war memorials), and ceremonies (the Pledge of Allegiance, Memorial Day parades) are used to unify a diverse society, undergirding a shared history/mythology and national purpose directed by God, which all validates the power and purposes of the state.[3]

Religious nationalism is the form of civil religion that arises when a specific religion, such as Islam, Hinduism, or Christianity, is married to the fortunes of a particular nation-state. American civil religion has generally been non-sectarian and pluralistic, social values famously embodied in the impromptu remark of President Dwight Eisenhower: "Our form of government has no sense unless it is founded in a deeply felt religious faith, and I don't care what it is."[4] Note that Eisenhower's primary "religious" concern was the preservation of American government, not clarifying the nature of God. The sanctification of a political status quo is characteristic of civil religion. Unsurprisingly, the goal of American civil religion is to unite the varieties of religious devotion found in America under the umbrella of an all-inclusive, shared religious expression, such as "in God we trust," in which the noun "God" serves as a patriotic placeholder inviting each citizen to import whatever religious content he or she prefers. God language, being more malleable than Jesus language, becomes a tool for social engineering.

Christian nationalism, curiously enough, is a particularly narrow expression of civil religion that aims at a very contrarian goal. Far from seeking to unite a religiously diverse population, religious nationalism works to exclude anyone who is not a member of the dominant religious faith. Consequently, religious nationalism is actually a type of political sectarianism that is hostile to the religious pluralism found at the heart of American democracy. Christianity is used to divide people and rally kindred spirits for political, nationalistic purposes. Therefore, Christian nationalism insists that Christianity is the only true national religion, making America an exclusively Christian nation.[5] The concerted efforts of Christian fundamentalists to sift, analyze, and interpret every Founding Father's allusion to providence, faith, and the Bible, no matter how generic or ill defined   as if those allusions were explicit testimony to faith in the redeeming power of the gospel of Jesus Christ—is an especially grotesque symptom of this nationalistic, and very uncivil, obsession to propagate a national myth most conducive to their political beliefs.

I must confess (if you haven't guessed already) that I find all of these symbols of civil religion and Christian nationalism to be highly offensive. And it is not because I do not love my country. I do. Rather, it is because Christian fundamentalists confuse the chest-thumping tribalism of patriotic nationalism with the suffering servanthood of a crucified Savior who died for all the world. Obviously, people who love Jesus can also love their country; but patriotism is no measure of Christian devotion. In fact, they are two different states of mind that are typically fueled by conflicting value systems. Think, for example, of the numerous ways that German Christians displayed their patriotism in the 1930s and 1940s by combining the cross with the swastika after Hitler's rise to power. Nazi flags were prominently displayed in every church sanctuary where pious German Christians worshiped Jesus and, at the same time, gladly confessed their devotion to the Führer as God's anointed leader.[6] These men and women were extremely patriotic, but did their patriotism honor Jesus? Did conformity to the Third Reich cohere with citizenship in the kingdom of God?

Is there any essential difference between the Independence Day service I attended and those patriotic services conducted by German Christians extolling the virtues of Adolf Hitler? Are crosses embroidered in red, white, and blue fundamentally different from crosses draped with swastikas?

No. They are not.

Regardless of the differences between Nazi Germany and modern America, all of these symbols are equally partisan demonstrations of a religious nationalism (or is it nationalistic religion?) offered up by equally sincere—and equally misguided—people convinced that their country, alone among all countries, enjoys a special relationship with God, that their nation is God's anointed instrument for accomplishing God's purposes in history. The kind of passion that deliberately conflates Christ's cross with nationalism and civil religion is also the brand of unthinking zeal that loudly protests any criticism of the confusion, while remaining blind, deaf, and dumb to the substance of the critique. The issue at stake is not that one nation's political program is evil while the other's is virtuous—for we should never forget that one group's political virtue is often another group's horrible despotism, depending on when, where, and how a person was born and raised—but that both sets of symbols hijack the meaning of Jesus's cross for its own political purposes. The gospel is being harnessed to pull a heavy nationalistic bandwagon. But Jesus Christ will not be hijacked. Regardless of the nation, or whoever's national anthem that band happens to be playing, the resurrected Jesus will not carry anyone's yoke of partisan politics, not even America's.

Jesus died and rose again in order to establish the kingdom of God on earth, and that kingdom is never represented by any earthly nation, no matter what its character is. I realize that many Americans will be insulted by my comparisons with Nazi Germany, thinking that the moral chasm separating us from them makes these two expressions of Christian nationalism as different as light is from darkness. Yet, aside from the Christian patriot's dubious assumptions about American virtue, taking umbrage at my conclusion is to miss the point entirely, illustrating how easily national allegiances and cultural embeddedness can override faithfulness to God's reign on earth. The heart of the matter is this: Can any nation, anywhere and at any time, regardless of its culture or political system, claim to be God's chosen people, uniquely commissioned to carry out God's kingdom mission in this world? From a disciple's perspective within the kingdom of God, the only possible answer to that question is no.

The only difference between crucifixes wearing swastikas and crosses embroidered in red, white, and blue is a matter of time, geography, social conditioning and political allegiance. The first symbol reflected the mindset of the mid-twentieth-century German Christian church; the second is a symptom of an identical illness within the twenty-first-century American church. Neither of them is agreeable with biblical Christianity or serious participation in God's kingdom.

The Biblical Roots of Exceptionalism

The many errors of Christian nationalism are rooted in a long-standing concept typically referred to as "American exceptionalism," a belief that the United States is a unique nation, created by God with a special role to play in world history. Accordingly, for many citizens of this country, American foreign policy is by definition God's foreign policy. The United States is carrying out God's work on earth, and we can think this way without the slightest hint of embarrassment over our myopic parochialism. In order to understand the roots of Christian nationalism, we must go back in time almost four thousand years, for the idea of an exceptional nation began, not with the English Pilgrims landing at Plymouth Rock or the Puritans settling in the Massachusetts Bay colony, but with the Old Testament story of Israel conquering the Promised Land. And even though the concept of American exceptionalism has become thoroughly secularized for many people today—concerning themselves with America's form of government, Manifest Destiny, and the mission of spreading democracy, devoid of all religious components—even this secularized tree has its exceptional roots embedded in rich religious soil.

According to the Old Testament, God initiates the story line of a divinely elected nation when he reaches out to a Bronze Age Sumerian by the name of Abram (soon to be renamed Abraham). For no reason other than his own choosing, God introduces himself to Abraham by announcing, "I will make you into a great nation, and I will bless you" (Gen. 12:2). God elaborates this promise to Abraham, now known as the Abrahamic Covenant, on several occasions (Gen. 12:1–7; 13:14–17; 15:1–7; 17:1–21; 22:15–18). Eventually, God fulfilled these promises and led Abraham's descendants, who come to be known as the people of Israel, into a collective covenantal relationship that was to make them a truly exceptional nation.[7] This step is taken in a second agreement (known as the Sinai Covenant), confirmed after Israel's deliverance from Egyptian slavery (Exod. 19:3–20:20). The people of Israel would become, through the

Abrahamic and Sinai covenants, God's own nation with a unique role to play in the salvation of the world.

But even as the Lord affirmed his commitment to Israel's special calling, he also reaffirmed his ongoing sovereignty over all the other nations of the earth. Yahweh initiates the Sinai covenant by saying, "Although the whole earth is mine, you will be for me a kingdom of priests and a holy nation" (Exod. 19:5–6). In calling ancient Israel to its peculiar status, Yahweh clarifies that he is not relinquishing his involvement in the histories of other nations. The whole earth is still his, and the Old Testament will regularly emphasize Yahweh's direct involvement in international affairs.[8]

A clear testament to God's dual concern for humanity appears in the book of Amos, a prophet who asserted both dimensions of God's kingship with equal certainty. Speaking to the Northern Kingdom of Israel, God said:

> You only have I chosen
> of all the nations of the earth;
> therefore I will punish you
> for all your sins. (Amos 3:2)

The prophet is crystal clear: *ancient Israel is the only nation God has ever selected to be his chosen people.* The biblical record is consistent on this score (Deut. 7:6–7). All other claims to national exceptionalism are fraudulent. There is only one possible candidate for the title "exceptional nation," and that is the ancient nation of Israel. Biblically informed people can argue for only Israelite exceptionalism.

Furthermore, the Sinai Covenant added important responsibilities to the promises made in the Abrahamic Covenant, for the new relationship forged at Mount Sinai took on the form of an obligatory covenant. An "if/then" clause was added to God's promises: *if* Israel obeyed, *then* she would be blessed; by implication, if Israel disobeyed, she would be punished (Exod. 19:5). Becoming God's exceptional nation brought great responsibility, including the certainty of divine judgement for Israel's unholy failings whenever she violated the laws of the covenant (Lev. 26:3–45; Deut. 28:1–30:20). Understanding the nature of God's obligatory covenant with Israel is crucial for any discussion of civil religion and religious nationalism today among countries claiming a Christian heritage.

Only *ancient Israel* and her leaders, judges, and kings have ever been promised divine blessings for national covenant faithfulness or punishment for national rebellion. These words have never been extended as a blanket promise that would be free for the taking by any nation presumptuous enough to grab God's favor for itself. That is not the way God's covenants work. Only God can decide whom he will favor. No modern prime minister, president, or parliamentarian can stand up and blithely announce, "We (nation X) will now become God's covenant people on earth!"[9] Consequently, the covenantal promises of blessings for obedience to the covenant and punishments for disobedience are addressed solely to ancient Israel.

It is also important to understand that the obedience at stake is not a general notion of national piety or civic righteousness, such as returning prayer to the public schools or lowering national divorce rates. What the covenant required was nationwide conformity to the Law, Israel's Torah, including the Levitical Code, the sacrificial and dietary laws, the maintenance of a priestly class, the construction of a centralized temple, and much more. Has America, or any other modern nation-state, embedded the Pentateuch into its legal system, established a purified levitical priesthood, and constructed a tabernacle or temple for animal sacrifice according to the Old Testament directives before claiming the blessed status of being God's chosen nation?[10] Not to my knowledge.

Passages such as Leviticus 26:3-45, Deuteronomy 28:1-30:20, and 2 Chronicles 7:11-22—a text I see emblazoned on a large roadside billboard every time I drive from my house into the nearest town, calling for America's return to God so that she will be blessed—which repeat the conditional promises of Israel's covenant, do not offer a blank check to any national group bold enough to cash in on God's account. The widespread failure to understand this point is symptomatic of the lackadaisical approach to Scripture reading shown by too many churchgoers who have never bothered to learn how to read their Bible. Think of how foolish it would be to eavesdrop on a phone conversation between two young lovers while imagining that their romantic cooings were actually intended for you. What sane person would argue that this eavesdropper's perverse twisting of that conversation was simply a matter of competing interpretations?

The Exception to Exceptionalism

But we are not yet finished with Amos. The prophet has more to say about exceptionalism as he goes on to disabuse Israel of its unmerited national arrogance. Israel made the mistake of taking pride in its covenantal status and boasting of its unique relationship with God, as if it were somehow a measure of its own achievement. So Amos reminds Israel that, while it may have been the exceptional nation living in covenant with God, it did not have an exclusive claim on God's interests. Israel was not as exceptional as it thought it was:

> Israel, I am the LORD God,
>> and the Ethiopians
> are no less important to me
>> than you are.
> I brought you out of Egypt,
>> but I also brought
> the Philistines from Crete
>> and the Arameans from Kir. (Amos 9:7, CEV)

Though God had never established a covenant with Egypt, the Ethiopians, the Philistines, or the Arameans, at vital moments in their histories he had been every bit as involved in their national lives as he had been in Israel's. There may not have been a prophetic explanation for the Philistine exodus from Crete, as Yahweh had explained Israel's deliverance from Egypt, but the same God was equally responsible for both. Israel's exceptionalism meant that it could receive specific insight into its national purpose and the manner of its fulfillment, but in making himself Israel's God the Creator had not surrendered one iota of his concern for anyone else. Yahweh remained free to direct any part of world history in any way he saw fit. In this respect, there is *no such thing as an exceptional nation.* Amos 9:7 implies that God works among all nations in ways that only he can explain. He is the cosmic director, though not the puppeteer, standing behind the stage of global history, attending to the role of every national character.

Thus, by claiming a unique, God-given role for the United States in world history, Christian nationalists commit a twofold mistake. First, they try to usurp the promises that God made only once to ancient Israel. Christian nationalism becomes the politics of fantasy, like the deluded stalker eavesdropping on someone else's romantic conversations. Second, in claiming to be the beneficiary of God's peculiar love and attention, America repeats Israel's sin of national arrogance, forgetting that God is involved in the history of every human group. No one can claim exclusive rights to God's editing of their nation's history books.

Claiming Exceptionalism Is Unexceptional

Christian nationalists typically justify this hijacking of God's promises by reading Israel's story mythologically rather than historically. Although the word "myth" implies that a story is fictitious, its most basic sense denotes a story that accounts for how things got to be the way they are, giving answers to our questions about meaning and purpose. National myths are stories "that convey commonly shared convictions on the purposes and the meaning of the nation," often extolling a nation's virtues by editing its history into a national mythology more ideal than real.[11] Ironically, conservative Bible readers, who believe that the book of Exodus records real historical events, can be the most prolific in transforming Israel's story line into the mythological paradigm justifying their own group's status as God's new chosen people.[12] According to this reading, Israel's exodus from Egyptian slavery (Exod. 1:1–14:29) and her conquest of the land of Canaan (see the book of Joshua) are taken as myths that describe the way God continues to deal with poor, oppressed people everywhere.[13]

Appropriating this "Israel mythology" has become commonplace in various strands of liberation, postcolonial, and black theology, all of which interpret God's rescue of enslaved Israel as a model of the work he also intends to do for the landless peasant classes of the world, the poverty-stricken victims of Western colonialism, and the descendants of slavery. According to this reading of the book of Exodus, God wants to lead all suffering people through their own Red Seas and Jordan Rivers, whatever hardships those aquatic obstacles may symbolize today, into a new Promised Land of liberation.

Mythologically harnessing Israel's Exodus story to the sufferings of contemporary groups and their collective aspirations is a well-established practice. To borrow the words of Stephen Grosby, this "myth of ethnic election" has been a major factor in forging and solidifying the national identities of many groups standing in the Judeo-Christian tradition.[14] The picture of a special people occupying a special land; once oppressed but now blessed; enjoying a protective relationship with God; called out for a special mission in this world—this picture will eventually become the paradigm for "Christian nationhood" in Western civilization and those non-Western nations influenced by Western colonialism. Let me offer a small selection of examples to make the point.

In medieval Europe, the early fourteenth-century pope Clement V issued a papal proclamation (*Rex Gloriae* in 1311) that compared the Gallic people of France to the nation of Israel. Their loyalty in defending the cause of Christ through the Roman church had clearly identified them as "a peculiar people chosen by God to carry out divine mandates, distinguished by marks of special honor and grace."[15] The Gauls were God's new Israel.

In his 1654 speech before the British Parliament, Oliver Cromwell compared the English revolution to God's deliverance of ancient Israel. According to Cromwell, "The only parallel of God's dealings with us that I know in the world . . . [is] Israel's bringing out of Egypt through a wilderness, by many signs and wonders towards a place of rest . . . the land of Canaan."[16] Identifying England with Israel remained commonplace throughout British history. The Victorian expansion of the British Empire was sanctified as the work of God's chosen people (now England) continuing to conquer the pagan lands of Canaan (now Africa and Asia). Britain's imperial appetite was spreading the gospel and extending the kingdom of God as both its missionaries and its armies delivered the English way of life to the darker recesses of a primitive, undeveloped world.[17]

The English Pilgrims and Puritans who colonized America's eastern seaboard were led by men of great vision whose imaginations were fueled by an intimate knowledge of the Old Testament. The combination of imaginative Bible reading within the context of fledgling settlements in a new land was like old-world steel striking against new-world flint, sparking the most elaborate descriptions of North America as God's new Promised Land. By fleeing persecution in England, these suffering colonists were being led out of Egyptian bondage, crossing their own version of the Red Sea by safely sailing across the Atlantic Ocean. The dark, untamed forests lying beyond the horizons of Plymouth and Massachusetts Bay metamorphosed into the land of Canaan, complete with godless Canaanites (Native Americans) waiting to be conquered and driven out, whether by the gospel or the sword. This new land would be transformed into the Puritans' "city on a hill," a Pilgrim version of Mount Zion, the new Jerusalem, a shining beacon of righteousness promised by God once his covenant people walked with him in obedience (Isa. 2:1–5; 27:12–13; 33:5–6; 60:1–5; 65:17–19).[18]

While the Puritans were still sailing across the Atlantic in 1630, their leader, John Winthrop, delivered a sermon entitled "A Model of Christian Charity," in which he quoted Israel's exclusive election promise in Amos 3:2 and transferred it to the Puritans, making them into the new covenant people. Winthrop explains:

> Thus stands the cause between God and us. We are entered into a covenant with him for this work. We have taken out a commission. . . . Now if the Lord shall please to hear us and bring us in peace to the place we desire, then

hath he ratified this covenant and sealed our commission. . . .The Lord will be our God and delight to dwell among us as his people and will command a blessing upon us in all our ways. . . . For we must consider that we shall be as a city upon a hill. The eyes of all people are upon us.[19]

Other nations, however, continually contested this American claim. In Scandinavia, N. F. S. Grundtvig (1783–1872), the nineteenth-century Danish intellectual, politician, churchman, hymn-writer, folklorist, poet, and historian would come to be known as one of the fathers of modern Danish nationalism. Combining his studies in Christian theology and Scandinavian folklore, he firmly believed that his homeland was God's new Israel for the modern world. Confidently writing that "all of human history points to it like the finger of God. . . . Denmark is history's Palestine," he looked forward to the Danish New Jerusalem.[20]

Grundtvig's association of a specific ethnicity with the true people of God was a nationalistic current that also infected German nationalist thinking long before the coming of the Third Reich. It helped to lay the groundwork for Hitler's fusing of Christianity with Aryan superiority. Thus, not long after Hitler's rise to power, Walter Grundmann (1906–1976), one of Germany's leading theologians, founded a monthly journal entitled *Christenkreuz und Hakenkreuz* ("Cross and Swastika"). In his first sermon after Hitler's appointment as the new German Chancellor in 1933, Grundmann proclaimed from his pulpit that Hitler had been raised up by God to fulfill the redemptive promises of Isaiah 1:26–27, turning Germany into God's new Mount Zion.[21]

I could go on citing more examples from across the centuries and other parts of the world, but space constraints mercifully require me to stop here. What can explain this repetitious but unwarranted confusion of Israel's story with other national stories throughout Western history?

Notice that every example repeats the same mistakes: not only do they redirect God's relationship with Israel onto another group (the error noted above), but they make no attempt to explain or justify the reapplication of God's covenant. On what basis can another nation stand in for ancient Israel and unilaterally appropriate God's covenant for itself? Implicit justification for this highhanded maneuver appears only by way of comparisons drawn between Israel's story and the history of the competing group (e.g., group X is oppressed just as Israel was oppressed; group X cries out to God just at Israel cried out to God, etc.). But creating parallels by cherry-picking the evidence does not warrant a description of nation X as God's "new Israel" any more than observing that my dog has a cute face with a mouth, nose, eyes, and ears proves that she must also be a human being since her master has a mouth, nose, eyes, and ears. Neither can we forget that these comparisons typically ignore the many inconvenient cultic and ceremonial expectations (priests, sacrifices, temple, etc.) laid on God's chosen people as conditions of his covenant blessing.

This entire Western current of "new Israelism" has always been a terrible mistake—with destructive consequences. Age has not sanctified it. Repetition has not improved it. American empire can never justify it. It is long past time for Christ's church to repudiate it.

All the nations of the world are exceptional in their own way. The French know that France is exceptional. Kenyans insist that Kenya is exceptional. Canadians promote Canada's exceptionalism. And they are all correct. Every culture, landscape, language, and national history contains its own unique features, well worth preservation and promotion, making its own contribution to the complexity of God's world.[22]

Unfortunately, many of these proud, nationalistic voices degenerate into pompous petulance by insisting that their brand of exceptionalism is the only legitimate exceptionalism. However, such objections merely testify to how very unexceptional sinners become when they sin. Without exception, we are all equally selfish, arrogant, boastful, proud, ready to exploit others, and reluctant to confess our many failings. There is a deeply rooted brokenness in fallen human nature that clamors after its own exclusive rights to the Creator, insisting that God is only on *my* side, endorsing only *my* way of doing things, making *me* the truly exceptional case. Individuals and nations alike dream of a God made in their own image, thinking their nationalistic, patriotic thoughts after them. God becomes the divine totem hanging only from the bow of their national ship, carved and painted to point the way forward while self-serving human hands guide the tiller and chart the course.

The Exceptional Church

With all that in view, whatever happened to God's covenant? Is there a divinely chosen, exceptional people anywhere in the world today? The answer is yes, though it may not be the answer we expect. God's one and only covenant people are now gathered together in the universal church of Jesus Christ, a community of faith spread throughout the world, made up of internationally dispersed "strangers and aliens," a countercultural people not of this world, citizens of God's heavenly kingdom on earth.

Yahweh takes an unexpected dogleg turn when fulfilling the promise that "all the peoples on earth will be blessed through Abraham" (Gen. 12:3; 22:18).[23] The Lord's sovereignty, creativity, and unstoppable desire to save all of creation regularly leads to a brand of "fulfillment" that could never have been anticipated by the original recipients of God's promises (see Heb. 11:8-16). But who are we to protest against God's way of doing things? Can anyone object and say, "No way, Lord. You can't do that"? God will be God, keeping his promises in whatever ways he chooses, exhibiting more beautiful hues of faithfulness, mercy, kindness, and grace than could ever be found in all the urgent scenarios concocted by the bloated industry of apocalyptic preachers, prophecy predictors, revelation readers, and starry-eyed dream merchants warning about the end times.

God has sovereignly redefined the composition of Israel. Abraham's descendants are no longer traced ethnically or biologically, for the Sinai Covenant has been superseded. As the prophet Jeremiah predicted, God has created a new covenant that changes the identity of the chosen people (Jer. 31:31). The sole requirement of this new covenant is faith and obedience to Jesus Christ, because it was established through Jesus's own life, death, and resurrection (Luke 22:20; 1 Cor. 11:25; 2 Cor. 3:6; Heb. 8:1-13; 9:15; 12:24). Anyone receiving this messiah as their resurrected Lord and Savior becomes a member of the Christian church, God's new community of new covenant people, where all nationalities, races, and people groups are wrapped up together in the cosmic banner of God's eternal kingdom. The trajectory of Yahweh's assurance that "all the nations of the earth will be blessed" through Abraham reaches out to include a global, multiethnic community of Christian faith.

The apostle Paul explains this unanticipated promise-fulfillment story line in several of his letters.[24] The children of Abraham are now identified, not by their Jewish bona fides, but by their commitment to Jesus Christ as the world's messiah (Rom. 4:11-12, 16-25; Gal. 3:6-9; 6:16). God ultimately fulfills the promise to make Abraham "the father of many nations" (Gen. 17:4-7) by creating an international family of faith. The new Israel consists of Jews, Greeks, Italians, Palestinians, Cambodians, Vietnamese, Nigerians, Americans, and many more who trust in the resurrected Jesus as King of Kings and Lord of Lords, worshiping him in a kaleidoscopic interracial swirl of redeemed humanity, praising Jesus as the cosmic Christ "in whom all things hold together" (Col. 1:15-20).

The book of Revelation captures this interracial diversity of God's new Israel with the repeated refrain about "a great multitude that no one could count, from every nation, tribe, people, and language" (see Rev. 5:9-10; 7:3-9; 14:3-7). This redefinition becomes explicit in Revelation 7: John hears about

12,000 people being chosen from each of the twelve tribes of Israel (7:3–8).[25] The resulting 144,000 represent the ideal gathering of God's covenant people. But when John finally turns to look at this congregation of righteous Israelites, he sees an international, multicolored, interracial mass of humanity extolling the wonders of the glorified Lamb of God (7:9–12). The twelve tribes have blossomed into all tribes. The caterpillar of Yahweh's exceptional nation has metamorphosed into the butterfly of Christ's extraordinary universal church.

God's goal in the Sinai Covenant was to make Israel "a treasured possession . . . a kingdom of priests and a holy nation" (Exod. 19:5–6). Several New Testament writers pick up this Old Testament language and reapply it to the Christian church, insisting that the covenantal characteristics of holiness, election, priesthood, and a royal kingdom have finally been realized in the body of Christ (1 Pet. 2:5, 9–10; Rev. 1:6; 5:9–10; 20:6). Even the apostle Paul's common reference to the local church as a gathering of "the saints," or "the holy ones," draws from God's Mount Sinai promise to make Abraham's descendants "a holy nation" (Rom. 1:7; 1 Cor. 1:2; 2 Cor. 1:1; Eph. 1:1, 18; 3:18; 5:3, 27; Phil. 1:1; Col. 1:2, 12; 3:12; 2 Thess. 1:10; see also Jude 1:3; Rev. 13:7; 16:6; 18:24; 19:8). All of God's intentions for a chosen people, an exceptional nation, a holy city set on a hill, a light shining in the wilderness, and a new Mount Zion have been collated, combined, attested, and confirmed in one group and one group only—the New Testament people of God.

Rejecting the Falsehoods of Nationalism and Civil Religion

Unsurprisingly, the Christian community's status as God's chosen nation raises the familiar challenge of conflicting loyalties for Jesus's disciples. What relationship does citizenship in God's kingdom and loyalty to the body of Christ have to one's nationality and the nation's practices of civil religion? Nation-states easily style themselves as alternative versions of the church, appealing to the worst (as well as the best) qualities of human nature: they offer much-needed camaraderie, objects of devotion, opportunities for service, and a sense of greater purpose for the individual. The important German jurist and political theorist Carl Schmitt (1888–1985) understood this very well, insisting that "all significant concepts of the modern theory of the state are secularized theological concepts."[26] The nation takes on God-like qualities as the corporate higher power calling for its citizens' allegiance. It clamors for the spiritual and psychological devotion expected of a worshiping congregation. The bent toward a national messiah complex is all but inevitable, and our innate desire to bow down before something greater than ourselves (while slyly remaining self-focused) finds satisfaction in civil religious sacraments and liturgies such as saluting the flag and sacrificing our children on the altar of military service.

Few Americans may self-consciously idolize their country, but that is one of the predictable outcomes of civil religious devotion. Every American president since George Washington has invoked the Almighty's providential direction of American progress, some more explicitly than others. For instance, one year after 9/11, on September 11, 2002, President George W. Bush, speaking at Ellis Island, said that "the ideal of America is the hope of all mankind. That hope still lights our way. And the light shines in the darkness. And the darkness will not overcome it. God bless America." In January 2003, the same president delivered his second State of the Union address and comforted the nation by assuring us that "there is power—wonder-working power—in the goodness, and idealism, and faith of the American people."

Both speeches offered an especially heavy dose of American civil religion, and I was shocked as I listened. The first address quoted from the New Testament, John 1:5, which declares the incarnate Logos, the eternal Son of God, to be the Savior of the world, "the light shining in the darkness" that will never be overcome. The second reference to "wonder-working power" lifted a line from a Christian hymn "There Is Power in the Blood," a song praising the resurrected Jesus for shedding his blood on the cross in order to save humanity. As a Christian, I was deeply offended by the president's deliberate confusing of the redemptive work of Christ with America's role in the world. Identifying the American people and their ideals with Christ's suffering for the world was a blasphemous belittling of the Savior that no amount of patriotism can excuse. The United States is not the savior of the world. Only Jesus Christ can provide a truly meaningful hope to humanity, as both John's Gospel and Lewis E. Jones, author/composer of "There Is Power," rightly understood.[27] But blurring the boundaries of country and Christ, both engulfed by the same saving mission, is a natural process for civil religion.

The power of civil religion to convert reprehensible blasphemy into admirable patriotism is, perhaps, most clearly shown in the way America memorializes warfare. I have lost count of the Memorial Day worship services I have attended where military veterans were extolled as model saviors offering their lives in order to save others. Fallen soldiers are molded into the likeness of Christ, "dying to redeem their countrymen."[28] Monuments such as Arlington National Cemetery, the Tomb of the Unknown Soldier, and many others across the nation become "sacred sites" worthy of pilgrimage. Battlefields are preserved as "hallowed ground" that is sanctified by the shed blood of those who died. The fruit of a nation's mourning becomes the civil religious unity produced by memorializing blood sacrifice.[29] Nothing infuses such nativist, xenophobic potency into civil religion as much as the nation's march to war and the patriotic ceremonies that keep the marching bands playing.

Unfortunately, this ability to transform combat soldiers, who are trained to maim and to kill a dehumanized enemy, into Christ-figures modeled after the Nazarene, who never raised a finger to defend himself against unlawful attack and execution, is a testament to the blinding, mind-numbing effects of civil religion as it short-circuits spiritual maturity and all rational powers of discernment.[30] Ironically, the very profane General George Patton understood the distinction between the work of Christ and modern warfare better than most Christian patriots do when he said: "Nobody ever won a war by giving up his life. He won a war by making some other poor bastard give up his life."[31] Exactly. Which is why the Christian gospel is as ill-suited to the patriotic platitudes of civil religion as a swan in a seersucker suit. "From the standpoint of civil religion, war is the nation's most important ritual."[32] What more needs to be said in explaining its evils and the imperative for God's people to steer well clear of it? Classrooms of young people made to recite the Pledge of Allegiance are being led onto the devil's playground where innocents are groomed as nationalists and introduced to the deceptive allure of war.

The church of Jesus Christ does not need nationalist patriotism, war, or bloodshed in order to find its sense of purpose, which is exactly why the church must always stand in principled resistance to nation-states, nationalism, and civil religion. Stanley Hauerwas puts it well when he says that being asked to die for the state should have the same appeal—for any right-minded Christian—as being asked to die for the phone company.[33] Yet, how many American Christians are even willing to risk being mocked for their faith in Jesus, much less being martyred for their identification with the body of Christ? It is the shed blood of Christ's martyrs that has sanctified the boundaries of truly hallowed ground throughout the world, not the bleak killing fields produced by any nation-state's war-making, whatever the justification.

Following the Savior of All Nations

Jean-Jacques Rousseau (1712–1778), one of the architects of modern civil religion, devoted a chapter of his book *The Social Contract* (1762) to working out the role of civil religion in the modern nation-state. He was adamant that true Christian faith will always be detrimental to the state because the Christian citizen's devotion is offered up to the kingdom of God rather than to the nation. Consequently, Christian faith will destroy the nation's unity by undercutting civil religion, since the church compels a broader allegiance: loyalty to the international community of fellow believers. Rousseau thus insisted that any state hoping to survive had to begin by outlawing the Roman Catholic Church, for it was the greatest enemy of civil religion.[34] It is not surprising that Roman Catholics have often suffered attack from nationalist, anti-Catholic movements because of their divided loyalties and international concerns.[35] The fact that similar accusations have seldom been launched against the Protestant church should be a source of unending shame for every descendant of Martin Luther and John Calvin.[36] Ironically, leaders of the Third Reich had a firm grasp of Rousseau's dilemma when they witnessed the German Christian Church openly debating whether or not its members could pray for fellow Christians in countries opposed to Germany's war efforts.[37] After all, since Germany was God's chosen nation, the idea of a "universal church" was farcical.[38] Such are the species of perversions given birth once the church allows itself to be co-opted by nationalistic civil religion.

Bank tellers have explained to me that the best way to identify counterfeit currency is to become intimately familiar with the real thing. Although Christian nationalism and American civil religion present themselves as touchstones of Christian piety, they are counterfeit expressions of faith in Jesus. When one searches for a corporate identity worthy of one's complete allegiance, only citizenship in the kingdom of God can meet the test as the genuine article. Neither Jesus nor the New Testament ever suggest that patriotism or national identity make any contribution to Christian discipleship. Hence the challenge for Christians appears in realizing that allegiance to the kingdom of God has nothing to do with nationality, partisan politics, or social conformity. Just the opposite. Typically, when real Christian faith is put into practice, it proves destabilizing to our narrow tribalism and the conformist pressures of America's religion of civility.

Living day by day in the Spirit-filled reality of obedient discipleship is the only effective antidote to the many deceits of civil religion and Christian nationalism. For Americans, the deprogramming begins once we realize that God's most important work in the world does not emanate from the spread of democracy, capitalism, or the Americanization of other societies, but from the innumerable courageous and self-sacrificial acts of humble Christian witness performed by anonymous men, women, and children around the globe. The angels rejoice as these courageous witnesses have their names inscribed in the heavenly book, whether or not the evening news media ever report their stories (which they would probably get wrong anyway). When the identities and accomplishments of history's great rulers, vast empires, and most powerful militaries are swept away by the sands of time, forgotten by everyone but wizened professors of ancient literature, the resurrected Jesus will continue to rejoice with his faithful disciples—devoid of all national flags, military salutes, or paeans to American virtue.

Grafted into the body of Christ, I discover that I have more in common—at least, in matters of substance—with my brothers and sisters in Christ around the globe than I do with most of my fellow Americans. Rousseau was quite right to identify Christianity as the principal threat to his beloved civil religion. What does this tell us about the state of American Christianity today?

Discussion Questions

1. The author insists that both nationalism and civil religion are in conflict with Christian faith. Discuss the different reasons given for this claim. Why do you agree or disagree? Justify your position by interacting with the arguments presented in this chapter.

2. The New Testament explains how the Old Testament's promises to Israel are now realized in the Christian church. What does this mean for the modern state of Israel and those Christians devoted to Israeli nationalism? What are the practical implications of the global Christian church being the "exceptional nation" through which God works in the world today?

3. List the many differences that distinguish Christ's death on the cross from a soldier's death on the battlefield. Why do you think that these very different types of "sacrifices" are so often confused by Christian leaders?

Additional Reading

Adams, David L., and Ken Schurb, eds. *The Anonymous God: The Church Confronts Civil Religion and American Society*. St. Louis: Concordia, 2004.

Boyd, Gregory A. *The Myth of a Christian Nation: How the Quest for Political Power Is Destroying the Church*. Grand Rapids: Zondervan, 2005.

Hauerwas, Stanley. *After Christendom: How the Church Is to Behave If Freedom, Justice and a Christian Nation Are Bad Ideas*. Nashville: Abingdon, 1999.

Lieven, Anatol. *America Right or Wrong: An Anatomy of American Nationalism.* Oxford: Oxford University Press, 2012.

Wilsey, John D. *American Exceptionalism and Civil Religion: Assessing the History of an Idea.* Downers Grove, IL: IVP Academic, 2015.

————. *One Nation under God? An Evangelical Critique of Christian America.* Eugene, OR: Wipf and Stock, 2011.

Chapter Nine

Does Kingdom Service Permit Military Service?

I was raised in a military family. My father joined the Army after high school in order to fight the spread of communism in Korea. He told me that when he finally returned home, he and a buddy were going to track down John Wayne and set him straight. Wayne's Hollywood depictions of warfare and combat were *nothing* like the real thing; they had been lied to. Pvt. Crump had shipped out to become John Wayne Jr., but he returned home a ragged and disillusioned twenty-year-old, aged well beyond his years. The Korean War convinced my father that humping an eighty-pound pack, carrying a rifle, and shivering in wet, cold, and dirty foxholes was for chumps. So he applied to aviator's school and learned to fly helicopters. No more foxholes for him, just 125 combat missions in Vietnam and a final return visit to postwar Korea maintaining the DMZ (the demilitarized zone along the border between North and South Korea). He retired after twenty-three years of active service.

I did most of my growing up on military bases scattered across the United States. As a child, I roamed the large tracts of undeveloped woodland set aside for troop maneuvers and occasionally joined in with platoons marching in formation down the dirt road I happened to be playing along, stepping in time with the drill sergeant calling out the tempo, chanting in rhythm with his column of boot-camp boys.

During my senior year of high school, I decided to join the Army after graduation, hoping that I would be sent to Vietnam. My father had been there twice, though he refused ever to talk about his war experiences or answer my pleas for stories or details about either of his wars. In fact, he rarely talked about much of anything around the house. And it was not difficult for us kids to notice that he eventually stopped participating in family outings like picnics or excursions to the nearby Cascade Mountains. Most of what little I knew about his war experiences I learned from my mother: mainly about how he had been shot down several times, which was why he suffered from a serious back injury that would eventually keep him in nearly constant pain. He did tell me of one incident: after a crash landing, he heaved a copilot over his shoulder and ran with him to a medevac hovering on the opposite side of a rice paddy. As the waiting crew hauled them both inside, the door gunner marveled that my father remained unscathed by the gauntlet of heavy enemy fire he had attracted while running from one side of the paddy to the other. But that story was about all I ever knew.

I was devastated when he was ordered to return for a second tour of duty. Even though my teenage mind had begun to feel some affinity for the anti-war movement, my heart was still with Dad. So that's why I decided to join the Army after high school and volunteer for Vietnam (not realizing that the reduction of American forces by that time meant that I had a better chance of being sent to Timbuktu). What better way to connect with my emotionally distant father, I thought, than to share in the same war? Maybe we could swap stories someday. At least, that was my adolescent strategy for finding an ever-elusive connection with my old man. If sharing in the same war wouldn't do the trick, what would?

I informed my mother about my scheme, feeling certain that Mom and Dad alike would swell with pride as they gave me the thumbs up. Several days later my father walked into the family room, in spit-shined black boots and crisply creased fatigues as always, while I was finishing my homework in front of the television (my favorite place to study).

"I hear you plan to join the Army," he said.

"Here it comes," I thought to myself. He is going to tell me how proud he is.

"Yep," I replied. "I'm going to volunteer for Vietnam, like you."

"No, you won't."

I could not believe my ears.

"What?" I asked. "Why not? I want to join up like you did."

"You're going to college," he answered. "Start school. Take your chances on the draft like everybody else. If you're drafted, you go. Otherwise, start college in the fall and get a degree."

He turned around and walked away—and that was that. The major had spoken. End of conversation. My plans to join the Army and march off to war ended more quickly than they had begun. You could have knocked me over with a feather. Years would pass before I would begin to understand the reasons for my father's tersely communicated decision.

Volunteering for Violence

I typically ask my students to conclude their biblical interpretation papers with a paragraph or two describing the practical significance of the passages they have studied. If they believe in the authority of the Bible, and they take the meaning they have discovered in these texts seriously, what difference would it make to the way they lived their lives? Several years ago an eighteen-year-old freshman wrote this:

> I am currently doing Army ROTC. My dream has been to lead men in the way that God would want me to, which is being an example of Christ and service. Just as Christ did with his apostles, I want to teach young men and guide them in their life. I hope that God leads me in this service to soldiers and to my country.

This young man expressed an admirable goal in wanting to be Christ-like, but I suspect that he had never stopped to reflect on the basic presuppositional issue underlying his career dreams: Does Jesus ever lead his disciples to join the military and direct others into war? The fact that many Christians, ancient and modern, have done exactly that does not answer the question. Many well-meaning people have insisted that God was directing them into any number of dubious activities. Remember the Crusades?

I suspect that it is becoming clear to the reader that I am an advocate for Christian pacifism—not for passivity but for nonviolence.[1] Living a nonviolent life is as essential to the character of kingdom citizens as is faith in Jesus, loving your enemies, and praying for those who curse you. Pacifism is a nonnegotiable posture for anyone who follows the crucified Lord, the one who "did not retaliate when they hurled their insults at him; and when he suffered, he made no threats" (1 Pet. 2:23). Therefore, based on my understanding of Scripture and early church history, I believe it is as likely that Jesus would direct his disciples to become combat-ready troopers as it is that he would guide them into filming pornography or burning crosses on black citizens' lawns at the behest of the local chapter of the Ku Klux Klan. Just as oil and water do not mix, neither will "seeking first the kingdom of God" ever direct a disciple into training for the ways of war.

Every nation's military establishment exists for only one reason: to destroy things and kill people. Armaments and armies are about as useful as a bird dog with a head cold once they are divorced from the possibility of using them. Jesus never came close to leading the apostles toward a military recruiter's office; in fact, he pointed them in the opposite direction.

I am not a naïve utopian who imagines that warfare will ever be scrubbed from human history. That is never going to happen, at least not until Jesus returns. The Lord warns us that this world will always suffer from "war and rumors of war" (Mark 13:7), but this bleak assessment of human history does not tell us anything about God's possible involvement in the conflicts. Greedy, nationalistic, fanatical human beings are perfectly capable of spurring themselves on to bloodshed without any help from God. Without a modern-day Jeremiah to stand and pronounce, "Thus saith the Lord," we cannot know what God may or may not be doing in any given place at any specific time with any particular people. Jesus's prediction about the inevitability of bloodshed is descriptive, not prescriptive, and it should never tempt the citizens of God's peaceable kingdom to abandon their essential role as "peacemakers" (Matt. 5:9) who love their enemies and live nonviolently. This fallen world will never be free from war, but every war should be free of Christians.[2]

Jesus gives his people crystal-clear instructions. The world travels one way. Disciples must travel another. The second-century apologist Tertullian insisted that Christians are people who would rather be killed than kill, even in self-defense.[3] Such a pacifist resolve is not offered as a strategy for international relations or a recipe for better domestic politics. This resolve is Christ's ethic for his church, and it is normative for all God's people, regardless of the world's opinion. Human history will continue to be a very bloody story, but those who have been washed in the blood of the Lamb are forbidden to have any part in shedding human blood anywhere, at any time.

The fundamental question is not whether a war—and by implication one's participation in that war and the military apparatus that makes war possible—can ever be just; in this respect, just-war theory is irrelevant to Christian decision-making.[4] The real question is: Is a Christian allowed to kill, volunteer and train to kill, become an instrument of violence, or have a hand anywhere in moving the gears and pulling the levers of a killing machine? Is it possible for true citizens of the kingdom of God to love their enemies, pray for those who curse them, and turn the other cheek while they are preparing, studying, training, and maintaining an expertise in unleashing death, violence, and destruction on those enemies and their families?

I think not.

What about the Centurions?

Earlier chapters on the kingdom of God, the teaching of Jesus, Romans 13, and 1 Peter have already addressed most of the New Testament material relevant to this conversation. Thus we saw in our study of Romans 13 that kingdom citizens are forbidden from participating in otherwise legitimate state actions (Rom. 13:4) when those actions involve revenge, violence, or anything other than "living at peace with everyone" (Rom. 12:14, 17-21). However, there is still one commonly raised question when anyone objects to Christians joining the military that still needs a response: What about the Roman soldiers mentioned in the New Testament? They are not commanded to resign their posts in order to follow Jesus or to join the church. Can we read their stories as a biblical endorsement for Christian soldiers today?

Despite the fact that this question was one of Augustine's favorite arguments in favor of Christian military service, its continuing popularity is a bit mystifying. According to the logic of this argument, the church also should embrace sorcerers, astrologers, and witches without requiring them to abandon their magical practices, since the Gospel of Matthew describes the three Magi who visited the baby Jesus (Matt. 2:1-12) without ever criticizing their unsavory occupations.[5] In fact, sorcerers and wizards should be welcomed into the Christian communion more eagerly than soldiers since the Magi went so far as to "worship" Jesus in Bethlehem (v. 11).

Returning to the question of New Testament soldiers, three stories call for attention, two in the synoptic Gospels and one in the book of Acts. The first is the Gospel account of a centurion's servant healed by Jesus at the request of his deeply worried master (Matt. 8:5-13; Luke 7:1-10). Both Matthew and Luke describe the centurion's faith as standing in stark contrast to the otherwise lackluster reception Jesus receives in the region surrounding Capernaum (Matt. 8:10-12; Luke 7:9-10). This pious Gentile soldier, whose desperate faith elicits a miracle, serves as both a paradigm of faith in Jesus as well as an indictment of Israel's reluctance to welcome her Messiah. In what appears to be a teachable moment in this man's life, Jesus does not tell him to quit the military.

Second, the Gospel of Luke mentions a group of soldiers who are part of the inquisitive crowd that searches out John the Baptist and asks what they must do to avoid God's impending judgment (Luke 3:7-14, esp. v. 14). John tells the soldiers: "Don't extort money; don't accuse people falsely, and be content with your pay." Here is a perfect opportunity, we are told, for John to warn soldiers against military service, but he doesn't do so.

Finally, the most important story is in Acts 10, where Peter meets with the centurion Cornelius, a pious man who appears to be a "god fearer," a Gentile adherent to the Jewish synagogue. Cornelius responds positively to Peter's preaching, receives the Holy Spirit, and by implication is received into the church. But he is not told to leave the Roman army as a precondition to baptism or acceptance into the local Christian community. Apparently, we can assume that the church in Caesarea was open to disciples serving in the military.

While these are all reasonable questions, the inferences drawn from these texts suffer from a number of problems. First, on the literary level, we cannot assume that either Matthew or Luke intended either of these stories to address the question of disciples serving in the Roman army. A story that strikes us as "a perfect opportunity" to address the concerns troubling our minds may only serve to remind us that our priorities were not necessarily shared by the Gospel writers.

Second, it is always tenuous to draw conclusions about an author's beliefs by ruminating over the things he does not say. At best, such rumination can produce an argument from silence, the plausibility of which depends on the hypothetical reconstruction offered to buttress its assumptions. I admit that I will offer a few such suggestions myself, but they involve far more likely assumptions given what we know about the post–New Testament church. However, even if my arguments from silence are rejected, the overall case being made will stand independently of them.

Notice that the centurion who came to Jesus pleading for his servant was not given any ethical instruction whatsoever. If Jesus did anything more than commend the centurion's faith, the written tradition was not interested in letting us know about it. At best, we may assume that *if* the centurion persevered in becoming a follower of the resurrected Jesus, he eventually joined a local church, in which case it is reasonable to assume that the contradictions inherent in Christian military service (see the evidence below) would have been addressed as he was catechized into kingdom citizenship. These are a much more reasonable set of likelihoods.

Cornelius's situation was similar. It is reasonable for us to make the same assumptions about his eventual instruction in discipleship after he joined the community of believers in Caesarea. Luke's point in telling this story in Acts 10 was not to comment on the viability of Christian soldiers, but to demonstrate God's revolutionary inclusion of believing Gentiles within the new covenant community without the traditional, Jewish requirements of circumcision and full adherence to the law.

Third, concerning the soldiers addressed by John the Baptist, we must remember that John was the forerunner of Jesus, the messenger who prepared the way. He was not the fulfillment. Jesus went so far as to say that "whoever is least in the kingdom of God is greater than John" (Matt. 11:11–15; Luke 7:24–28). Only Jesus brings the kingdom and initiates his disciples into the mysteries of that kingdom. In fact, John's exhortation to the crowd, including tax collectors and soldiers, in Luke 3:7-14, far from being a new or radical ethic, is simply a restatement of the ancient Old Testament's prophetic witness about social justice among God's people. Furthermore, neither the Old Testament nor much of second-temple Judaism—including John the Baptist, in all probability—had any qualms about God's people taking up arms for Yahweh. Jesus is the one who draws the line for a new ethic, not John.

Fourth, the apostle Paul may preserve a relevant practical consideration. Paul answers a question posed to him by the church at Corinth by telling the people that "each one should remain in the situation which he was in when God called him" (1 Cor. 7:20). Apparently, some members of the church were wondering whether their newfound life in Christ meant that they should quit their jobs or change their living situations. Paul tells them to stay where they are, doing whatever they were doing before the Lord called them. Of course, the unstated presumption, which we examined earlier in this book, is that a believer can never disobey the Lord Jesus even when obeying him means disobeying an earthly master, employer, or government official. We have already examined the suffering that could arise from this tension in the life of a Christian slave, for instance, who was owned by an unbelieving master. Again, it is reasonable to assume that the same tension, with all of its negative consequences, confronted the soldier who was converted to Christ and joined the Christian community. He could remain a soldier, but he could never disobey the Lord's command not to kill. If his kingdom citizenship put him in a perilous situation with a commander for disobeying an order, he would submit to Roman authority by suffering his punishment—undoubtedly execution—for the cause of Christ.

Roman soldiers could not simply walk away from their military commitment. Resigning was not an option. Telling a soldier to abandon his imperial obligation was nothing at all like Jesus calling Peter to abandon his nets and fishing boat (Mark 1:16-18). During this period, early dismissal from the ranks happened only feet first or as the result of a serious health problem. There was no such thing as conscientious objector status and no Canadian sanctuary for soldiers who had gone AWOL. What little we do know about Christian soldiers disobeying orders and asking to be released from the army because of their religious scruples are all stories that end in martyrdom.[6]

The Witness of the Early Church

I suspect that some readers are wondering how feasible all of this was in the ancient world. Christians who would not serve in the army getting away with refusing to defend their homeland? Christian soldiers choosing death rather than obeying a commander's orders to march into combat and kill another human being? And all of this civil disobedience sprang from an idealistic ethic against violence? Is there any evidence that the early church actually lived out these ideals in real life?

Fortunately, there is a sizable body of literature left to us by leaders of the early church that sheds considerable light on this subject. The research is vast, with scholars often arriving at contradictory conclusions after purportedly studying the same sources. It can all be very confusing for the nonspecialist. Some authorities insist that the argument made here is incorrect, that early Christian authors were *not* uniformly opposed to a disciple's participation in war or military service. Phillip Wynn, the author of *Augustine on War and Military Service*, is representative of this view: "The most meaningful general statement to be made about early Christian attitudes toward war and participation in it is that no such general statement can be meaningfully made."[7] According to this school of thought, different ancient authors advocated different positions and wrote accordingly, and even those who were opposed to military service based their objections on the all-pervasive nature of Roman idolatry, not on the evils of shedding enemy blood.

Unfortunately, Wynn's bibliography does not include two important works conclusively demonstrating that he, and those who share his opinion, are mistaken. In fact, professors George Kalantzis and Ronald Sider both demonstrate that *all* extant Christian literature written before the fourth-century reign of Constantine *unanimously forbids* disciples from either joining the military or shedding blood if they are already enlisted.[8] Kalantzis and Sider have made the ancient literature readily available to the modern reader in an excerpted format. Leaving no stone unturned, they both thoroughly dismantle the opposing arguments of those who believe that they find contradictions in the evidence. In fact, every extant Christian author from the first three centuries of church history affirms the same message with the same voice.[9] Sider summarizes the evidence: "Nine different Christian writers in sixteen different treatises say that killing is wrong. No extant Christian writing before Constantine argues that there is any circumstance under which a Christian may kill."[10]

The text most frequently cited by these ancient authors in support of their antimilitary, antikilling position is Matthew 5:38-48. Jesus's injunction for disciples to love their enemies and turn the other cheek is referred to by "at least ten different writers in at least twenty-eight different places" in support of the pacifist position.[11]

Kalantzis similarly insists:

> [T]here is no polyglossia among the Christian writers. With remarkable uni-
> vocity they speak of participation in the Christian mysteries as antithetical to
> killing, and the practices of the army, whether in wartime or peacetime. The
> dominical command to love one's enemies and pray for one's persecutors is
> a common thread woven throughout these documents.[12]

Evidence exists that, by the late second century, there were Christians in the
Roman army, and the numbers of Christian soldiers appears to have increased
into the latter half of the third century. What we do not know, however, is how
many of those soldiers, like Cornelius, were converts to the Christian faith.
Furthermore, the possibility of a disparity existing between the principles advanced by church leaders, on the one hand, and the actual behavior of congregational members, on the other, should not surprise anyone who has served
in church leadership. How many churchgoers today carefully abide by every
doctrine and ethical practice enjoined by their pastor, priest, or bishop from
the pulpit? The presence of Christian soldiers in the Roman army prior to the
fourth century is an interesting historical observation, but it does not coun-
termand either the words of Jesus or the application of that teaching by every
known pre-Constantinian writer.

It should also be noted that, given the vast size of the Roman Empire
and the regional nature of its conflicts, it was entirely possible for a soldier
to go through his career without ever stepping onto a battlefield or shedding
blood; in that case, a converted soldier could conceivably adhere to church
teaching and maintain his pacifism.[13] On the other hand, how he reconciled
regular participation in the mandatory, military cultic practices, including
emperor worship, while maintaining his avowedly Christian conscience is
another question altogether. But since when does a failure of discipleship,
no matter how widespread, become the reason for nullifying the words of
our Lord?

Origen's book *Against Celsus* (ca. AD 248-49) provides interesting evidence
of how widespread the Christian refusal to join the army had become by the
third century. Apparently, at least in Celsus's neck of the woods, the teachings
of church leaders on this point were followed rather broadly. Celsus, a pagan
critic of Christianity, complained that if everyone behaved like the Christians,
the Roman army would quickly dwindle in size to the point where it could no
longer defend the empire against its enemies (*Against Celsus* 8.67-70). Even if
we assume a certain amount of exaggeration on Celsus's part, his accusation

indicates that Christians' refusal to join the Roman army was the norm, not the exception.

Being a loyal Roman patriot, Celsus also complained that it was hypocritical of the church to enjoy the many benefits provided by the empire while refusing to share in the burden of its defense (8.72–75)—an argument that has a very contemporary ring. Origen replied that Christians make a much more significant contribution to the empire's protection and stability through the spiritual combat conducted by disciples as they pray for the emperor, intercede for his armies, and pray against the demonic forces wanting to unleash chaos against the state.[14]

Although the church fathers also appealed to other aspects of Scripture and theology in making their antimilitary arguments, this is enough detail for our purposes. Here is a brief summary of these writers' conclusions:

- Christians were forbidden to join the military, whether in peacetime or in time of war.[15]
- Under no circumstances could a Christian soldier kill, commit acts of violence, or participate in the idolatrous religious practices endemic to military life.[16]
- If a Christian soldier was ordered to fight, shed blood, or take part in idolatry, he was obligated to disobey orders and accept the consequences, since his primary allegiance was to the Lord Jesus Christ, not to Caesar.[17]
- Church members who violated these instructions were to be put out of the church.[18]

Once Constantine had publicly embraced Christianity (ca. AD 312), the unanimity of church leaders opposed to Christians joining the military came to an end. An increasing number of authors began to think about how a Christian could be a member of the army and even go to war while remaining an ostensibly obedient disciple and a faithful member of the church. So, why do I focus attention only on the pre-Constantinian writings? Is it arbitrary to ignore the later evidence?

I do not think so.

Although I am not one to say (as some suggest) that Constantine's conversion led to the near extinction of authentic Christianity, it did generate a significant paradigm shift that opened new pathways for Christian ethics, paths that I believe led the church far away from the teachings of Jesus and the apostles.[19] Once the enterprising would-be emperor began declaring his battlefield victories to be the work, not of the old Roman gods, but of the new Christian God, Jesus Christ, a doorway that had long been locked, barred, chained off, and welded shut against Christian use was suddenly thrust open by imperial fiat. Jesus Christ was supposedly blessing the converted Christian Caesar on the field of combat while he slaughtered his enemies. Who would stand up and call Constantine a liar? What theologian dared to contest the seemingly brute facts of imperial history? It was obvious, or so many believed, that under the right circumstances, Christ did approve of Christians fighting and killing after all.

Like the attractive fruit once dangled squarely in Eve's line of sight, this development was too tempting to resist. The previously persecuted church was given a chance to stand arm in arm with the establishment wielding power. Some traditionalist voices continued to speak out against military service, but once leaders such as Augustine began interpreting Constantine's conversion and the resulting "Christianization" of the empire as the fulfillment of biblical prophecy, the harnessing of God's people to the wild, unbroken horses of bloodshed and warfare was complete.[20] A newly Christianized war-wagon was off and running.

Creating Young Killers

> What is the spirit of the bayonet?
> To kill! Kill! To kill without mercy, Drill Sergeant!
> What makes green grass grow?
> Blood! Blood! Bright red blood, Drill Sergeant![21]

Yelling at the top of their lungs, hundreds of young recruits charge full steam ahead, rifles with fixed bayonets at the ready, pointing at the distant targets. Young men and women in drab fatigues run as fast as they can until they collide with the man-sized target dummies, plunging eight-inch steel bayonets in with all their might. Then they pull the bayonet out and thrust it in again and again, piercing the dense targets made to mimic a human body.

Each recruit has just enacted killing another human being, not with a "clean" kill shot at forty yards, but by puncturing lungs, ripping through kidneys, slashing open stomachs and intestines repeatedly. You can almost hear the artificial victims gasping their last breath.

"Kill! Kill! Kill!" is shouted by each one, men and women alike, with every repeated stab.

"Blood! Blood! Blood!" yelled over and over again at the drill sergeant's commands.

"Without mercy! Without mercy! Without mercy!"

My friend Chaplain (Col.) Herman Keizer has told me, "Without question, I did the most trauma counseling during and after bayonet training." I don't doubt that.

Chaplain Keizer is a retired Army chaplain with thirty-four years of active-duty service. Twice wounded in Vietnam, he knows the rigors of combat and has learned to manage his own experiences with PTSD. He has also been generous enough to talk with me at length about his years in the military chaplaincy.

It should not surprise anyone to learn that this standard exercise in basic training (until recently), where young recruits physically enact the process of running a large knife blade into the human body, might traumatize a would-be soldier.[22] The goal of basic training, after all, is to immerse the novice soldier into a new world, unlike anything most of them have ever experienced before, and to turn civilians into combatants ready to kill. That goal is accomplished by breaking down individuals, stripping them of any prior sense of purpose, priorities, or morality, so that they can be rebuilt from the ground up into soldiers, that is, the potential killers that the military needs them to be.

For instance, according to Kayla Williams, a veteran of the Iraq war, "It's scary to think about how much being in the Army has changed me. That experience couldn't leave even the strongest person the same."[23] In other words, even the strongest person *will* be broken down and reshaped to military specifications. Ms. Williams admits that, at least for a time, she even obeyed orders to torture Iraqi prisoners.[24] After all, many inventive minds and a great deal of creativity, time, and energy have all been invested in the creation of a training process that predictably yields the desired results.[25]

The intensity of modern basic training is intended to develop the mental and physical toughness required to perform well and to survive on the field of combat. Much of today's training evolved in response to a study conducted by Brigadier General S. L. A. Marshall throughout and immediately following World War II. Much to everyone's surprise, Marshall discovered that "only 15 to 20 percent of the American riflemen in combat during World War II would fire at the enemy."[26] As remarkable as it may sound, the other 80 to 85 percent of American ground forces either occupied themselves so that they were unable to use their rifles, or they purposely aimed to miss, firing into the air or not bothering to aim at all. Though some have contested his findings, Marshall's results have been independently verified time and again.[27]

The explanation for Marshall's unexpected discovery is rather straightforward. The vast majority of human beings have an innate and powerful revulsion to killing another person. In fact, this revulsion runs so deep within the human psyche that Lt. Col. Dave Grossman describes it as "a force stronger than drill, stronger than peer pressure, even stronger than the self-preservation instinct."[28] Regardless of the danger, when it actually comes time to pull the trigger or plunge in the bayonet, the vast majority of people will hesitate or refuse altogether. I credit this humane instinct to God's gift of conscience planted in every human being.

Modern basic training is the military's response to these immutable facts of human nature. The challenge boils down to this: How can we train masses of young people to violate their gift of conscience? After all, how many commanding officers would be delighted to learn that 80 to 85 percent of their fighting force will always aim to miss? The modern characteristics of boot camp in the post-Marshall military evolved in response to these concerns. They culminated in what we have today, an intensively designed, comprehensive environment that is always working to condition people reflexively to do things that normally they would rarely be able to do: kill others like themselves on command. Some veterans refer to it "as 'programming' or 'conditioning' . . . a form of classical and operant conditioning (à la Pavlov's dog and B. F. Skinner's rats)."[29] Depersonalization, sleep deprivation, brutality, dehumanization of the perceived "enemy" (as Huns, Krauts, Chinks, Slopes, Gooks, Japs, Ragheads, Hajis, etc.), severe punishments to enforce arbitrary rules, combined with "disorientation followed by rites of reorientation according to military codes" all contribute to "a process of slow, continuous, and almost imperceptible indoctrination."[30] Subsequent studies have shown the remarkable effectiveness of these newer methods of combat conditioning. During the Korean War the average rate of fire had risen to 55 percent; by the time of the Vietnam War it was as high as 90 to 95 percent.[31]

Is it any surprise, then, that the majority of combat veterans wrestle with psychological trauma, when they were trained and conditioned to do something that violates their God-given conscience? Doing it reflexively, not reflecting on what they are doing? Once military conditioning has successfully overridden that part of our conscience that says "Do not kill," the surrealistic intensity of actual combat supplements that conditioning in horrific, unanticipated ways, leading many soldiers to depart even further from what they once believed was right and wrong. For the vast majority of veterans, however, their innate humane conscience will eventually reassert itself. It is only a matter of time. This is why Grossman concludes that "at least 98 percent of all soldiers in close combat will ultimately become psychiatric casualties."[32]

Dr. Jonathan Shay, the author of *Achilles in Vietnam: Combat Trauma and the Undoing of Character*, confesses to "the pain that I feel when I witness in our veterans the ruin of moral life by the overwhelming coercive social power of military institutions and of war itself."[33]

Vietnam veterans have confessed to Dr. Shay:

> I'm horrified at what I turned into. What I was. What I did. I just look at it like it was somebody else. . . . Somebody had control of me.[34]

> I was a f*****g animal. . . . When I look back at that stuff, I say, "That was somebody else that did that. Wasn't me. That wasn't me." War changes you, changes you. Strips you, strips you of all your beliefs, your religion, takes your dignity away, *you become an animal*. . . . Y'know, it's unbelievable what humans can do to each other.[35]

> I'm horrified at what I turned into.[36]

Such expressions of remorse are not unique to the survivors of any particular war. Similar testimonies have been repeated many times over by the veterans of every modern war.

Chaplain Keizer puts his finger on the core problem: "When you train men to go to war, you are training them to do things in a totally different moral context than most of us live in. When you come out of that [military] community, how do you make sense of the [civilian] world you're in now?" Many veterans, like my father, will wrestle with that moral conundrum for the rest of their lives, trying to fit the broken pieces of their lives back together again. The consequences are the psychologically and emotionally crippling effects of what has come to be called "moral injury," a seemingly irreparable guilty conscience.[37]

Chaplain Keizer has seen it many times: "The temptation to go against your conscience in wartime is really bad. . . . If you sin against your conscience, you commit moral suicide."[38] Tragically, the moral suicide regularly committed in combat is often translated into literal suicide at home. ABC news is only one of many sources to report that, since 2001, more veterans have committed suicide at home than have ever died in combat, an average of eighteen to twenty-two deaths per day.[39]

The conscience is a masterful escape artist. We can bind it, gag it, tie it up, and try to bury it away as deeply as possible inside the bowels of a calloused psyche, but eventually it always claws its way back up into the light of day. And it invariably brings with it all of the immoral acts we committed during its absence, acts that we thought had been left behind in the darkness.

Taking a Stand

Jeffrey Brown is another man I am proud to call my friend. Jeff enrolled at Calvin College with a full-ride ROTC scholarship. Several years into his program, however, Jeff came to the firm conclusion that faithfully following Jesus Christ was incompatible with service in the US Army. As a young man of deep conviction, Jeff paid a steep financial price for his decision to resign from ROTC. He anticipated the large debt burden that he will now carry for years as he slowly repays his military loans on a social worker's salary. The component I found most disturbing about Jeff's story was the harassment, insult, and ridicule that he endured from his commanding officer, a man who called himself a Christian. "He put me down in ways that made me feel horrible," Jeff confessed. But then, that was entirely in keeping with standard military training.

Jeff described his dilemma: "As I grew more in my Christian faith, I found that what I was learning in the military disagreed with everything the Holy Spirit was teaching me about following Jesus. It doesn't make any sense in the military to live after the fruit of the Spirit." The hypermasculinity, machismo, denigration of women (typically referred to as "sluts" or "bitches"),[40] and the "us vs. them" mentality fostered between soldiers and the civilian world all violated everything Jeff was coming to understand about Christian morality. It didn't matter whether or not it was for an apparently good cause—like defending the nation. It was all behavior condemned by Jesus, and Jeff was unwilling to live a schizophrenic life.

"You have to be a soldier at all times," Jeff explains. "But when you do that, you take away the ability to live into the person God wants you to be. They [the Army] give you a set of virtues, ideals, creeds, everything. Soldiers are united under a new faith, a new ethic, a new moral compass."

Jesus warns all of his potential followers: "No one can serve two masters. Either he will hate the one and love the other, or he will be devoted to the one and despise the other" (Matt. 6:24). "That servant who knows his master's will and does not get ready or does not do what his master wants will be beaten with many blows" (Luke 12:47). Jeff eventually knew that he had to choose between the competing demands being made on him by the Army's kingdom and by God's kingdom. I am happy to say that he chose life as a faithful citizen in the peaceable kingdom brought by Jesus. He counted the cost, paid the price, and will one day hear his Lord say, "Well done, good and faithful servant" (Matt. 25:21, 23).

This all-too-brief survey barely scratches the surface of some complicated issues. I realize that the handful of testimonies I have provided are vastly outnumbered by a chorus of militaristic, nationalistic voices raised in the average American church. But that is all the more reason to let these minority voices be heard. Remember that Jesus also warned us that "wide is the gate and broad is the road that leads to destruction, and many enter through it. But small is the gate and narrow the road that leads to life, and only a few find it" (Matt. 7:13–14). The truth of a matter is never determined by majority vote.

There are also nuances yet to be explored in the evaluation of military noncombat roles, such as the work of medics and chaplains. Perhaps equally devout disciples can have legitimate differences of opinion on whether such work is permissible or not. Do medics and chaplains bring light to the darkness, or do they merely aid and abet the violence that Jesus condemns? However one answers that question, I believe that at least one thing is crystal clear: *faithful disciples may not pledge allegiance to Jesus Christ and then have anything to do with facilitating bloodshed.* Furthermore, it should go without saying that no kingdom citizen can ever train for combat without knowing that, in this age of a global Christian church, they will almost certainly be responsible for destroying the lives and families of overseas brothers and sisters in Christ who have been similarly indoctrinated, coerced, and sacrificed by the nationalist propaganda instruments of their own government authorities. Christ will never lead the kingdom of God to war against itself. I suspect that the demonic legions have fallen all over themselves in mockery and celebration every time one Christian has killed another throughout the history of human warfare because the church failed in its teaching duties: that is, extolling loyalty to the nation-state or a political ideology rather than faithfulness to God's kingdom.

John Wayne's Hollywood Lies

As the years passed, I eventually learned about my father's frequent nightmares and the times he had nearly strangled my mother to death as she crept into bed after he had fallen asleep. Fortunately, she always woke him before it was too late, and he would apologize in a panicked voice, describing how he had been back in Korea. In that scenario, she had slithered her way into his nightmare as an enemy "chink" who was creeping into his dark trench, knife clenched between her teeth.

I heard about his struggles with depression and my mother's frustrated attempts to find group counseling for combat veterans, and I slowly came to understand why he did not want his oldest son to volunteer for the Army. Fortunately, people were beginning to talk about the reality of PTSD (Post-Traumatic Stress Disorder, though many nowadays prefer to drop the word "disorder") among combat veterans. More recently, a handful of psychologists working with veterans of the wars in Iraq and Afghanistan have begun to describe a related issue, one they call "moral injury": the haunting, sometimes debilitating, guilt caused by violating one's sense of morality.[41]

My father, a man of deep and abiding faith in Jesus Christ, had lived for many years, I am certain, in a desperately lonely wrestling match against both PTSD and moral injury. With these two syndromes attacking like a pair of tag-team wrestlers, outnumbering him two to one and never letting him rest, he found himself seriously overmatched. Patriotism, commitment to duty, belief in both the global threat of world communism and the moral superiority of American democracy had led him into circumstances and actions that had slashed at his conscience and broken his psyche. Now he lived haunted by monsters he never could have imagined as an eighteen-year-old volunteer fresh from the sawmills of Coos Bay, Oregon, a boy who only wanted to be like John Wayne and defend his country.

Unfortunately, the John Wayne effect continues its deceptive, destructive work today. Too many romanticized movies spreading glorified, sanitized images of warfare continue to mislead young men and women down a pathway that leads eventually to the gaping mouth of hell on earth—the battlefield. We also, shockingly, live in an age where the gore of warfare has been glamorized so as to offer its own big-budget, bloody appeal to young, testosterone-driven males, whether on the silver screen or a computer monitor. I will allow the novelist Tim O'Brien, another Vietnam combat veteran, to testify as the last witness against these Hollywood lies.

A true war story is never moral. It does not instruct, nor encourage virtue, nor suggest models of proper human behavior, nor restrain men from doing the things men have always done. If a story seems moral, do not believe it. If at the end of a story you feel uplifted, or if you feel that some small bit of rectitude has been salvaged from the larger waste, then you have been made the victim of a very old and terrible lie. There is no rectitude whatsoever. There is no virtue. As a first rule of thumb, therefore, you can tell a true war story by its absolute and uncompromising allegiance to obscenity and evil.[42]

Discussion Questions

1. Have you or any members of your family served in the military and had combat experience? Are you able to share something about what that was like?

2. What questions has this chapter raised for you as you think about the relationship of Christians to the military and warfare? What further investigation can you do?

3. What can the local church do to help returning combat veterans reenter civilian life and learn to live at peace with their memories of war?

Additional Reading

Bourke, Joanna. *An Intimate History of Killing: Face to Face Killing in Twentieth-Century Warfare*. New York: Basic Books, 1999.

Brock, Rita Nakashima, and Gabriella Lettini. *Soul Repair: Recovering from Moral Injury after War*. Boston: Beacon, 2012.

Grossman, Dave. *On Killing: The Psychological Cost of Learning to Kill in War and Society*. Rev. ed. New York: Back Bay Books, 2009.

Hauerwas, Stanley. *War and the American Difference: Theological Reflections on Violence and National Identity*. Grand Rapids: Baker, 2011.

Hays, Richard B. *The Moral Vision of the New Testament: Community, Cross, New Community; A Contemporary Introduction to New Testament Ethics*. San Francisco: HarperCollins, 1996. (See especially chap. 14, pp. 317–46, on the interpretation and application of Matthew 5:38–48.)

Kalantzis, George. *Caesar and the Lamb: Early Christian Attitudes on War and Military Service*. Eugene, OR: Cascade Books, 2012.

Nadelson, Theodore. *Trained to Kill: Soldiers at War*. Baltimore: Johns Hopkins University Press, 2005.

Sider, Ronald J., ed. *The Early Church on Killing: A Comprehensive Source Book on War, Abortion, and Capital Punishment*. Grand Rapids: Baker Academic, 2012.

Chapter Ten

God Hates Poverty

I well remember my conversation with the middle-aged man who approached me after I preached a Sunday morning sermon, entitled "God Hates Poverty," in his church. I had recently returned from east Africa, where I was visiting my daughter, Fiona, who was busy working with several orphanages scattered throughout the slums of Nairobi, Kenya. It was not the first time I had witnessed poverty up close and personal in the developing world, but it was particularly memorable. Perhaps it was the length of my stay combined with the opportunity to observe how easily my daughter lived and served among the poorest of the world's poor that caused this trip to leave a particularly deep impression. Perhaps it was also my visits to local churches that were flourishing in the middle of poverty-stricken neighborhoods. Sharing in the joyful and heartfelt worship offered up by my Kenyan brothers and sisters in Christ had sparked a deeper round of reflection on my own responsibilities to the Christian family that is scattered around the world, many of whom must contend with a brutal daily struggle for survival.

I began my sermon that morning with a few pictures showing Nairobi's slums, the people who lived there—their homes, schools, churches, and their orphans. The body of my sermon explained the main points I address in the rest of this chapter, explaining why every Christian needs to understand that God hates poverty and that he expects his people to do something about it.

As the gentleman approached me, I could see the tears running down his cheeks. He grabbed my hand and said, "You have convinced me. I see that God's word does, in fact, teach the things you say it does about my responsibility to the poor, but I have a problem. I have been politically conservative all my life, and even as I say this, every conservative bone in my body rises up to fight against these new ideas. I don't know if I can change. What should I do?"

With this final sentence, the stream of tears burst into heavy sobs.

At no point had I suggested that conservatives necessarily ignore the poor. In fact, I had not used any political references in my message at all, but something in Scripture had struck this man as contrary to his political identity. I was eager to find out what it was.

My new acquaintance had begun to recognize two issues he had never seen before. First, his eyes were opened to the fact that some of his attitudes about wealth, poverty, and generosity had more to do with his sinfulness than they did with following Jesus. He recognized that continuing as Christ's disciple meant that he must change certain attitudes and behaviors that had become second nature to him. Second, he had begun to gain some insight into how his attitudes about the poor were not formed by Scripture but had been instilled by his environment, his family background, his friends, associates, and the various news outlets woven into the fabric of his daily life—all uniformly reflecting specific social, political, and economic opinions that, until now, he had assumed were synonymous with Christian values.

I applauded him for recognizing the conflict between his cultural Christianity and the truth of God's word. Many believers never have their eyes opened to that distinction, and none of us ever becomes so saintly as to recognize all the daily falsehoods we unwittingly confuse with the truth of the gospel. We all have peculiar ways of diluting God's word with our own homemade, cultural pablum.

We had begun a momentous conversation. I suggested that we get together for lunch or coffee and dig more deeply into the issues at stake. But when I asked for his phone number so that I could get in touch, he hesitated and said that he would call me. So I gave him my number, but, for whatever reason, he never called. Our conversation ended as quickly as it began. I can only hope that the work initiated by the Holy Spirit that Sunday morning has continued fruitfully in other ways, but I suspect not.

A Growing Divide between Rich and Poor

Scripture is clear on this subject: God hates poverty—especially when it exists within the kingdom of God—and he expects his people to work to eliminate it. Traditionally, Western churches have considered poverty to be a problem separating the developed from the undeveloped (or "developing") nations of the world. Yet the Western church increasingly finds itself confronting the problems of wealth and poverty within its own communities, in dimensions not seen since the early part of the twentieth century, during the so-called age of the Robber Barons that preceded the collapse of Wall Street in 1929 and the subsequent Great Depression.[1]

Paul Craig Roberts, the assistant secretary of the treasury under President Ronald Reagan, was one of the original proponents of the "trickle-down," supply-side theory of economics (called Reaganomics in the past, more commonly "neoliberalism" today) that has held sway over American economic policy for the past thirty-plus years.[2] In his book *The Failure of Laissez Faire Capitalism and Economic Dissolution of the West*, Roberts, of all people, now warns that "the Robber Barons have been resurrected" in twenty-first-century America.[3] Citing information collected by the US Central Intelligence Agency, Roberts argues that America has "the worst"—that is, the most unequitable—distribution of income of any nation in the developed world.[4] In fact, the widening income gap between the richest and the poorest Americans is greater than the wealth gaps found in Iran, Nigeria, Nicaragua, Cambodia, Thailand, Kenya, Russia, China, Senegal, Turkmenistan, and Jordan. The richest 20 percent of Americans control 84 percent of the nation's wealth. America's wealthiest 400 families, all billionaires, control as much wealth as the bottom half of the nation's population combined (approximately 175 million people).[5] While more of the country's wealth accumulates in the bulging pockets of billionaires, more and more Americans slide irretrievably into dire poverty. In fact, over six million more Americans have fallen below the poverty line since 2014. In his massive study *Capital in the Twenty-First Century*, Thomas Piketty goes even further in demonstrating that free-market capitalism, by its very nature, perpetuates an uneven playing field, enabling the rich to grow richer while hindering the poor in their efforts to climb the ladder of success.[6] Capitalism does not automatically create equal opportunity for everyone. Just like the pigs in George Orwell's dystopian novel *Animal Farm*, wealthy owners of capital are always more equal than everyone else.

Poverty, even American poverty, can exact a heavy price from those who bear its burdens. For instance, as America's poverty rate has increased over the past 20 years, a woman's average life expectancy has decreased in more than 300 counties around the country.[7] Among member nations of the Organisation for Economic Co-operation and Development, as of 2014, the United States ranked twenty-sixth in infant mortality.[8] In 2008 the same organization reported that the United States had the highest level of income inequality among all member nations.[9]

While the ever-swelling pool of America's poor live shorter and more difficult lives, the wealthiest Americans find creative new ways to unburden themselves of their (typically inherited) piles of money while redecorating palatial mansions and lavishing themselves with obscene excess. They may, for instance, check the time by glancing at their new $736,000 Franck Muller wristwatch while using one of their $700,000 Mont Blanc jewel-encrusted pens to write another check for the newest $50 million yacht (if they can tolerate the two-year waiting list).[10]

Certain secular pundits may dismiss these gross disparities as endemic to the ways of this world. The rich get richer while the poor get poorer. So what else is new? It's a dog-eat-dog world. The Greek historian Thucydides (c. 460 BC–c. 395 BC) observed that the "strong do as they wish, while the poor suffer as they must."[11] But is this an acceptable attitude for God's people? How should a disciple of Jesus Christ evaluate such vast economic disparities? Can they patriotically applaud a capitalist economic system that helps to perpetuate this wealth gap? More particularly, can Christians merely shrug their shoulders and accept the status quo when both the rich and the poor claim to be members of the same universal church? Can the rich and the poor sit together in the same worship services (as if this would ever happen), pray side by side, shake hands, pass the peace, and then go their separate ways?

There Were No Needy Persons among Them

Short phrases can sometimes prove long on significance. Take, for example, the first seven words in Acts 4:34. Describing the embryonic community life emerging among the Christian disciples in Jerusalem, Luke, the author of Acts, highlights the fact that "there were no needy persons among them." In other words, no church member was ever required to go without life's necessities. Fellow community members simply would not allow this to happen.

On the immediate, literary level, the whole of Acts 4:32–37 continues an earlier description of the church's communal practices first found in Acts 2:42–47, which makes the same point. The key portion for our purposes appears in verses 44–45:

> All the believers were together and had everything in common. Selling their possessions and goods, they gave to anyone *as he had need.*

There were "no needy persons" among the early Jerusalem Christians, not because the rich and powerful were the only people interested in hearing about Jesus, or because no poor people happened to join the church (see Acts 6:1). Rather, the Jerusalem church was an economically diverse group of people in which the wealthier members voluntarily took responsibility for supplying the needs of all those who would otherwise go without. Those who had more than enough freely shared with those who had less than required. We see this principle in the way Luke elaborates community practice in Acts 4:32, 34–35:

> All the believers were of one heart and mind. No one claimed that any of his possessions was his own, but they shared everything they had. . . . *There were no needy persons among them.* For from time to time those who owned lands or houses sold them, brought the money from the sales and put it at the apostles' feet, and it was distributed to anyone *as he had need.*

After reading Luke's summary of the early Christian social life in Acts, I cannot help but recall the famous Marxist dictum: "From each according to his ability, to each according to his need." Except that the book of Acts proves that Marx was not coining an original adage; rather, he was channeling the New Testament and plagiarizing from the earliest followers of Jesus. This is not a Marxist principle; it is a Christian principle, and it requires a Christian community for its implementation. Marx's idealistic attempt to apply specifically Christian community standards to the whole of society was a misstep that we will revisit before this chapter is over.

Voluntary generosity was the Jerusalem church's original antipoverty program. It was an impulse that sprang naturally from their Jewish heritage, where benevolence programs coordinated through the local synagogue had deep-seated, ancient roots.[12] The earliest Jesus followers composed a new brand of synagogue, so it was natural to continue the social practices already familiar to them. Daily food distribution to the community's widows, described in Acts 6:1–7, similarly was born of traditional Jewish piety. Furthermore, when a severe famine struck the province of Judea in the late 40s AD, the church in Syrian Antioch (nearly five hundred miles north of Jerusalem) "decided to provide help for the brothers living in Judea, *each according to his ability*" (Acts 11:29), the earliest example of international aid provided by one Christian community to another.

Organizing in order to satisfy the living requirements of brothers and sisters who had fallen through the fissures of a broken world and had become mired in poverty's hardships was a normative value for the citizens of God's kingdom. People who owned property sold portions of what they had in order to share the proceeds with those who had little or nothing.[13] Those who were fortunate enough to own two homes transferred the title and house keys of one home over to the homeless family who ate beside them at the communion table. Those who were wealthy enough to rattle around in spacious homes they had long since outgrown reconsidered their lifestyle and took steps to simplify, to downsize, freeing up excess property and income to share with others. Paul's eventual traveling companion and fellow apostle, Barnabas (Acts 14:14), is first mentioned in Acts for implementing such creative downsizing. He sells a piece of property and contributes all of the proceeds to the church for poverty relief (Acts 4:36–37).[14]

Luke then deliberately contrasts Barnabas's freewheeling generosity with the satanically inspired miserliness of his fellows, Ananias and Sapphira (Acts 5:1–11). Nothing in Luke's account of the church's communal generosity suggests that there was any coercion involved. No authority figures were strong-arming people to surrender their goods. Gifts were offered voluntarily. The only pressure was social, and however strong that social pressure may have been, every person's response remained their own. The Ananias and Sapphira of Acts 5, however, revealed their stinginess and duplicity by lying about the value of their property and secretly retaining some for themselves, while claiming to have shared it all (v. 2). More interested in *looking* generous than in actually *being* generous—like most of us, in fact—they nominated themselves as poster children for the demonically inspired life. The Holy Spirit fosters empathy, hospitality, and generosity. Selfishness, on the other hand, signals like a bright red warning light that a person's conscience remains shipwrecked on the reef of satanic seduction. The stark contrast between the Barnabas story and the Ananias and Sapphira story is no accident.[15] Luke's literary art provides specific illustrations of a crucial fault line separating the impostors, who only pretend to follow Jesus, from the authentic citizens of God's kingdom. Joyful, intentional, sacrificial sharing with the poor is one tangible sign separating genuine confessions of Christian faith from the many counterfeiters who depend on cheap grace as a way to remain cheap.[16]

God's Mission for Israel Is Fulfilled

But there is more to glean from these seven words in Acts 4:34: "There were no needy persons among them." A second literary dimension of the text ties Luke's antipoverty theme into God's ancient plans for the people of Israel. We know this because Acts 4:34 is a direct quotation from the rendering in the Septuagint (the Greek translation of the Old Testament) of Deuteronomy 15:4: "There should be no poor [or needy] among you." That some English translations of Deuteronomy refer to "the poor" rather than "the needy," as in the book of Acts, obscures the fact that the Greek wording in both passages is identical.

God took one opportunity in all of human history to form a nation, design the framework of its legal system, and describe how to create a just society reflecting divine ideals for human society. That nation was ancient Israel.[17] Even though we cannot draw any simple, across-the-board parallels from Israel's agrarian culture to our modern, technological society, we can try to distill the underlying principles found at the heart of God's instructions and translate them into workable applications for today that aim at the same social goals. One distinctive cornerstone of Israel's legal system was its social-welfare laws, an array of regulations intended to weave a social safety net guaranteeing a measure of economic equality among all of God's people.[18] Deuteronomy 15 cuts to the heart of the matter in declaring God's intentions for these welfare regulations: there is no reason for anyone to remain poor and needy in the land of Israel (vv. 4, 7, 11).

But God's expectations were not foolishly utopian. Deuteronomy 15 recognizes that some measure of poverty is inevitable in this world, even in the Promised Land, admitting that "there will always be poor people in the land" (v. 11).[19] But the land of Canaan would be sufficiently fruitful that a surplus could always stand ready for redistribution to the needy. Thus the appropriate response to poverty was never to shun needy people or leave them to their own devices—as if poverty were a punishment for sin. Instead, seeing another person in need should be the stimulus for creative action to meet that need.[20] So God says:

> If there is a poor man among your brothers . . . do not be hardhearted or tightfisted toward your brother. Rather be openhanded and freely lend him whatever he needs. (Deut. 15:7-8)

God's mandated generosity could be expressed in a variety of ways. Deuteronomy 15 discusses the importance of forgiving debts, lending money interest-free, and sharing generously with those in need. But two particular "laws of generosity" provide especially helpful insight into God's desire for economic and social equality. These are the gleaning laws (Lev. 19:9-10; Deut. 23:24-25; 24:19-22) and the Jubilee Year (Lev. 25:8-55).[21]

The gleaning laws dictated that farmers did not produce crops only for themselves; rather, they planted, tended, grew, and harvested their crops for the entire community. Within certain limits, the fruit of every farmer's labor was freely available to the poor; it was never private property in the sense that the grower could do with it as he pleased. *The poor had a right to their fair share*.²² In fact, sometimes when the Old Testament prophets castigated the rich for stealing from the poor, they were condemning wealthy landowners for ignoring these gleaning laws, excluding the poor from their property while keeping all of the harvest for themselves (Isa. 3:14).

It was God's law that any hungry person could enter a neighbor's field, orchard, or vineyard and collect as much food as he or she could carry away by hand (Deut. 23:24-25). There were to be no "Private Property, Keep Out!" signs in the Promised Land. There was no such thing as truly private property. Grandpa Abraham had no business sitting on the front porch, shotgun in hand, waiting to blast away at the pesky vagrants who plucked at ears of corn as they walked past his fields. In fact, Jesus and his disciples took advantage of this law on at least one occasion (Mark 2:23). Although their gleaning got them in hot water with the Pharisees, it was because they were gleaning on the Sabbath, not because they were snitching from a stranger's wheat field.

Furthermore, when harvest season finally arrived, every farmer had to leave an unharvested margin around the edge of each field (Lev. 19:9). This portion of the crop was left for the wild animals and the poor, and the people were free to take away as much as their hands could carry. In addition, the farmer and his harvest workers could only make one trip through a field, vineyard, or orchard in order to reap a harvest. Fruit trees and grapevines could be beaten only once. There were to be no second or third passes over the same ground in order to collect more fruit. Whatever produce ripened in the days ahead, after the initial harvest, whatever fruit fell to the ground afterwards, whatever grain was dropped or overlooked the first time—all must be left behind for wildlife and the poor (Deut. 24:19-22).²³

Notice that these regulations did not dictate how wide a field's margins must be. That decision was left up to the farmer, who was encouraged to remember that the Lord promised great blessing to everyone who shared generously with the needy (Deut. 15:4-11; 24:19, 22). The poor were expected to collect their own harvest, though the disabled might have someone do it for them; but they could (at least ideally) rest in the knowledge that the more prosperous members of society were always working on their behalf. Clearly, the poor had rights. Every manufacturer understood that he or she was working for the good of the entire community, that a certain measure of his or her production belonged to other members of the neighborhood simply because they needed it.

The Jubilee Year served an even more extensive purpose than the gleaning laws. As Israel moved into the land of Canaan, the people were reminded that none of the land actually belonged to them. Israel remained the steward of God's real estate, assured that they would be blessed as long as they used the land properly and obeyed the Sinai Covenant (Deut. 8:6-11; 15:4-7; Lev. 25:23; Josh. 1:6-8).[24] When the land was first apportioned among the tribes of Israel, Yahweh guaranteed equality by allotting to each tribe exactly what the tribe needed: larger portions of land were given to the larger tribes, and smaller portions to the smaller tribes (Josh. 12:6-7; 13:6-19:51). Eventually, local leaders oversaw the division of land among the tribal families, and these allotments remained the permanent property of each family.

Families might fall on hard times, but whatever business dealings led to a family's loss of real estate, their deprivation could only be temporary. Every fifty years, all debts were cancelled, all indentured servants were liberated, and all land was restored to its original owners (Lev. 25:8-13, 23-28, 39-43). God required the regular redistribution of his real estate so that the rich, who were more adept at business, could only become rich for so long, while the poor man who had bad fortunes or less skill in his business dealings could remain deprived of the property that was rightfully his for only so long. Every half century the national restart button was pushed so that all land owners returned to ground zero, so to speak. Wealth and property were redistributed in order to maintain equality.

Modern Western notions of ownership and private property have no place in this biblical worldview. Ownership always entailed social obligation. Property owners were not free to do whatever they pleased with their property. It was actually the Romans who developed the concept of private property that we are familiar with today, allowing property owners to dispose of their belongings in whatever way they saw fit, without the constraints of social, communal, or environmental responsibilities.[25] Our individualistic society, founded on the governmental protection of personal property rights, is based on a thoroughly pagan notion of ownership most akin to Israel's selfish behavior in the dark days of its lawlessness, when "every man did that which was right in his own eyes" (Judg. 21:25, KJV; cf. Deut. 12:8).

Unveiling both of these strands of literary connection to Acts 4:34, one in the New Testament and another in the Old Testament, reveals that *Luke is describing the early Christian church as God's faithful community where the economic and social goals for the covenant people are now finding fulfillment.*[26] We do not know how faithfully the laws of gleaning and Jubilee were practiced throughout Israel's history, but Luke wants his readers to know that obedient Israel now exists as citizens of the kingdom of God, disciples of Jesus Christ who are "one in heart and mind," where "no one claims that any of his possessions are his own" (Acts 4:32). Such empathy and communal generosity are held out to us as normative characteristics of kingdom citizenship.

There Should Be No Needy Christians Anywhere

We do not know what poverty relief practices may have been implemented as the church expanded its reach beyond Judea throughout the Roman Empire. I would argue, however, that it is safe to assume that the generous habits of the Jerusalem community were perpetuated in every Christian assembly where core members were drawn from the Jewish synagogue. Every Pauline community, for instance, was formed around believing Jews who followed Paul after he was driven from the local synagogue (Acts 13:5, 14–52; 14:17; 16:1; 17:1–4, 10–13; 18:1–8, 19–20, 24–28; 19:8–10, 17–20). There is no reason to think that their vision of community care would have differed significantly from that of the Jerusalem church (cf. Paul's instructions to Timothy about how the church should care properly for its widows in 1 Tim. 5:1–16). It is reasonable to assume that there would be broad continuity between the benevolent impulses of second-temple Jewish ethics and their practical outworking in the earliest generations of the Christian church all throughout the Roman Empire.

The one place where Paul teaches at length about the importance of sharing with the poor continues very neatly along the trajectory laid out in the book of Acts. In Galatians 2:10, Paul recalls the admonition given to him at the Jerusalem Council (Acts 15:1–29) that he "should continue to remember the poor," the very thing that Paul claims he "was eager to do."[27] After all, Paul had been a Pharisee and thus knew well the Jewish traditions of communal poverty relief; furthermore, Paul was an apostle of the resurrected Lord, and he now saw issues of wealth and poverty through the lens of kingdom citizenship and the eschatological reversal of values taught by Jesus.[28] The crucial text here is 2 Corinthians 8:1–9:15, where Paul reminds the Corinthian church about their responsibilities to the famine relief collection he was gathering for their brothers and sisters in Judea (see Rom. 15:25–28; 1 Cor. 16:1–4), another international endeavor in which churches in modern-day Turkey and Greece sent money to the poor Christians in Israel-Palestine. Several elements of Paul's instructions make an important contribution to this study.

First, Paul commends the Macedonian churches for the way in which both their actions and attitudes have been shaped by the kingdom's reversal of values. He says: "Out of the most severe trial, their overflowing joy and their extreme poverty welled up in rich generosity" (2 Cor. 8:2). Severe trials have produced overflowing joy, and extreme poverty has yielded rich generosity. The kingdom's eschatological, ethical reversal strikes again. The Macedonians rejoice in their poverty as they suffer for Jesus, and this otherworldly joy moves them to share what little they have with brothers and sisters in Christ who are suffering in foreign lands far across the Mediterranean Sea. They are living upside-down, counterintuitive lives where their own poverty is transformed into a hothouse of empathy, nurturing extraordinarily generous hearts eager to relieve the suffering of others. Racial, ethnic, linguistic, and cultural differences were all irrelevant in this task. The only bond that mattered was their common faith in the resurrected Jesus.

Second, Paul's churches further illustrate that all gifts were offered willingly, not under compulsion, and that the principle operating in the Jerusalem church continued to function in his churches: from each according to her ability, to each according to her need. Paul says,

> They gave as much as they were able, and even beyond their ability. Entirely on their own. . . . I am not commanding you. . . . Now finish the work, so that your eager willingness to do it may be matched by your completion of it, according to your means. For if the willingness is there, the gift is acceptable according to what one has, not according to what he does not have. (2 Cor. 8:3, 8, 11–12)

Third, Paul describes the standard that drives his charitable work and measures its success: equality throughout the church, not only locally but internationally.

> Our desire is not that others might be relieved while you are hard pressed, but that there might be *equality*. At the present time your plenty will supply what they need, so that in turn their plenty will supply what you need. Then there will be *equality*, as it is written: "He that gathered much did not have too much, and he that gathered little did not have too little." (8:13–15)

Paul's definition of equality is explained by his quotation of Exodus 16:18, describing God's instructions for how Israel was to collect the heavenly manna during their wilderness wanderings. Large families gathered larger amounts of manna, while small families collected smaller amounts. No families were allowed to accumulate more than they required, but neither did any families come up short by having less than they needed. In this sense, everyone was equal.[29]

It is striking that Paul applies this principle of equality to the international body of Christ. The book of Acts first describes how the church in Jerusalem safeguarded every member's equality by ensuring that all resource needs were met locally. Then the church in Syrian Antioch shared resources with the church in Judea (Acts 11:29-30). Paul further extends this ethos to embrace the entire family of God around the world when he takes up a collection from churches scattered throughout Asia Minor, Macedonia, and Achaia in order to assist the Judean community. The Jerusalem church had a unique role to play as "the mother" community, symbolizing Judaism's gift of the gospel to the Gentile world. But Paul also had a special interest in using this collection to repair the strained relationships between his own predominantly Gentile communities and the "Judaizing" faction, hostile to Paul and his mission, centered in Jerusalem (Acts 15:1-2, 5, 24; Gal. 1:6-3:29; 4:17-20; 6:12-18). But nothing in his instructions to the Corinthians suggests that his vision of *equality* is limited to this single effort for Judea. The theological motivations described in 2 Corinthians 8-9 are universal, gospel truths, applicable to every local church in all times and places. The global church is one body, one family. As long as any disciple in any part of the world goes hungry, lacks decent shelter, or suffers from other needless deprivations of the essentials of life, all other Christians who have more than enough to cover their daily necessities should joyfully draw from their excess to share resources with their sick, hungry, imprisoned, unclothed, and neglected brothers and sisters in Christ around the world. The New Testament vision for all the people of God is one of *worldwide equality*.

The Church as a Place of Equality

That seven-word sentence in the book of Acts—"There were no needy persons among them"—shows itself to be very long on both theological and practical significance. If space allowed, we could pursue the economic issues raised in this verse by delving into Jesus's teachings in the synoptic Gospels, especially the Gospel of Luke.[30] We could also look at the non-Pauline letters, together with the book of Revelation—all New Testament resources that provide multiple confirmations of the financial attitudes discovered here in the books of Acts and 2 Corinthians.[31] As I conclude by summarizing a few practical applications from the biblical teaching, I should offer a note of caution about how easily confusion arises when modern authors fail to pay attention to the New Testament's intended audience. We cannot forget that kingdom ethics are addressed to kingdom citizens.

The kind of generosity that ensues from "there are no needy folks among God's people" provides hardcore evidence to the real presence of God's kingdom in this world, testimony to the Holy Spirit's miraculous transformation of selfish sinners into generous givers. As such, it is not a generosity that can be expected, much less required, of anyone and everyone. Too many biblical scholars jump immediately from the biblical material into grappling with broad economic applications, asking questions like, "How do we build a world of economic equality where poverty disappears?" The problem with this approach is that the economic question can only be answered in conjunction with related concerns about personal character, issues such as: How do we teach everyone in society to turn the other cheek? To forgive every offense? Never to hold a grudge? To lend to anyone who asks without thought of repayment? The economic and the character questions are all cut from the same bolt of cloth.

As I have repeated throughout this book, Jesus's kingdom ethics are not applicable to everyone carte blanche, despite the boon they would bring to anyone who dares embrace them. Kingdom morality is the fruit that springs from the obedience of faith. Failure to grasp this spiritual connection between faith and practice is the cardinal methodological mistake running throughout the works of many advocates for social transformation, whether it be Karl Marx's vision of international, communist equality, Walter Rauschenbusch's nineteenth-century Social Gospel movement, or contemporary Latin American works in liberation theology.[32]

Audiences matter. I cannot take the coach's advice to my son's wrestling team and apply it straightaway to my daughter's ballet class. Little girls in tutus do not need instruction in a half-nelson takedown. Neither can we take the Spirit's instruction to the church of Jesus Christ and lay it upon a society that ignores the Spirit because it does not know Jesus. In fact, history shows that, even among those who *do* claim to experience the work of the Holy Spirit, it is well-nigh impossible to uniformly act out kingdom generosity and universal sharing with any long-term consistency. The church has its hands full simply trying to be The Church, the authentic body of Christ, as the Lord intends it to be, without the additional burden of working to transform the whole of society. As Stanley Hauerwas has repeated throughout his career, the church's job is to be the church, illustrating before the watching world how different life can be in the kingdom of God in contrast to everything else.[33]

Typically, it is those very Christians who are most intent on rebuilding the structures of this world according to the church's specifications who eventually allow the world to reshape God's church according to its own specifications. The temporal powers that be are nothing if not practical, but God's extremely impractical, upside-down kingdom ethics are not made for universal acceptance, at least not in this fallen universe, where sin continues to play a starring role and always drives a hard bargain with anyone—no matter how well-intentioned—who wants to be counted a success.

Neither the Bible nor the church can provide this world with a Christian economic system. There is no such thing.[34] No one "biblical plan" offers itself as the remedy to our global or national economic woes. Neither capitalism nor socialism fills that bill. This practical lacuna is not the result of God's instructing a deliberately sectarian church to keep itself separate from the world, but of the world's stubborn insistence on keeping itself separate from the transformational work of the Holy Spirit. God's plan for universal economic redemption begins with pledging allegiance to the kingdom of God by surrendering to the lordship of Jesus Christ. Personal conversion is the first step in moving toward a new society, a new nation, a new world where there are no more needy people among us. And this step cannot be legislated or planned. However, this is not a recipe for hopelessness or social apathy. The fact that all people, regardless of their kingdom citizenship, personally possess both (1) the image of God and (2) a fallen, sinful nature has two important implications for everyone who stubbornly continues to dream of one day living in a poverty-free world.

First, the church must continue to challenge itself. All believing communities will regularly struggle, fall short, and disappoint in their stutter-step attempts to become the generous, hospitable, international community where poverty is fought and equality is sought for all of God's people. But our temporal failures can never become the excuse for abandoning God's call. Every disciple must persevere in the journey of following hard after Jesus and gradually becoming the transformed kingdom citizen who happily sells his or her possessions in order to share with a brother or sister in need (Acts 2:45).

Second, though some readers may misinterpret my perspective as a brand of sectarianism, they would be wrong. All human beings, regardless of their kingdom membership, are created as the image of God. Because the universal impress of the *imago Dei* exists prior to anyone's leap of faith in Jesus Christ, disciples must confidently seek out occasions where collaborating with secular organizations can provide effective alternative ways to combat poverty. It is entirely possible for the image of God to burn brightly in someone who lives outside God's kingdom, while the Holy Spirit is barely able to strike a match in the cold hearts of others who live inside the kingdom. As long as God's people are never asked to compromise their witness to Christ or his kingdom values, there is no reason for the church not to form coalitions with other public and private agencies that share a common humanitarian focus. God loves all people, after all. Our common humanity appears in God's image, and this universal image promiscuously calls out to its own wherever and whenever the *imago Dei* suffers, is broken, goes hungry, shivers with cold, wastes away from neglect, dies needlessly from treatable illness, and goes unrecognized by those of us who should know better. Fortunately, there are many beautiful image-bearers in this world—of all creeds, faiths, and nationalities—who are joining hands to share in this mission of poverty relief. As important as it is, personal benevolence alone will never adequately meet the needs of everyone who requires help.[35] Larger coalitions of public, private, religious, and nonreligious organizations are the only way to tackle problems as vast and intractable as poverty. The philosopher J. D. Trout has written that "fighting poverty with charity is like fighting a battle with weekend warriors."[36] Kingdom citizens should be among the first to join up and help tackle the broader organizational and political issues that perpetuate global poverty and inequality.

Next Steps

Finally, at the risk of being not specific enough for some but too specific for others, let me conclude by offering a few practical suggestions on how this very limited peek into the New Testament perspective on generosity and poverty should shape Christian behavior today.[37]

First, all local churches are responsible to ensure that every member's needs are being met. "From each according to her ability; to each according to his need" should have a place in every church's vision statement as members worship, pray, celebrate, confess, repent, forgive, and pursue God's mission in this world. Pastors, elders, local ministerial associations, and others can all seek for God's guidance as they work creatively to develop new ways of making the New Testament vision of economic equality a lived experience within the local church.[38] We should take the message of Deuteronomy 15 as seriously as the Jerusalem church did. Unfortunately, as Craig Blomberg laments, "serious application of this principle to contemporary churches would require such radical transformation of most Christian fellowships that few seem willing even to begin."[39] But that does not mean there cannot be a faithful remnant of the select few who are determined to follow Jesus no matter the cost. Be one of them. The church must take whatever steps are necessary to care for, empower, employ, house, and protect the poor, needy, and less fortunate members of their communities.

Second, the local church must continually look beyond itself and reaffirm its citizenship in the international kingdom of God. Every needy believer in every part of the world sounds a spiritual clarion call for material assistance from other members of Christ's Body. This requires that disciples educate themselves about the economic conditions of our cities, states, nations, and the rest of the world. Kingdom citizens are called to be world citizens, knowing something about the condition of God's people scattered among the nations of the globe, especially in places afflicted by poverty, hunger, famine, disease, natural disaster, warfare, and persecution. No Western Christian can rest easy while knowing that there are Sudanese believers languishing in refugee camps, or East Indian disciples starving because of persistent crop failures, or Palestinian Christians suffering the daily cruelties of an illegal Israeli military occupation. We must educate ourselves. As far as Jesus is concerned, we are bound more closely to fellow believers on the opposite side of the globe than we are to the people of our own country—or even to our immediate family (Mark 3:31-35). Just as the kingdom of God spells the end of nationalism (see chapter 8, above), it also marks the beginning of a necessary internationalism.

Third, Ben Witherington offers sound advice when he observes that "the emphasis of the New Testament lies not on the acquisition side of things . . . but on sacrifice and divestiture. Instead of a prosperity gospel, modern affluent Christians mostly need to hear the gospel of divestiture and self-sacrifice."[40] Reevaluating our budgets and our lifestyles in order to make more of our resources available for helping others is sure-fire evidence of the Holy Spirit's work in our lives. Many helpful resources are available to assist anyone who is seriously wrestling with practical "next steps" in shedding more of his or her materialism and acquisitiveness.[41]

Fourth, the American church must stop assuming that capitalism is God's own heavenly economy.[42] Some form of regulated capitalism may be the optimal economic system available to this fallen world, but no system that extols the primacy of individual liberty (unencumbered by community or environmental responsibility), private property (divorced from social obligation), the profit motive (seeking higher levels of accumulation), and competition (where winning means beating out everyone else) can ever be embraced by the Christian church. Rather than surrendering to the capitalist propaganda working to baptize the free-market system, kingdom citizens must learn to operate in the world as it is without drinking the capitalist Kool-Aid and surrendering their consciences to the all-pervasive norms of a capitalist society. Religious advocates of capitalism, such as the Roman Catholic theologian Michael Novak, have gone to great lengths to defend it as the system most pleasing to God and congenial to the gospel. Yet, as so often happens in such apologetics, Novak's enthusiasm for capitalism far outstrips his commitment to God's kingdom or his ability to let Scripture speak for itself.[43]

It is, however, worth pausing to note an interesting feature of such canonical, procapitalist texts as Novak's *The Spirit of Democratic Capitalism* and F. A. Hayek's *The Road to Serfdom*.[44] Advocates of modern capitalism are generally antagonistic toward government regulation and state funding of public-welfare programs. Yet, at several points both Novak and Hayek admit that there are circumstances where precisely this kind of government intrusion is necessary for the maintenance of a healthy society.[45] Capitalist devotees rarely acknowledge these stark departures from contemporary capitalist orthodoxy.[46] I believe this is worth noting in connection with what we have seen about the way Israel's legal code unapologetically interferes with personal property rights. Recall that Israelite landowners were legally prohibited from disposing of property as they pleased. They were obligated by law to share both their capital and their produce with the needy so that Israel's public welfare system served as a mark of national identity. There is no good reason for any disciple to think it a matter of Christian principle to decry government programs that assist the poor. That is capitalist ideology, not biblical thinking. The church should be asking itself, "What might be the twenty-first-century analogs to Israel's laws on gleaning, debt forgiveness, community tithing for the poor, sabbatical years, etc.?" We then need to engage in creative conversations about the implementation of the various way that we can urge the public and private sectors of society to work together in relieving poverty locally, nationally, and globally.

Thus Christian social activism will (a) begin within the community of faith and work outwards, (b) never become confused with humanistic optimism, whether from the right or the left, (c) always remain fused with personal witness to the Lordship of the resurrected Jesus, (d) not become discouraged at human failure, remembering that final "success" awaits the Parousia, and (e) happily cooperate with other private and public interests to bring about real change for all people.

Adam Smith, often considered the father of capitalism, lamented that the Christian church was "the greatest obstacle to the emergence of the capitalist economic order."[47] After all, the Christian habit of caring for the poor thoroughly undermined the competitive, entrepreneurial spirit essential to capitalist development. How surprised Mr. Smith would be today if he could see how easy it was for large sectors of the Western church to turn their backs on the poor, replacing grace with competition and service with success as the preeminent values in life.

Not long ago, two old friends of mine took an opportunity to open their home to a young woman in need of temporary housing. They told her that what was theirs was now hers for as long as she needed their help. They were members of a local megachurch and anxiously attended their next weekly small-group Bible study in order to ask for prayer that they might be able to share the love of Jesus with their young friend. Much to their surprise, the group unanimously challenged them on the wisdom of their decision. Everyone else in the group insisted that they would never do such a thing as open their home to a stranger.

"What if she steals from you?" they asked. "What if she breaks or ruins something? You don't know what she might be capable of!"

Fortunately, my friends had the spiritual maturity to ignore the collective evil expressed by these so-called fellow Christians (see chapter 7, above). Unfortunately, the all-too-comfortable Western church is filled with many modern Ananiases and Sapphiras who continue to spout the ancient, demonic temptations of selfishness that choke out sharing and hospitality like noxious weeds bent on ruining a beautiful vegetable garden.

Do not listen to such discouragement. It is the voice of Satan speaking. Be like my friends who took the opportunity to share the love of Jesus with a woman in need.

Recall the history of the ancient church. In AD 362, the Roman emperor Julian complained that devotion to the ancient gods was withering away due to the exemplary levels of Christian benevolence being shared with strangers and the poor all throughout the empire![48] Be a part of resurrecting that expression of the church.

Be like Barnabas. Share what belongs to you promiscuously; give to anyone who asks; make sure that there are no needy among you; educate yourself in the sufferings of others around the world; and watch what the Lord will do as you plant your seeds of grace.

Discussion Questions

1. What steps can you take in your personal finances to free up more resources for sharing with others?

2. What parts of your beliefs and thinking processes need to change in order for you to become a more generous, charitable person?

3. How is your local church involved in helping the poor? What can you do to take a more meaningful role in that ministry?

4. If we really understood that we do not rightfully own anything, that everything we have is a gift from God, and that the Lord expects us to use these
   God-given resources in order to meet the needs of others, how would you
   change? What specific steps can you begin to take now in order to make
   that change?

Additional Reading

Bell, Daniel M., Jr. *The Economy of Desire: Christianity and Capitalism in a Postmodern World*. Grand Rapids: Baker Academic, 2012.

Blomberg, Craig L. *Christians in an Age of Wealth: A Biblical Theology of Stewardship*. Grand Rapids: Zondervan, 2013.

Gay, Craig M. *With Liberty and Justice for Whom? The Recent Evangelical Debate
over Capitalism*. Grand Rapids: Eerdmans, 1991.

Sider, Ron. *Rich Christians in an Age of Hunger: Moving from Affluence to Generosity*. Nashville: Thomas Nelson, reprint 2015.

Witherington, Ben. *Jesus and Money: A Guide for Times of Financial Crisis*. Grand
Rapids: Brazos, 2010.

Chapter Eleven

"Blessed Are Those Who Suffer Because of Me"

"The New Testament is a brutal destroyer of human illusions. If you follow Jesus and don't end up dead, it appears you have some explaining to do."[1]

After stumbling on this quote in a review of Terry Eagleton's book *Reason, Faith, and Revolution: Reflections on the God Debate*, I had to run out and buy it. Leave it to a Marxist-atheist not only to articulate a wonderfully ironic defense of Christian faith but to confront the blatant inconsistencies on display in the Western (and especially the American) church as it persistently separates what it claims to believe from what it actually does. Is Eagleton wrong in charging that "for the most part [American Christianity] has become the creed of the suburban well-to-do"?[2]

I don't think so.

An insatiable desire for personal comfort is the main culprit preventing a good many professing Christians from following through on living out the ethics of Jesus as citizens of the kingdom of God. The well-to-do seldom transgress the social and economic norms that have created and sustained their well-to-do-ness. To do otherwise would be comparable to shooting yourself in the foot. How many millionaires advocate higher income taxes because they want to care for the poor by building a stronger social safety net? Not many. Instead, both the rich and the not-so-rich all tend to worship at the same altars of prosperity, altars that have been cleverly cloaked in the pious Christian trappings of heavenly blessing.

Our principal idols are the Bobbsey twins of security and success, societal ideals that bewitch the people of God just as they do everyone else. I confess that I find their charms alluring, for no one's desires for a charmed life animate me as energetically as my own do. My ability to empathize with others is seldom as highly attuned as my instincts for holding onto what is mine and avoiding the pain of losing it. Yet we have seen that these all-too-human instincts of self-aggrandizement run contrary to the upside-down kingdom values taught and modeled by Jesus. The gospel of God's kingdom never promises what many of us are hoping for: worldly security and success. On the contrary. We have already seen that following after Jesus promises to turn every disciple into an illegal alien, an inconvenient stranger traversing a difficult pilgrimage through an inhospitable foreign land, an outcast rejected by family and former friends whose only certainties in this life are the faithfulness of God, the grace of our Savior and the transforming presence of the Holy Spirit.

The second-century church father Tertullian (circa AD 155–240) spoke from experience when he warned that martyrdom, the sacrifice of one's life for Jesus, was the only legitimate option for Christians living in a pagan world.[3] American paganism may be more subtle than the civic religion of the Roman Empire, but it is every bit as real and all-pervasive—something I trust this book has demonstrated. Today's Western Christian will never be asked to shed an animal's blood while praying for a divinized president, but the sly ubiquity of American paganism—constantly energized by marketing firms, advertising agencies, political campaigns, military recruiters, shopping malls, self-help movements and positive thinking, prosperity-gospel megachurches—puts the twenty-first-century disciple in greater spiritual danger than Tertullian could have imagined. Whatever brand of paganism a Christian confronts, the unavoidable outcome of genuine discipleship will always be suffering. We may not be called literally to die for Jesus, but suffering in one form or another will inevitably mark the journey of God's faithful pilgrims.

It is no accident that the book of 2 Timothy insists that "all those who want to live a godly life in Christ Jesus will be persecuted" (2 Tim. 3:12). Paul, languishing in a Roman prison cell as he awaited execution, did not mince words. There are no ifs, ands, or buts about it. All kingdom citizens who make obedience to Jesus their life's goal will suffer some form of pain and opposition. The apostle understood what Jesus meant when he congratulated the disciples by saying, "Blessed are you when people insult you, persecute you and falsely say all kinds of evil against you because of me" (Matt. 5:10–12). Obeying the Lord of an inaugurated kingdom with upside-down values will always appear ineffective, misguided, naïve, narrow-minded, simplistic, uppity, antisocial, anticonservative, unprogressive, unreasonable, unrealistic, irrational, unsophisticated, and more than worthy of rejection, opposition, sneering, laughter, guffaws, head-shaking, and even violence by those who live outside the kingdom. "Rightly witnessed to the gospel so transforms the social vision of those who receive it that the result appears ... to be a form of craziness."[4]

The New Testament warns God's people in stark alternatives about the high price of following Jesus:

> [Jesus said,] If the world hates you, keep in mind that it hated me first. If you belonged to the world, it would love you as its own. As it is, you do not belong to the world, but I have chosen you out of the world. That is why the world hates you.... If they persecuted me, they will persecute you also. (John 15:18-20)

Jesus warns us in advance that his fate is prophetic: "Whoever wants to be my disciple must deny himself and take up his cross and follow me. For whoever wants to save his life will lose it, but whoever loses his life for me and for the gospel will save it" (Mark 8:34-35). Here is the ultimate expression of God's kingdom reversal. Losing our lives for Jesus, both literally and figuratively, is the only way kingdom living can happen. We know that we have followed the right path when we arrive at our own personal Calvary, where we allow the Father's love to carry us through the loss of everything else. The alternatives are clear and simple: follow Jesus and suffer persecution or avoid persecution by not following Jesus.

We should be alarmed if we have never suffered in any way for the gospel, for the New Testament logic is unavoidable: those who are *never* persecuted for their faith *are not* following Jesus, *are not* living righteous lives, and cannot be citizens of the kingdom of God. If we have never been mocked, smirked at, or dismissed; never been shunned, ignored, inconvenienced, or passed over for promotion; never been accused of being out of touch, unrealistic, or ridiculous; never been labeled narrow-minded for insisting that Jesus is the only way to God; have never lost a friend because our love for Jesus became a barrier rather than a bridge—then there is insufficient evidence to convict us on the charge of Christian discipleship. We are either impostors playing at kingdom citizenship or are among the most infantile disciples imaginable.

Rupert Shortt's eye-opening book *Christianophobia: A Faith under Attack* surveys the contemporary systematic persecution of the Christian church in nineteen countries around the world.[5] He reminds us that the twentieth century saw the torture and execution of more Christian martyrs than the previous nineteen centuries combined.[6] Knowing that we are surrounded by such a vast cloud of Asian, Middle Eastern, African, Latin American, and Eastern European witnesses to true faith (see Heb. 12:1), Western believers should warmly embrace the social slights, personal insults, and career hiccups that a Christian confession may occasionally generate in our society. Being a kingdom citizen in the

United States may prove inconvenient at times—though many people get along very well avoiding even a minimal level of discomfort—but it never demands that we shiver and starve in a dank prison cell before being beaten to death by an angry mob. Despite the Christian media's paranoid complaints about the discriminatory onslaught of "secular humanism," the American church remains remarkably comfortable, its tax-exempt status firmly intact. We haven't the foggiest notion of what real religious persecution feels like in this country. This is the inconvenient irony of Western Christianity: those sectors of the church who complain the loudest about being "under attack" are among those least capable of producing the evidence needed to convict them of discipleship.

The Church Tries to Reverse the Reversal

When it comes to the prospects of suffering for the gospel, the American church commits two mistakes that distort a proper understanding of its role in this world: first, Christians wish to occupy a privileged place in society; second, Christians want to live "triumphantly" here and now, immediately possessing all the power and authority exhibited in Christ's resurrection.

The first error is most clearly seen in the so-called culture wars supposedly waged between what passes for a Christian worldview and secular humanism.[7] What this obsession with spiritual warfare reveals, however, is not secularism's efforts to extinguish Christianity, but the church's assumption that Christianity has a right to unchallenged preeminence in the public square. This cultural conflict is not evidence of a cosmic struggle between light and darkness as the televangelists proclaim. Its roots are much more mundane and secular, for this so-called culture war is actually the last gasp of an antiquated confusion between church and state once referred to as Christendom, that is, the merging of Christianity with a nation's social, political, and cultural life such that the church and its teachings dominate public affairs, confusing Christian discipleship with state citizenship.[8] The current cultural combat is not concerned with a genuine defense of Christian faith, but is fomented by the church's misplaced desire to assert social and political dominance over society at large. Personally, I cannot blame nonbelievers for resisting these efforts.

How curious it is, then, to observe that neither Jesus nor Paul (or any of the other New Testament writers, for that matter) ever expresses the least bit of concern about seeing the church assert control over the social, cultural, or political landscape in their own day and age. The apostle Paul was surrounded by an utterly pagan Greco-Roman society awash in idolatry, immorality (from a Christian viewpoint), and bloodthirsty political maneuvering; yet he never so much as hints at the need for his communities to devise a strategy for taking over Rome's politics, social customs, arts, or mores. In this respect, Paul was following his master, for as Christopher Bryan correctly notes, Jesus did not show any interest in changing, much less controlling, the temporal forms of political power in his day either.[9] Instead, Jesus and Paul focused on creating a new, alternative community that would shine as a light to the world, showing the spiritually curious where they might discover the kingdom of God in the midst of this world's corruption.

In a pluralistic society such as America's, why should Christian prayers, holidays, and ceremonies be prioritized above those of other religions? Why should displays of the Ten Commandments, crucifixes, and nativity scenes receive pride of place on state lands and facilities without equal representation from Jewish, Muslim, Buddhist, or Hindu symbols? The honest answer is that there is no reason for Christian ceremonies or insignia to receive any state-sponsored preferential treatment. And being denied such prioritized benefits does not constitute discrimination, much less persecution. The fact that many Americans believe otherwise, and are willing to fight tooth and nail over small-minded concerns like manger scenes and Christian prayer in public schools, merely demonstrates how the American church is still trying to capitalize on the historical momentum generated by past centuries of Western Christendom, even as that momentum grinds to a halt. This explains the oddity of a country like the United States, which has never had an established state church and hence never officially participated in Christendom, nevertheless experiencing a culture war where Christian people assume that they are justified in imposing their religiously based moral code, spiritual sensibilities, and religious symbols on the rest of the nation.

We should not be the least bit surprised when non-Christian people resist the church's efforts to exercise such power over them. Unfortunately, when the predictable resistance appears, the church typically responds by crying "persecution," "discrimination," and "anti-Christian bias" when, in fact, prejudice and suppression are working the other way around. The church frequently behaves like the worst sort of petulant child, crying "foul!" when Christians are the ones kicking every other player in the shins.

To offer only one recent example, the US Air Force Academy in Colorado Springs, Colorado, has been the scene of a continuing dispute over religious freedom. Ever since the late 1990s, evangelical Christians (both students and faculty) had exercised a free hand not only in talking about their faith among friends (which everyone should be free to do) but in forcing Christian indoctrination on subordinates and fellow students.[10] Cadets who did not want to attend chapel were set apart and marched to their barracks in a formation dubbed the "heathen flight." Those uninterested in converting to Christianity report being insulted and penalized by upperclassmen who abused their authority to forcibly proselytize. Jewish cadets tell of being labeled "Christ-killers" and being told that the Holocaust was revenge for the death of Jesus. For a number of years, one of the favorite jokes at the Academy went like this: Question—"Why do Jews make the best magicians?" Answer—"Because they can go into a building and vanish in a puff of smoke." As the controversy became more public, Christian leaders played the victim card, offering further testimony to how the church has conformed itself to American culture by adopting its popular cult of victimhood. Spokesmen like James Dobson described the dispute as another example of persecution against the church. Congressman John Hostettler stood on the floor of the US House of Representatives to lament: "The long war on Christianity in America continues."[11] People who call themselves Christian while behaving so thuggishly demonstrate that they know little if anything about the kingdom of God.[12] They have made themselves so at home with the narcissistic, bullying tactics of this world that they can only be strangers and aliens to the ways of Jesus. Remember, Jesus said, "Blessed are you when people insult you . . . *because of me*" (Matt. 5:10-12). Being criticized as an insufferable jerk does not merit the Lord's blessing. It has nothing to do with suffering for the gospel.

A recent study probing levels of hostility directed against Christians in America sheds an interesting light on what the Religious Right has managed to accomplish as they prosecute their culture war at the Air Force Academy and the rest of the nation, especially as Christian leaders continue to complain about unfair discrimination against the church. Two professors from North Texas University, George Yancey and David Williamson, published the results of their nationwide research in the book *So Many Christians, So Few Lions: Is There Christianophobia in the United States?*[13] Unsurprisingly, Professors Yancey and Williamson discovered low levels of hostility against Christianity among those who hate all religion; this is not anti-Christian sentiment but a universal antireligious bias. These folks are equal-opportunity despisers, directing their ire against every belief in a Supreme Being. Christians who complain about suffering from this type of generic, antireligious hostility are simply warming up for the day when they will probably shirk Jesus's yoke altogether, as he expressly warned his followers that hostility was inevitable.[14] So, why complain about it? Rejoice that we have finally been given some evidence to confirm our confession and convict us of discipleship.

Much more importantly, Yancey and Williamson's work demonstrates that fundamentalist, evangelical, conservative Christianity—call it what you will, but for simplicity, let's stick with the "Religious Right"—has successfully confused the public's perception of the Christian faith and the liberating gospel of Jesus Christ with its conservative, right-wing, Republican politics (44). It is noteworthy that their study reveals very little hostility toward Christianity per se or toward the moderate ("liberal") church in America (33, 47). Rather, those who express anger and negativity toward Christianity explicitly define the target of their anger as the *Religious Right* (44, 47, 110–11, 138). In fact, many respondents assumed that Christians and Republicans were simply different labels for the same group (52). There was a strong tendency

> to conflate Christians with Republicans. . . . For respondents like these, *Christianity is a conservative political ideology*. . . . Anti-Christian hostility in the United States is primarily animosity directed toward conservative Christians. . . . It may be more accurate to talk about anti-conservative-Christian hostility than anti-Christian hostility. (4, italics added)[15]

In light of these data, Yancey and Williamson felt the need to modify the standard definition of Christianophobia to fit the American situation. For their discussion, Christianophobia "refers to an unreasonable hatred toward and fear of conservative Christians" (12, 11). The majority of their respondents, however, would insist that their fears are hardly unreasonable, since the political activities of the Religious Right demonstrate (to their minds) that the goal of American Christianity is to exert political and social control over the entire country (25–27, 45, 52–53, 109)—in effect, to establish an American Christendom, enforcing sectarian, religious values on believers and unbelievers alike. Whether or not such fears are reasonable is not the point. The point is that this has actually been the message broadcast by the Religious Right over several decades, and the nation has been listening.

So, where is the historical Jesus, the message of the cross, and the good news of God's kingdom in the midst of all this contentiousness? I know what it looks like when a friend rejects the gospel of Christ, with a whiff of superiority, because he will not admit to being a sinner who needs Jesus as his Lord and Savior. I know what it means to be judged an oddity for believing such twaddle myself. And, undoubtedly, some of the generic religion haters surveyed bear a degree of animus against Christian acquaintances who lovingly told them that they were sinners who needed to repent and follow Jesus. But nothing in Yancey and Williamson's findings suggests that the personal issues at stake in saying yes or no to the resurrected Jesus have any measurable role in American Christianophobia.[16] In fact, the truth of the gospel and the upside-downness of Jesus's kingdom values appear to have *nothing at all* to do with the high level of hostility many Americans feel toward the Christian faith. The monumental national and ecclesial tragedy crying out for recognition is that the Religious Right has managed to obscure the central message of the crucified, resurrected Jesus beneath a never-ending soundtrack of over-heated partisan rhetoric lamenting the dangers of "secular humanism" and "liberal politics."[17] They have pursued a no-holds-barred strategy to reach their partisan goals and have successfully accomplished what can only be described as a demonic victory. They have blacked out the good news of God's kingdom from public perception like a hellish eclipse of the Son. Such betrayers of God's kingdom have no business complaining about their bogus "persecution."

Wanting Resurrection without the Cross

The second error keeping much of the America church stunted in spiritual immaturity is the theological handmaiden to the first mistake. Too many churchgoers are looking for an easy detour around the road of Jesus's suffering and death so that they can speed-walk into the power and glory of his resurrection and ascension. In theological terms, they want to opt out of living in the church militant (composed of disciples here and now who struggle to deny themselves, resist the devil, say no to temptation, grieve over their disobedience, suffer opposition from the world and live counterintuitive, upside-down lives for the sake of being like Jesus) in order to rest victoriously in the church triumphant (the glorious assembly gathered up into heaven where they share in Christ's eternal reign).[18] Take notice sometime how many Christian churches, ministries, books, and retreat centers—especially on the Religious Right—describe themselves with the triumphant vocabulary of power, victory, glory, miracle, and success. It is endemic to the American scene.[19]

The problem, however, is that our heavenly Father does not allow his children to get rid of their yucky vegetables by feeding them to the pet dog under the dinner table so that they can immediately chow down on a double portion of dessert. There is a divinely ordained, historically determined sequence to the spiritual development of God's people, and it requires death before resurrection, burial before ascension, faithfulness among the church militant before exaltation with the church triumphant.

The Cambridge compendium *Suffering and Martyrdom in the New Testament* contains an insightful essay by Morna Hooker that traces the theme of "salvation as participation" throughout Paul's writings.[20] Professor Hooker explores the way the apostle not only describes Jesus as the church's substitute, the one who *acts on behalf* of God's people, but how he is also presented as our representative, the one *in whom the church participates* by sharing in his experience of obedience. Therefore, to share in the benefits of Christ's salvation, every disciple must personally identify with Christ, first in a step of faith and baptism, then by deliberately sharing in the personal experience of his sufferings. Suffering must precede glory.

Such participation is not automatic; it requires will and deliberation. Granted, the frequent references to the mutual indwelling of Christ with the believer, that is, "Christ in you"/"you in Christ" (Rom. 6:3–11; 8:1; 12:5; 16:3, 7, 9; 1 Cor. 1:30; 15:22; Col. 1:20, 27) point to a mystical union that locates every believer on the cross at Calvary (Rom. 6:3, 5, 6, 8; Gal. 2:20; Col. 2:20; 3:3), inside the tomb where Jesus was buried (Rom. 6:4), in Jesus's resurrection appearances before the public (Rom. 6:4, 5, 8), and, finally, ascended with him into heaven (Eph. 2:6; Col. 3:1). Yet Paul provides an even more elaborate discussion of how the believer's union with Christ is both mystical and existential—a current lived experience. Paul thus reminds the Romans of both the historical sequence and the temporal overlap of God's already/not-yet kingdom as the disciple experiences life in two realms simultaneously:

> The Spirit himself testifies with our spirit that we are God's children. Now if we are children, then we are heirs . . . if indeed we share in his suffering in order that we may also share in his glory. (Rom. 8:16–17)

First, note the language of participation, of a shared experience. The believer will experience in the flesh what Jesus already experienced himself. Genuine disciples are bound together with Christ in a common, lived experience—not an identical experience, but a shared experience. We will not all have nails hammered through our wrists, but we will all acquire our own stories of tears, rejection, loss, and heartache because our decision to follow Jesus, in one way or another, puts us at loggerheads with the ways of this world.[21]

Second, observe the unavoidable sequence of events: believers will share in Christ's glory *if and only if* they have first shared in his suffering. Suffering with Christ in this life is a precondition to glory in the next. A life devoid of suffering met in the course of following Jesus is clearly not a life lived in union with the crucified one. As a result, a totally pain-free Christianity has no reason to expect anything like victory, power, or glory in the future.

Finally, we should not overlook the ambiguity introduced by the presence of the Holy Spirit. The gift of the Spirit is evidence of Jesus's victory over death, yet that victory is not complete in this world because every Christian must still die. Expecting a life of unending triumph, glory, and power in this fallen world forgets that the earthly Jesus discovered his power in weakness, his triumph in defeat, the gift of life at the moment of his death.[22] God's kingdom has come, but it is not yet uncontested. We live in the time of overlap. Yes, we can see miracles, but unless Jesus returns today (which is always possible) we all must age, watch our bodies deteriorate, get sick, see loved ones die, and molder away in the grave. This world is not yet the place for pain-free celebration. That awaits the final resurrection.

The gift of the Spirit will always prove a conundrum to the thoughtful believer. On the one hand, the Spirit testifies that he can only reside within God's child. Therefore, whoever has God's Spirit is obviously a citizen of his kingdom. On the other hand, Paul goes on to whack every supposed child of God over the head with a colossal conditional ("if") clause (v. 17). We are God's children, heirs to Christ's glory, if—*if*—we share in the burden of Jesus's sufferings. Mystical union with Jesus always shows itself in the way Christ's love receives the world's antagonism in a disciple's life. Only those who can empathize with Jesus's sufferings by telling their own painful stories can safely say that they know Christ. As Morna Hooker concludes:

> This Gospel is not a mere objective fact to be believed, but a way of life to be accepted. Christian discipleship means identification with the Crucified Lord. . . . Those who follow this path of faith must be prepared to share the humiliation and suffering that it brings, if they wish to experience also the glory that God gives.[23]

Paul's second letter to the church in Corinth[24] contains a particularly poignant description of how the apostle viewed his own discipleship as both a living participation in the sufferings of Jesus and an opportunity to see his difficulties through the lens of the kingdom's upside-down values. In describing the hardships he endured, Paul says,

> We are hard pressed on every side, but not crushed; perplexed, but not in despair; persecuted, but not abandoned; struck down, but not destroyed. We always carry around in our body the death of Jesus, so that the life of

Jesus may also be revealed in our body. For we who are alive are always being given over to death for Jesus' sake, so that his life may also be revealed in our mortal body . . . because we know that the one who raised the Lord Jesus from the dead will also raise us with Jesus and present us with you to himself. (2 Cor. 4:8-14)

Paul's pains did not supplement Jesus's sufferings, but they were visible evidence of Paul's participation, of his union—both mystical and experiential—in his Savior's life. Confident in the reality of his union with his Lord, Paul accepted arrest, imprisonment, beatings, shipwreck, rejection, slander, betrayal, abandonment, and all manner of abuse as tangible, living, breathing, warm-blooded moments of encouragement and reward because it proved that he was living in God's kingdom.

Life is revealed in death. Strength is experienced in weakness. Winning occurs in the moment of losing. Yes, life in God's kingdom looks crazy.

Ensuring That We Not Reverse the Reversal

Before closing this chapter, I should clarify precisely what I mean by Christian suffering, which is, *experiencing hardship that is specifically a result of following Jesus.* I will share the advice offered by one of the church's most profound teachers on this subject, the nineteenth-century Danish Christian thinker Søren Kierkegaard.[25] Drawing from his own lifetime of discipleship, biblical and theological study, prayer, reflection, and personal tragedy, Kierkegaard provides in his writings a treasure chest of wisdom and insight into this subject. His handbook on discipleship, *Practice* [sometimes translated "Training"] *in Christianity* (published in 1850), had a significant influence on Dietrich Bonhoeffer's exposition on being faithful to Jesus, *The Cost of Discipleship*.[26]

Kierkegaard argues that three characteristics distinguish the suffering generated by faithful citizenship in God's kingdom: first, suffering for Jesus is voluntary; second, such suffering conforms us to the model of Jesus's suffering on the cross; third, from a natural, worldly perspective, suffering for Jesus makes little if any sense. It may even appear worthy of criticism to those around us. To use one of Kierkegaard's favorite phrases, it presents us with "the possibility of offense."

First, *suffering for Jesus is voluntary*. It is not voluntary in the sense that Christians have the freedom to select from a spiritual menu: choose one from column A—be the kind of Christian who doesn't suffer for Jesus; or one from column B—be the kind of Christian who does suffer for Jesus. No, discipleship does not work that way. Suffering for the gospel is voluntary only because following Jesus is a choice. No one who chooses to live in God's kingdom can opt out of suffering for their faith, but I can always choose to renounce my kingdom citizenship. Abandon Jesus. No more need to suffer. It's simple.[27]

There are a hundred and one ways to walk away from the Lord Jesus while still pretending to follow him. I need not become a Satan worshiper. All I have to do is dial in my compromises to the desired comfort level. Driven by my need to fit in and become one of the crowd, like a calf afraid to be separated from the herd, I simply shave off the faithful peculiarities that make a kingdom citizen stand out in this world. For instance, I can keep my mouth shut and stop talking about Jesus, his gospel, the need for repentance and obedience, the requirement of a changed life, and the claim he makes to be Lord of every person's life here and now. These basic topics can antagonize many of my fellow churchgoers as well as my irreligious friends. Sometimes faithful disciples can suffer hostility from within the church as well as from without. So all I have to do is identify which pieces of my loyalty to Jesus cause others to see me as inconveniently different, to treat me as an oddity (even if only a mild oddity), and then make sure that no one ever sees, hears, or smells those traits in me again. Voila! I am no longer an odd "other" but one of the gang. I can go along to get along.

On the other hand, I can choose to remain faithful to all the multifarious ways that loving and following Jesus make me an outsider to this world's status quo (and oh, how easily that status quo infiltrates the church!). I may suffer internally as I grieve over my sinful behavior when others chide me to forget about it, telling me that I was justified. Everyone does it. What's the big deal?

Or I can choose to love my enemies, which can quickly turn my countrymen into new enemies because I will not march in their patriotic parades of hatred, xenophobia, discrimination, racism, and warfare.[28] Instead, I can walk across the racial, national, tribal, social, class, and economic boundaries that my fellow citizens warn me to steer clear of. I can welcome the outsider, make the immigrant feel at home, invite "sinners, tax-collectors, and harlots" to share a meal with me, as Jesus did (Mark 2:15-16; Luke 5:30; 15:1).

Understanding the voluntary nature of suffering for the Lord also helps to distinguish universal human suffering from specifically Christian suffering. Human suffering is unavoidable, for it is woven into the tattered fabric of our mortal existence in this frayed and broken world. Everyone, Christian and non-Christian alike, will suffer from disease, accident, natural disaster, the death of loved ones, arthritis, and shingles. But too many preachers abolish this distinction by coddling their congregations into imagining that every inconvenience is an affliction born for Jesus.

There is a significant difference between Christian suffering and suffering Christianly. Fortunately, any universally human suffering can be redeemed for a spiritual purpose when it is endured in faith. Several New Testament writers offer advice on how to channel life's hardships into the development of godly character (Rom. 5:3-5; James 1:2-4). They teach us how to suffer Christianly.[29] However, even though trusting patiently in Jesus as I undergo chemotherapy is a beautiful expression of godly character, it is not suffering for my faith. The fact that this confusion has become commonplace is further testimony to how widespread is the church's neglect of the kingdom of God. Having so little genuine Christian suffering to pray about, pastors and parishioners alike conspire to smuggle a mangy dog into the manger. Praying for Aunt Minnie's bunions (as good as that may be) becomes the equivalent of asking Jesus to protect the oppressed who are being stepped on and maligned because they will not betray their Lord. Kierkegaard rightly laments the church's efforts to reverse God's kingdom reversal in this way. He repeatedly warns throughout *Practice in Christianity*:

> Christendom [misses the point] with regard to what is specifically Christian suffering . . . to such a degree has Christendom enjoyed preaching this whole rigmarole of earthly adversities into the category of specifically Christian suffering. Authentic Christian suffering has been abolished, [such as] suffering "on account of the Word" (Matt. 13:21), for "righteousness' sake" (Matt. 5:10). . . . Ordinary human sufferings have been dressed up to be Christian sufferings—what a masterpiece of upside-downness! What is decisive in Christian suffering is voluntariness and *the possibility of offense for the one who suffers.*[30]

Second, *Christian suffering makes us more like Jesus,* conforming us to the cross. Jesus teaches his followers that they must follow his lifestyle of self-denial, which will lead them to carry their own cross of suffering (Mark 8:34; Luke 14:27). Luke even adds the word "daily" (9:23) to Mark's saying in order to clarify the fact that faithful disciples will carry this cross of self-denial every day of their lives.

What does this mean?[31]

We can see by now that self-denial is the only way any sinful human being can cultivate an obedient and productive life in the kingdom of God. Jesus, after all, is both the first and the exemplary citizen of that kingdom. My natural human urges are working overtime in their attempts to sabotage any plans I make to live out the upside-down values taught and modeled by Jesus. Not everyone will struggle in the same way, but struggle we will. Fortunately, the Father gives us the gift of the Holy Spirit to remake our character so that the Lord's standards of ethical reversal become a real possibility for us.

I have to confess that loving my enemies and doing good things for those who hate me do not come easily (Matt. 5:43-48; Luke 6:27, 35). Neither does the sort of generosity that gives freely to anyone who asks without requiring repayment (Matt. 5:42; Luke 6:30). Nor do I hand out gifts so promiscuously that one hand loses track of what the other hand is doing (Matt. 6:3). I excel at keeping mental accounts on who owes me what and how much.

In all of these areas, and more, Christian discipleship only develops through a rigorous, daily discipline of saying no to my natural, sinful inclinations and saying yes to the Holy Spirit's impulses to make me more like Jesus. This is what Christian obedience looks like.

The cross was the Father's ultimate earthly goal for his Son. Allowing himself to be arrested unjustly on trumped-up charges, beaten, humiliated, and nailed to a cross to die in agony was the climax of Jesus's own self-denial, the climax to his own life of obedient discipleship. "Take up your cross daily" is a metaphor that sets the bar for Jesus's expectations of every other citizen in God's kingdom. We strive to be like him. True disciples obey the Father as Jesus did, no matter how painful or costly that obedience proves to be, even if it eventually exacts the ultimate price of losing our lives, too.[32] This expectation is nonnegotiable. Following Jesus is not like buying a condo, where I can choose between basic, mid-level, or deluxe units (some can get the Jacuzzi, while others may opt out). No, everyone is asked to pay the same price for the same product, for Jesus explicitly warns that those who insist on "saving their life," by holding on to their plans for success rather than submitting to God's plans for service, will finally "lose their life" (Mark 8:33-35; Luke 14:27; Phil. 2:4-8). I cannot be a part-time disciple. Though I often try, I find that it never works out well. Suffering for Jesus in some way is the fruit of choosing obedience rather than disobedience.

Jesus warns all would-be followers that the "gate is narrow and the way is hard that leads to life, and those who find it are few" (Matt. 7:14, ESV). Being a Christian was never intended to make for an easy life (at least in worldly, material terms). Kierkegaard eloquently explains:

> Hardship is the road. Far be from us also this hypocritical talk that life is so varied that some are walking along the same road without hardships, others in hardships. . . . Doubt about the task [of discipleship] always has its

stronghold in the idea that there could be other roads . . . but since hardship is the road, the hardship cannot be removed without removing the road, and there cannot be *other roads*, but only *wrong roads*.[33]

A crucified King has only one type of servant: a cross-bearer walking with him over a rocky and narrow path.

Third, *Christian suffering tempts the sufferer to be offended at the seeming craziness that Jesus requires.* This "possibility of offense" is, I believe, Kierkegaard's most important contribution to our understanding of New Testament faith.[34] Because God's kingdom establishes a counterintuitive, upside-down set of values leading disciples to reach ethical decisions in conflict with social norms, obedient believers will often find themselves tempted to think that Christ's demands are unreasonable, his requirements ridiculous. At this moment of imminent offense, we teeter at a crossroads. We can (a) choose to harbor the growing sense of God's injustice and look for an alternative "easier" way to follow Jesus, which is really the same as canceling our journey altogether. Or we can (b) push through this human preference for indignation, our eagerness to judge God by our own sinfully skewed standards, and choose to persevere in faith, believing in God's promises. Christian faith is always a movement beyond the temptation to be offended by Jesus and to quit the journey. But faith overcomes offense with Job's own resolve: "God may kill me, but still I will trust him" (Job. 13:15, CEV).

Commenting on Jesus's parable in Mark 4:3-20 and focusing on those who make a start in the kingdom but then "fall away quickly when trouble or persecution comes because of the word" (v. 17), Kierkegaard remarks on how easily people mistake Christianity for the way to comfort and convenience:

> The fact that tribulation and persecution come on account of the Word is the self-contradiction in which the possibility of offense is present. . . . They go to the Word to seek help—and then come to suffer on account of the Word. The help looks like torment. . . . Everyone who stands outside must say: He must be mad to expose himself to all that. . . . Now the issue is: will you be offended or will you believe? If you will believe, then you will push through the possibility of offense and accept Christianity on any terms . . . then you say: Whether it is a help or a torment, I want only one thing, I want to belong to Christ, I want to be a Christian.[35]

For those who know and experience the eternal promises of God's kingdom, it is a privilege to suffer, whether directly or obliquely, for the Savior who gave his life for us. The kingdom realigns our estimate of worth and value, what brings us joy and what causes grief. Serving Jesus, no matter the consequences, becomes the disciple's raison d'être, the basis of fulfillment and satisfaction. The New Testament book of Acts describes how the apostles, jailed by their Jerusalem opponents for preaching in the name of Jesus, walked away from their accusers "rejoicing because they had been counted worthy of suffering disgrace for the Name" (Acts 5:41). Western Christians may never risk imprisonment or public humiliation, but we can still share in the apostles' rejoicing whenever we risk the negative consequences of living our lives like foreigners who will not bend before the hostile winds of a blowhard world. We can stand straight to bolster the cause of justice wherever we see injustice. We will remain honest in an environment of duplicity. We will speak up for the voiceless whenever we witness their exploitation. In this dystopian world of post-9/11 America, God's kingdom citizens will be the first to reach out to, befriend, and defend their Muslim neighbors, together with anyone else feeling threatened in our increasingly hostile society, and share God's unconditional love with them all. And we will do these things, come what may, because as citizens of God's eternal kingdom, we choose "to fix our eyes not on what is seen, but on what is unseen. For what is seen is temporary, but what is unseen is eternal" (2 Cor. 4:18).

Discussion Questions

1. Have you ever experienced anything you would call "persecution" or suffering for Jesus? If so, how did your situation illustrate the three characteristics of Christian suffering discussed in this chapter?

2. In how many different ways have you found yourself trying to "reverse the reversal" in order to avoid Christian suffering? What do you need to change about your life or attitudes?

3. How can you help your local congregation and its leadership shine more brightly as a distinctive community of people faithful to the kingdom of God?

Additional Reading

Barth, Karl. *The Call to Discipleship*. Translated by G. W. Bromiley, edited by K. C. Hanson. Minneapolis: Fortress, 2003.

Bonhoeffer, Dietrich. *The Cost of Discipleship*. Translated by R. H. Fuller. New York: Macmillan, 1963.

Horbury, William, and Brian McNeil, eds. *Suffering and Martyrdom in the New Testament*. Cambridge, UK: Cambridge University Press, 1981.

Hovey, Craig. *To Share the Body: A Theology of Martyrdom for Today's Church*. Grand Rapids: Brazos, 2008.

Kierkegaard, Søren. *Practice in Christianity*. Translated and edited by Howard V. Hong and Edna H. Hong. Princeton: Princeton University Press, 1991.

Whitfield, Joshua J. *Pilgrim Holiness: Martyrdom as Descriptive Witness*. Eugene, OR: Cascade, 2009.

Chapter Twelve

Being a Kingdom Church

I walked out of the police station in a daze after ten hours in custody. I was exhausted and dehydrated, fumbling now with five different plastic bags made of the slipperiest material I'd ever held in my hands. Each bag contained a different piece of my personal belongings, all confiscated when I was initially booked, fingerprinted, and photographed. One crucial item was missing, however, my eyeglasses, which had been smashed when a half dozen policemen lifted my body into the air and threw me to the pavement face first with my arms twisted behind my back. Several knees dug into the small of my back, while gloved hands grabbed my legs. A heavy boot was planted on my head, firmly pressing my face into the concrete.

My exit from the station was channeled down a human corridor of police standing shoulder to shoulder, extending from the station doors to the sidewalk. I had taken only a few steps when a crowd of fifty to seventy-five strangers let out a raucous cheer, giving me a standing ovation. The same greeting was repeated every time another protester was released that night. I was now one of the "NATO one hundred," the moniker given to those of us who were arrested in May 2012 by the Chicago Police Department while marching in a peaceful and nonviolent protest against NATO militarism, particularly America's use of NATO forces for its own military adventurism.

Before I could begin to process what was happening, a vibrant-looking young woman approached, holding a steaming bowl to my face with both hands as if it were a burnt offering.

"Don't worry. It's vegan," she said with a reassuring smile.

The look on the woman's face almost convinced me to take the bowl of hot food, despite the fact that I am a confirmed carnivore. I politely declined but asked if I could have a bottle of water instead.

"Of course," she said.

Her long, flowing skirt twirled in the humid evening air as she turned away. Another young woman approached, with an equally big smile, holding open a large brown paper bag. She asked if I needed anything—cigarettes, gum, aspirin, or whatever. No sooner had I assured her that I was fine than a man in his mid-twenties with a bushy black beard, scruffy hair, and coal black eyes approached with a look of dead earnestness.

"May I have the chance, please?"

I wasn't sure what he was asking, but before I could think to respond, he wrapped both arms around my shoulders and gave me a long, firm bear hug.

The first woman returned with a bottle of water, and I downed it in one long gulp. There had been a drinking fountain in my cell, but the fountain and the water were hot, dank, and dirty. It was still the hottest day of the year, and my thirst was anything but satisfied. Even at 2 a.m., the humidity felt oppressive.

Two men, one in his late twenties and the other, I guessed, in his early forties, approached with clipboards. They introduced themselves as members of the National Lawyers Guild, an ad hoc collection of attorneys offering their services pro bono to all those who had been arrested by the Chicago police over the past several days. They both took down my personal information—in order to have duplicates, I suppose—asked me to describe the details of my arrest, explained the nature of our attorney-client privilege, and then emphasized that under no circumstances was I to discuss my case with anyone from the police department or the prosecutor's office. I was not even to tell my story to family or friends.

The police had looked to me like an army of storm troopers from the dark side, many on horseback, all outfitted from head to toe in black Kevlar body armor, carrying clubs and heavy Plexiglas shields, all advancing without provocation against the group of peaceful protesters. They had marched toward us, forcing an unnecessary confrontation that resulted in the injury and arrest of innocent citizens who were doing nothing more than exercising their constitutional rights to peaceable assembly and freedom of speech.[1]

My primary memory from that night, however, was not about the police but about the supportive community that was waiting to greet me in the streets. An extensive collection of like-minded people from across the country had come together to work toward a shared purpose that was born of common values. A part of that purpose included taking care of each other. They had pooled their resources, anticipated what people's needs might be after release from a police station, offered their services—including professional services— free of charge and took care of those who needed their help. Providing food, comfort, encouragement, legal counsel, and moral support, these generous citizens made it clear that they appreciated the efforts of anyone who followed the dictates of their conscience in the cause of peace and was willing to suffer the negative consequences.

Strengthening the Community of Kingdom Citizens

My brief but significant experience of spontaneous community that hot Chicago night offers a good corollary to the central role that should be filled by the Christian church in the implementation of Jesus's kingdom ethics in this world. As the community of flesh-and-blood citizens inhabiting God's kingdom, the church is called to be the birthplace and the supportive family that assists faithful disciples in both the blessings and the risks awaiting anyone daring enough to obey Jesus's upside-down model of loving God.

In fulfilling this mission, God's kingdom community will be characterized by a number of essential features, none of which are electives from which we may pick and choose as we like. Rather, they are each defining *traits that identify the church as church*, as opposed to its being a curious religious/social club. First, every kingdom community will be awash in biblical teaching that explains how Christ not only died for us but also how he lived for us in order to exemplify the way of salvation. A community of the redeemed will worship and adore the Lord Jesus for his gracious sacrifice, and it will exemplify his teaching and ministry throughout the regular affairs of daily life.

Consequently, the material contained in this book should not be unfamiliar to members of the body of Christ. On the contrary, all of these lessons should be old hat for anyone who regularly attends a Christian church, as familiar as a child's nursery rhyme to even the youngest novice disciple. Wherever Jesus's teaching is new or unfamiliar, remedial measures need to be vigorously implemented by church leaders, for the community obviously has not fulfilled its responsibilities. Anyone inclined to reject Jesus's gospel lessons as objectionable or unrealistic requires mentoring by more mature disciples who can explain the importance of following Jesus faithfully from their own personal experience. As both Martin Luther and Søren Kierkegaard insisted, in this world the true church is always the church militant, never the church triumphant. Whenever the church becomes a byword for prosperity, comfort, and success, or offers nothing more than a blasé ceremonial blessing draped over a safe, middle-class life proceeding without inconvenience or interruption, then the church has ceased to be the church. Those who refuse to embrace the difficulties of authentic discipleship need a good talking to, an occasion on which they are told, gently but firmly, that their behavior belies their confession. Jesus warned the boastful disciples who were seeking recognition for their gifts of prophecy and miracles:

> Not everyone who says to me, "Lord, Lord," will enter the kingdom of heaven, but only those who do the will of my Father who is in heaven. Many will say to me on that day, "Lord, Lord, did we not prophesy in your name, and in your name drive out demons and perform many miracles?" Then I will tell them plainly, "I never knew you. Away from me, you evildoers." (Matt. 7:21-23)

We dare not forget that the Father's will, previously described by Jesus in Matthew 5-7, never says anything about working miracles, exorcisms, or delivering prophecies. Rather, true disciples reveal themselves as those who are poor in spirit (5:3), meek and merciful (5:4-7), behave as peacemakers (5:9), are persecuted for the sake of Jesus and his gospel (5:10-12), never carry grudges (5:21-26), always speak the truth and keep their word (5:33-37), love, serve, and pray for their enemies (5:28-48), share generously with anyone in need without ever demanding repayment (6:1-4), forgive all those who sin against them (6:14-15), and make faithful kingdom citizenship the number-one priority of life (6:33).

No one can follow the Lord Jesus by moving exclusively along broad, smooth, level, six-lane highways festooned with convenience stores, gas stations, restaurants, and health spas. Jesus warns us in advance that he rarely travels those routes. His preferred pathways are dusty, narrow, steep, rocky, inconvenient, lacking in amenities, and often dangerous. No one can complain that they weren't warned. Jesus commands us to "enter through the narrow gate. For wide is the gate and broad is the road that leads to destruction, and many enter through it. But small is the gate and narrow the road that leads to life, and only a few find it" (Matt. 7:13-14).

Serving among such faithful Christian communities entails the cultivation of a normative Christian self-understanding throughout the entire body of Christ that focuses on *the ultimacy of life in the kingdom of God*. The focal point of a disciple's identity is life in Christ, not nationality, gender, sexual orientation, career, hobbies, levels of personal consumption, leisure-time pursuits or political activities. This self-understanding will express itself as community members (a) consistently think, believe, and behave according to the upside-down values of God's kingdom; (b) remember that this world is not the believer's true home, that we are only pilgrims here, strangers passing through a fallen world on our way to a perfected, eternal home; (c) learn not to value what the rest of this world values so that we remain free of its deceptive power—for us "to live is Christ, and to die is gain" (Phil. 1:21); (d) remember that we are always sinners saved by grace, even as we are being sanctified through experience. This means that following Jesus—at some level, in some way—will commonly run contrary to our natural inclinations. When my faith in Jesus *never* makes me the oddball in the board room, then I know that I have lost my way somewhere along the line.

Human nature, being what it is, will frenetically poke and prod each of us, looking for a way to turn this advice into the framework for a new game of spiritual one-upmanship. But kingdom communities will consciously foster an environment that rejects legalism and works-righteousness while making grace-filled obedience to a forgiving Savior central. We will bear each other's burdens, rejoicing with those who rejoice and mourning with those who mourn (Rom. 12:15), not guffawing at those who bungle or turning green with envy at those who succeed. Richard Burridge makes an important observation in his book *Imitating Jesus: An Inclusive Approach to New Testament Ethics*, when he notes that, whereas Jesus's ethical instruction is always rigorous and demanding, his actual treatment of repentant sinners, including his doubtful disciples who often fail him, is always gracious and forgiving.[2] Anyone who genuinely wants to follow Jesus can always have another chance—another chance to do the hard things he tells us to do. Jesus is like the patient parent who anxiously anticipates the day when his child will walk all the way to school by herself; but as long as the child remains an infant, he lovingly cheers her on at every feeble act of faith, no matter how imperfect, one faltering step at a time. But he never excuses her from the task of walking.

Moments of fellowship and mutual support in such communities will extend well beyond the typical chitchat about ball games and vacation plans. It will include regular stories of how our friends have taken risks, suffered setbacks, and been shunned by others in their efforts to live for Jesus. The church community will be able to recite the details of miraculous interventions, dramatically transformed lives, amazing answers to prayer, and the refreshing presence of the Holy Spirit—all of which occurred because faithful brothers and sisters were serious about the risky business of following Jesus.

Conversely, there is no reason for God's kingdom people to expect similar behavior from those living outside of the kingdom or to shun unbelievers for violating the norms of kingdom living. Unfortunately, this is an ancient confusion that many in the church perpetuate today. When the apostle Paul condemned sexual immorality within the Corinthian church (1 Cor. 5:1–5), he urged the community to discipline the guilty parties by banning them from the fellowship until they repented and changed their ways (vv. 2, 5, 11). Discipline was a tool for redemption. The church, however, grabbed the wrong end of the stick and mistakenly assumed that Paul's admonition "not to associate with sexually immoral people" (v. 9) meant that they should not have any dealings with people outside of the Christian community. This is always the easier—and more self-righteous—decision to make. However, Paul offers a quick correction:

> I have written you in my letter not to associate with sexually immoral people—not at all meaning the people of this world who are immoral. . . . In that case you would have to leave this world. . . . What business is it of mine to judge those outside the church? Are you not to judge those inside? God will judge those outside. (1 Cor. 5:9–13)

The church suffers from a massive delusion when its members think they are justified in refusing to do business with "sinners" outside of the community. Are we to assume that Paul, the tentmaker (Acts 18:3), never sold a tent to local shoppers in the marketplace because they, like everyone else in the ancient world, prayed to their household-ancestor deities before family meals?[3] I doubt that very much. Consequently, *Christians are not being persecuted* when they suffer the legal consequences of such self-righteous discrimination against those unlike themselves. Whatever the penalties may be for this misguided misbehavior, none of it has anything to do with following Jesus of Nazareth, the man who feasted with sinners, tax-collectors, and prostitutes.

Finally, a community of kingdom citizens will work to break down the traditional, destructive liberal/conservative political dichotomies by doing evangelism and proclaiming historically orthodox theology while *simultaneously* encouraging widespread countercultural kingdom living and social activism among its members. The modern American evangelical church's unhelpful identification of historic orthodox theology with conservative Republican politics, while it identifies and links liberal, unorthodox theology with progressive Democratic politics, has always been a poisonous misrepresentation that is damaging to both ends of the political spectrum. The kingdom of God can never be identified by way of anyone's political Rorschach test, as though we can project a new tax policy or foreign affairs initiative on the screen and then discover God's will in the fine details.[4] Real disciples simply will not fit into anyone's partisan mold because Jesus's kingdom mindset is not of this world.

I once told a colleague that he had given me one of the nicest compliments of my life when he said in exasperation that he could never predict where I would come down on a controversial social issue. I smiled and said, "Thank you. I hope that is because I am trying to think biblically, not politically."

I am still trying.

The church must continually plug its ears to the numerous strategies that are offered for manipulating earthly power for kingdom purposes by grabbing the reins of government. The lie of that power is as old as the devil himself. Those who would co-opt the kingdom of God for their own partisan agendas need to listen again to Jesus's rebuke when that very temptation was first offered to him in the wilderness: "Away from me, Satan! For it is written: 'Worship the Lord your God, and serve him only'" (Matt. 4:10).

Admittedly, equally sincere disciples will not always agree on where the lines of kingdom faithfulness should be drawn. One of the intractable debates that divided the German Confessing Church in the days of the Third Reich was a stubborn disagreement over when resistance against the state was genuinely theological and confessional (and therefore justified) versus when resistance was merely political and not truly a result of faithfulness to the gospel (and therefore unjustified).[5] As a result, the Confessing Church never extended its critique of the Nazi government beyond its interference in church affairs; and it never criticized Nazi foreign or domestic policy. For example, Confessing Church leaders such as Pastor Martin Niemöller never opposed the Nazi anti-Semitism laws because the enactment of those laws did not interfere with normal church life.[6] After the war Niemöller confessed that his own anti-Semitism had blinded him to the demonic nature of the Nazi discrimination laws. Today it would be well worth the time for church members to prayerfully discuss—with Bible in hand and an unwavering focus on the personal character cultivated by kingdom citizenship—what the gospel's implications are for a Christian's response to the laws, policies, and actions of our own government. In how many ways has American Christianity been blinded to the right-minded implementation of God's upside-down kingdom values because of our own cultural conditioning?[7]

What about Effectiveness?

At this point I expect that more than a few readers are wondering whether living out Jesus's kingdom ethic in this way will doom the Christian church to forever sit on the sidelines when it comes to effecting real change in the world. How can the church's efforts at eradicating even the smallest part of humanity's suffering ever prove effective if we are wedded to Jesus's irrational, antipragmatic views of godly behavior? Some, such as the prominent twentieth-century theologian Reinhold Niebuhr, have concluded that, while Jesus's teachings offer a noble, personal ethic for individuals, it becomes irrelevant when engaging larger social issues, such as justice, war, peace, poverty, homelessness, or economics. Niebuhr insisted that the ethics of Jesus could never inform "a prudential social ethic."[8] Thus his teachings have no application "to the task of securing justice in a sinful world."[9]

I have tried to argue throughout this book that, on this point, Niebuhr and all those who follow him are mistaken—in at least two ways. First, Niebuhr repeats the common error of assuming that Jesus expected his kingdom ethics to be lived out by everyone—an expectation doomed to be unrealized. Second, the church always gets itself into trouble when it forgets who it is and what it is called to be, that is, the people who trust, obey, and imitate Jesus of Nazareth, the risen Christ—*all of the time, wherever they go.* There is no escape clause allowing disciples to abandon godly behavior while reverting to their sinful impulses as long as the shift in gears serves a noble cause. Instead, the challenge for kingdom citizens is to be "as shrewd as snakes while remaining as gentle as doves" (Matt. 10:16). One can be smart, informed, educated, even stubborn, deliberate, and hard-nosed while living an upside-down life.

What the world needs more than anything else is not a superior social ethic but the kingdom of God. It is not the church's responsibility to Christianize society but, first, to thoroughly Christianize itself as the collective of all God's kingdom people. That kingdom society, with all of its world-changing ethical, social, and cultural significance, expands only as more and more individuals surrender themselves to the lordship of Jesus Christ. We need to keep this order straight: we do not expand God's kingdom by changing the world; God changes the world through the good news of his kingdom and the resulting community of obedient disciples who share the gospel while living crazy, upside-down, self-sacrificial lives. In this way, Jesus's followers exhibit the blessing of God's alternative society for anyone craving an alternative to life in this dog-eat-dog world.

For the believer, gospel and ethics can never be separated; yet the church often forgets this link. Many among the Religious Right confuse gospel faithfulness with harsh condemnations of those, like secularists, humanists, gays, and other "deviants," who have yet to receive Jesus, behaving as if it were abhorrent to associate with sinners who remain sinful. On the other hand, more politically "liberal" believers frequently confuse their activism with gospel proclamation, forgetting that the good news of Christ requires verbal explanation. I once attended a denominational workshop for training in strategies of nonviolent resistance. The one strategy that was never mentioned (until I raised the issue) was how to look for fresh opportunities to talk about Jesus Christ in the middle of a demonstration, including conversations with both our compatriots in the current social coalition and those standing on the opposite side of the fence.

For anyone who believes in life after death, becoming a citizen of God's kingdom is the most important social transformation one can hope for in this world. Anyone who counters by suggesting that prioritizing the gospel somehow denigrates the importance of social, political, and cultural engagement has not been paying attention. How much do we really love others if we teach them to grow better crops or help them to climb out of poverty but remain needlessly mute about the Father's offer of eternal life through his one and only Son? Jesus asks every social activist, "How does a man benefit if he gains the whole world and loses his soul in the process?" (Mark 8:36, The Living Bible).

The answer is obvious.

Second, those worrying about effectiveness can forget that the power of the cross is revealed in its apparent foolishness. Calvary is the supreme moment of victory through failure. Though believers can never use the upside-down nature of God's kingdom to excuse silly, rude, or ignorant social proposals, we must always guard ourselves against the tyrannical need to fit in or to be taken seriously by the rest of society as our reason for compromising God's kingdom values. That is the road to ruin. This will mean that disciples are not always the most reliable partners in their social coalitions. Clashes are inevitable between kingdom values and the tactics often employed by others in working toward social change. For instance, disciples can never use or justify violence as a means to some greater end. Similarly, no matter how wonderful a candidate may be, kingdom citizens cannot be involved with the kinds of dirty tricks and smear tactics commonly used in political campaigns. Nor should we be surprised if our worldly allies sometimes drop us from their list of friends because they find our approach to problem-solving to be too naïve, soft, or ineffective. At the end of the day, disciples must ask whether we really believe what we profess about God's power and sovereignty over history, not as an excuse for doing nothing but as the necessary assurance for doing the right things in the right way while leaving the outcome to God.

Third, this pragmatic worry about effectiveness is also common to the popular "dominionist" approaches to Christian engagement circulating today, whether it appears in the neo-Calvinist, Kuyperian desire to redeem society via cultural engagement, the Religious Right's obsession with winning the culture wars, or the more recent populist movements such as the one striving to "reclaim the seven mountains of cultural influence" in America.[10] While all of these approaches to Christian social ethics are subject to the criticisms made above, they also make the additional mistake of assuming that the church must dominate the terms of public conversation and enjoy a comfortable majority in hospitable circumstances before it can truly be the church.

We have already seen that this misconception is as old as Christendom's confusion of Christian ethics with civic behavior, combined with the bizarre expectation that Christians need never suffer. The poet T. S. Eliot, whose theological ability unfortunately lagged behind his poetic muse, was another spokesman for this triumphalist view of Christian cultural engagement. In his book *The Idea of a Christian Society*, Eliot writes, without a hint of irony, that it is "intolerable" for Christians ever to expect "to lead a Christian life in a non-Christian world," since only a sufficiently Christian society provides "maximum opportunity for us to lead wholly Christian lives."[11] What a perverse twist on Christian servanthood to assume that the church's efforts at society's improvement should spring from its own self-interests and aversion to pain. This is an underhanded back-channeling of the human impulse to whittle down the kingdom's yoke—or to replace Jesus's hardwood yoke with one made of balsa wood—until it is barely the weight of a toothpick (Matt. 11:29-30).[12] It is a selfish ruse attempting to hide (whether consciously or not) the church's real concern: if society can be sufficiently Christianized, then Christians can comfortably conform to society's norms, avoiding the discomfort that comes with living as aliens in this world, and confusing kingdom living with Christian acculturation.

I am certain that the apostle Paul and all the members of his fledgling churches remained blissfully unaware of the fact they could never live "wholly Christian lives" because they were condemned to dwell in a paganized, Greco-Roman world. I suspect that Jesus would be shocked to discover that his ethical demands were grossly unrealistic and that expecting his followers to live accordingly would have to wait several centuries until Christianity became society's official religion.

Fourth, *Christian ethics cannot exist apart from Christ*, which means that living out a Christian ethic can never be divorced from a person's submission to Christ's lordship. Thus Jesus's expectations for kingdom citizens cannot be offered promiscuously as a general social ethic for world transformation. Christ's ethics are applied to the body of Christ living in the power of the Spirit. The church's first task is to actually be the church as defined by the Lord himself; to be that community of faith where no one goes without the essentials; where everyone's needs are met; where forgiveness, reconciliation, unconditional love, and mercy reign; where the poisonous fruit of nationalism, civil religion, and violence are always rejected; where the lost can find a new home and the marginalized can experience acceptance.

Then, shunning hypocrisy, knowing that we must live consistently everywhere and at all times, disciples are the same kinds of people with everyone else as they are "at home" with their brothers and sisters in Christ. We will be directed by the same concerns for justice, righteousness, nonviolence, honesty, fairness, mercy, and kindness everywhere in the world. Remembering that all people bear the same image of the same creator God, disciples can eagerly join hands and collaborate with anyone who shares similar goals for social, cultural, and political transformation.

But let's not be confused. Mohandas Gandhi was not working for the kingdom of God. He was a powerful champion of peace and justice for the Indian people, and a legitimate hero for all those committed to nonviolence. God's image shone brightly in his life, and its flourishing is always a beautiful thing to behold, well worth acknowledgment by the people of God. Undoubtedly, many followers of Jesus righteously collaborated with him as a vital expression of their own Christian discipleship. Yet, without some explanation of the gospel, without repentance and the confession of sin, without submission to the lordship of Jesus Christ, what Gandhi's movement accomplished was important humanitarian work that improved millions of people's lives, but it did nothing to enhance the kingdom of God.

What a tragedy that Gandhi's negative experiences with bigotry in the all-white churches of England and South Africa helped alienate him from the truth of the gospel. In any case, however praiseworthy our united endeavors at social, cultural, or political improvement may be, followers of Jesus Christ can never be fully satisfied with half measures, even beautiful half measures. For forgiven sinners who rest in the love and grace of Jesus Christ, only the eternal benefits of kingdom work will do.

Discussion Questions

1. In what area(s) of your life have you been most challenged by this book?

2. What specific steps will you take, or personal disciplines will you cultivate, to become a more obedient kingdom citizen in this/these area(s)?

3. In what ways does your local church/Christian community demonstrate that it is a genuine "kingdom community" as described in this chapter?

4. In what ways does your local church/Christian community still need to grow and mature in becoming the "kingdom church" described in this chapter?

5. How can you make a positive contribution to your church's growth as a family of faithful kingdom citizens?

Additional Reading

Cobb, John B., ed. *Resistance: The New Role of Progressive Christians*. Louisville: Westminster John Knox, 2008.

Dayton, Donald W. *Discovering an Evangelical Heritage*. New York: Harper & Row, 1976.

Ellul, Jacques. *The Politics of God and the Politics of Man*. Ed. and trans. by Geoffrey Bromiley. Grand Rapids: Eerdmans, 1972.

Hauerwas, Stanley, and William H. Willimon. *Resident Aliens: Life in the Christian Colony*. Nashville: Abingdon, 1989.

Sider, Ronald J. *Just Politics: A Guide for Christian Engagement*. Grand Rapids: Brazos, 2012

————. *Nonviolent Action: What Christian Ethics Demands but Most Christians Have Never Really Tried*. Grand Rapids: Brazos, 2015.

Stringfellow, William. *An Ethic for Christians and Other Aliens in a Strange Land*. Waco, TX: Word, 1973.

Yoder, John Howard. *What Would You Do? A Serious Answer to a Standard Question*. Scottdale: Herald, 1992.

Notes

Notes to the Preface

1. Gregory A. Smith and Jessica Martinez, "How the Faithful Voted: A Preliminary 2016 Analysis," *Pew Research Center*, November 9, 2016, available at: http://www.pewresearch.org/fact-tank/2016/11/09/how-the-faithful-voted-a-preliminary-2016-analysis/.

2. Trump's landslide among conservative Christian voters is even more striking when seen by way of national statistics. Forty-two percent of all eligible voters did not bother to vote in the 2016 presidential election; of the 58 percent who did vote, Hillary Clinton had 48 percent of the popular vote (about 3 million more popular votes than Trump), and he received 46 percent of the popular vote. Thus, Clinton tallied only 28.4 percent of all eligible US voters, while only 27.2 percent of all eligible voters voted for Trump. All in all, then, roughly three-quarters of all American voters did not vote for Donald Trump, whereas 81 percent of evangelical voters helped him win the presidency via the Electoral College (see Ryan McMaken, "26 Percent of Eligible Voters Voted for Trump," *Mises Institute*, November 9, 2016, available at: https://mises.org/blog/26-percent-eligible-voters-voted-trump).

3. For a convenient summary of what I judge to be only a few of Obama's unacceptable policy decisions, see Andrew J. Bacevich, "Barack Obama: Anatomy of a Failure," *The Spectator*, January 3, 2015, available at: https://www.spectator.co.uk/2015/01/barack-obama-anatomy-of-a-failure/; Peter Maass, "Obama's Gift to Donald Trump: A Policy of Cracking Down on Journalists and Their Sources," *The Intercept*, April 6, 2016, available at: https://theintercept.com/%202016/04/06/obamas-gift-to-donald-trump-a-policy-of-cracking-down-on-journalists-and-their-sources/; Matt Clarke, "Obama Administration Promises Transparency but Vigorously Prosecutes Whistleblowers," *Prison Legal News*, December 2, 2015, available at: https://www.prisonlegalnews.org/news/2015/dec/2/obama-administration-promises-transparency-vigorously-prosecutes-whistleblowers/; Adam Gallagher, "Obama's Dangerous Drone Policy," *The American Prospect*, September 29, 2016, available at: http://prospect.org/article/obama%e2%80%99s-dangerous-drone-policy.

4. William Stringfellow, *An Ethic for Christians and Other Aliens in a Strange Land* (Waco, TX: Word Books, 1973), 13 (italics in original).

Notes to Chapter One

1. Larry Hendricks, "Flag Soldier Died Deeply Conflicted," *Arizona Daily Sun*, March 10, 2007, available at: http://azdailysun.com/articles/2007/03/11/news/2007 0311_news_39.txt.

2. These two brave women of conscience were not the only ones who put themselves at risk by refusing to approve of or to apply torture. For instance, see Rebecca Gordon, "6 Heroes Who Refused to Torture," *Alternet*, February 10, 2015, available at: http://www.alternet.org/news-amp-politics/6-heroes-who-refused-torture. Fortunately, more names can be added to this short list, such as Colonel Morris Davis, originally assigned to be the chief prosecutor at Guantanamo Bay, who resigned in protest after witnessing the treatment of prisoners there. Nevertheless, the list of exemplary men and women of conscience during this dark chapter in American history is tragically short.

3. Kayla Williams (with Michael E. Staub), *Love My Rifle More Than You: Young and Female in the U.S. Army* (New York: Norton, 2005).

4. This was true during the administration of George W. Bush. Even though President Obama officially ended the use of torture by members of the government and its military, he continued the practice of "rendition," in which suspects are transported to cooperative foreign countries, knowing that they will certainly be tortured at American expense.

5. Many of the torture techniques used during the Bush administration were studied after American POWs returned home from the Korean War. Many of these men had been tortured into making false confessions repudiating America. As bizarre and illogical as it is, it was the US study of how and why North Korean torture proved so effective *in eliciting false confessions* that would become the basis for the "enhanced interrogation techniques" (i.e., torture) used by the American government to force "confessions" from "unlawful combatants" (another Orwellian euphemism).

6. Karl Barth, *The Church and the War* (1944; Eugene, OR: Wipf and Stock, 2008), 24.

Notes to Chapter Two

1. See George Stratton, "Some Preliminary Experiments on Vision without Inversion of the Retinal Image," *The Psychology Review* 3, no. 6 (1896): 611–17; "Vision without Inversion of the Retinal Image," *The Psychology Review* 4, no. 4 (1897): 341–60; and 4, no. 5 (1897): 463–81.

2. David E. J. Linden, Ulrich Kallenbach, Armin Heinecke, Wolf Singer, and Rainer Goebel, "The Myth of Upright Vision: A Psychophysical and Functional Imaging Study of Adaptation to Inverting Spectacles," *Perception* 28 (1999): 479. Linden et al. repeat the assertion that Stratton claimed to see the world in its proper orientation, with his goggles on, during the sixth day of his experiment. A careful reading of Stratton's notes, however, indicates that he claimed no such thing.

3. Unless otherwise noted, I am using the New International Version for Scripture quotations throughout.

4. See, e.g., Donald B. Kraybill, *The Upside-Down Kingdom* (Scottdale, PA: Herald Press, 1978); Allen Verhey, *The Great Reversal: Ethics and the New Testament* (Grand Rapids: Eerdmans, 1984).

5. Bruce Malina, *The Social Gospel of Jesus: The Kingdom of God in Mediterranean Perspective* (Minneapolis: Fortress, 2001), 1. "Kingdom of heaven" and "kingdom of God" are interchangeable constructions in the Gospel of Matthew.

6. Richard B. Hays, *The Moral Vision of the New Testament: Community, Cross, New Creation; A Contemporary Introduction to New Testament Ethics* (New York: HarperCollins, 1996), 14.

7. For a thorough analysis of this question, see David Wenham, *Paul: Follower of Jesus or Founder of Christianity?* (Grand Rapids: Eerdmans, 1995).

8. Hays's argument here reminds me of Rudolf Bultmann's erroneous claim that "the message of Jesus is a presupposition for the theology of the New Testament rather than a part of that theology itself." See Bultmann, *Theology of the New Testament* (New York: Charles Scribner's Sons, 1951), 1:3.

9. Hays, *Moral Vision*, 167. I believe that the excursus to chap. 7 (158–68), ostensibly giving further justification for Hays's Pauline starting point, thoroughly undercuts his position.

10. Hays, *Moral Vision*, 166.

11. Allen Verhey, *Remembering Jesus: Christian Community, Scripture, and the Moral Life* (Grand Rapids: Eerdmans, 2002); Glen H. Stassen and David P. Gushee, *Kingdom Ethics: Following Jesus in Contemporary Context* (Downers Grove: IVP, 2003; 2nd ed., Grand Rapids: Eerdmans, 2016); Richard A. Burridge, *Imitating Jesus: An Inclusive Approach to New Testament Ethics* (Grand Rapids: Eerdmans, 2007).

12. *Echrisen*, a verbal form of the noun *Christos*, is used in the Septuagint (abbreviated as LXX), the Greek translation of the Hebrew Bible.

13. *Euaggelizasthai*, "to preach the gospel," a verbal form of the noun *euaggelion*, the gospel/good news.

14. Gerhard Friedrich, "*euaggelizomai*," in *Theological Dictionary of the New Testament* (hereafter *TDNT*), trans. Geoffrey W. Bromiley (Grand Rapids: Eerdmans, 1964), 2:722–23.

15. *TDNT*, 2:724–25; see also Hans-Josef Klauck, *The Religious Context of Early Christianity: A Guide to Graeco-Roman Religions,* trans. Brian McNeil (Minneapolis: Fortress, 2003), 298.

16. S. R. F. Price, *Rituals and Power: The Roman Imperial Cult in Asia Minor* (Cambridge, UK: Cambridge University Press, 1984), 75, 220; Klauck, *Religious Context*, 286, 291–93.

17. *Son of man* is a Hebrew idiom meaning "human being"; see Job 25:6; Ps. 8:4; 144:3.

18. A verb form related to the noun *euaggelion*, in the Septuagint (LXX).

19. See Joel B. Green, "Kingdom of God/Heaven," in *Dictionary of Jesus and the Gospels*, ed. Joel B. Green, Jeannine K. Brown, and Nicholas Perrin, 2nd ed. (Downers Grove, IL: IVP Academic, 2013), 468, 476.

20. Albert Swing, *The Theology of Albrecht Ritschl together with Instruction in the*

Christian Religion by Albrecht Ritschl (New York: Longmans, Green, and Co., 1901), 178–79, 239–40; Albrecht Ritschl, *The Christian Doctrine of Justification and Reconciliation*, trans. H. R. Mackintosh and A. B. Macaulay (Clifton, NJ: Reference Book Publishers, 1966), 30–31, 296; see also Bruce Chilton, *Pure Kingdom: Jesus' Vision of God* (Grand Rapids: Eerdmans, 1996), 9–10; Green, "Kingdom of God," 469.

21. Ritschl, *Christian Doctrine of Justification*, 280.

22. Walter Rauschenbusch, *Christianizing the Social Order* (New York: Macmillan, 1919), 78–79; Benson Y. Landis, *A Rauschenbusch Reader: The Kingdom of God and the Social Gospel* (New York: Harper and Brothers, 1957), 111–19. For the influence of this social-reformist perspective on God's kingdom over the course of American history, see H. Richard Niebuhr, *The Kingdom of God in America* (New York: Harper and Row, 1937), 150–63.

23. Henry R. Van Til, *The Calvinistic Concept of Culture* (Grand Rapids: Baker, 1960; repr. 2001), 59.

24. Van Til, *Calvinistic Concept of Culture*, 44, 213.

25. Niebuhr, *Kingdom of God*, 56.

26. The quotation is from Eliot's *Christian Commonwealth, or the Civil Policy of the Rising Kingdom of Jesus Christ*, published in 1659; cited in Niebuhr, *Kingdom of God*, 131.

27. For an extensive recent treatment of this issue, see Richard T. Hughes, *Christian America and the Kingdom of God* (Chicago: University of Illinois Press, 2009).

Notes to Chapter Three

1. Johannes Weiss, *Jesus' Proclamation of the Kingdom of God*, trans. Richard Hiers and David Holland (Minneapolis: Fortress, 1971), 2.

2. Weiss, *Jesus' Proclamation*, 135.

3. The Kuyperian doctrine of "common grace" is a misguided attempt to account for the uninterrupted benefits enjoyed by a fallen world inhabited by fallen human beings who, nevertheless, remain bearers of the divine image. Human society can create such wonders as art, culture, and beneficial technologies because God's image continues to express itself in all humanity, not because the Creator somehow reinfused a universal common grace into his desolate, post-Fall creation.

4. For a more thorough discussion of the reversal theme in Jesus's ethics, see Allen Verhey, *The Great Reversal: Ethics and the New Testament* (Grand Rapids: Eerdmans, 1984), 11–21, 30–33.

5. John Calvin, *Commentary on a Harmony of the Evangelists, Matthew, Mark, and Luke*, trans. William Pringle (Grand Rapids: Eerdmans, 1956), 298–99.

6. Calvin, *Commentary on a Harmony*, 299.

7. Calvin, *Commentary on a Harmony*, 299, 301.

8. For the standard treatments of this duality, see George Eldon Ladd, *Crucial Questions About the Kingdom of God* (Grand Rapids: Eerdmans, 1952), 63–98; Werner G. Kümmel, *Promise and Fulfilment: The Eschatological Message of Jesus*, trans. Dorothea M. Barton (London: SCM, 1957); George Eldon Ladd, *A Theology of the New Testament* (Grand Rapids: Eerdmans, 1974), 64–80.

9. Edna Hong, *The Way of the Sacred Tree* (Minneapolis: Augsburg, 1983), 179, 189.

Notes to Chapter Four

1. Franklin H. Littell and H. G. Locke, eds., *The German Church Struggle and the Holocaust* (Detroit: Wayne State University Press, 1974), 128, 174; Victoria Barnett, *For the Soul of the People: Protestant Protest Against Hitler* (New York/Oxford: Oxford University Press, 1992), 11; Richard Steigmann-Gall, *The Holy Reich: Nazi Conceptions of Christianity, 1919–1945* (Cambridge, UK: Cambridge University Press, 2003), 69.

2. Winsome Munro, "Romans 13:1-7, Apartheid's Last Biblical Refuge," *Biblical Theology Bulletin* 20, no. 4 (1990): 161–67; see also the discussion of Romans 13:1-7 in section 2.1 of the historic *Kairos Document* issued by South African church leaders in 1985, available at: sahistory.org.za/archive/challenge-church-theological-comment -political-crisis-south-africa-kairos-document-1985.

3. Joel L. Alvis, *Religion and Race: Southern Presbyterians, 1946–1983* (Tuscaloosa: University of Alabama Press, 1994), 72; Mark Newman, *Getting Right with God: Southern Baptists and Desegregation, 1945–1995* (Tuscaloosa: University of Alabama Press, 2001), 21.

4. J. C. O'Neill, *Paul's Letter to the Romans* (Baltimore: Penguin, 1975), 209.

5. I do not intend any partisan political judgment here by using the word "conservative." I am simply drawing on its traditional and etymological sense: a *conservative* is one who tries to *conserve* the particulars of a given situation. It is entirely possible for political liberals to act conservatively.

6. Augustine, *The City of God* 19.17; see *Concerning the City of God against the Pagans* (London: Penguin, 1984).

7. The story and concluding miracle found in Matthew 17:24-27 concern payment of the half-shekel tax for the support and maintenance of the Jerusalem temple; it is a conversation about religious conformity, not civil obedience.

8. Wayne Grudem, *Politics according to the Bible: A Comprehensive Resource for Understanding Modern Political Issues in Light of Scripture* (Grand Rapids: Zondervan, 2010), 25 (italics in original). For a good overview of the history of interpretation and the differing schools of thought, see Joseph Fitzmyer, *The Gospel according to Luke X–XXIV*, The Anchor Bible (Garden City, NY: Doubleday, 1985), 2:1292-94.

9. *Kēnsos* is a Greek loan word from the Latin *census*, in Matt. 22:17; Mark 12:14.

10. Henry B. Swete, *The Gospel according to Mark* (London: Macmillan, 1898), 258–59; Vincent Taylor, *The Gospel according to Mark* (London: Macmillan, 1963), 1:479; 2:817.

11. In Syria the tribute was exacted from all men ages fourteen to sixty-five; see Gildas Hamel, *Poverty and Charity in Roman Palestine, First Three Centuries C.E.* (Berkeley: University of California Press, 1990), 144.

12. English translations that render the Greek word *kēnsos* as "tax," rather than "tribute" or "poll tax," and *dēnarios* as "coin" rather than "denarius," are obscuring the significance of Jesus's conversation.

13. Josephus, *War* 2.1; *Antiquities* 18.1. See also William Whiston, *The Works of Josephus, Complete and Unabridged* (Peabody, MA: Hendrickson, 1987).

14. Joel Marcus, *Mark 8-16* (New Haven: Yale University Press, 2009), 824.

15. Fitzmyer, *The Gospel according to Luke*, 1293.

16. Luke 23:2 refers to *phoros*, the proper Greek term for tribute/poll tax. Luke maintains the logical connection with Mark 12:14, however, by changing *kēnsos* to *phoros* in

Luke 20:22. Within Luke's story line, the witnesses at Jesus's trial are referring back to the entrapping question, "Is it lawful for us to pay tribute (*phoros*) to Caesar?"

17. Suetonius, *The Lives of the Twelve Caesars, Claudius* 25.4, trans. Philemon Holland (New York: Heritage Press, 1965). I. Howard Marshall explains that *Chrestus* and *Christus* were pronounced the same way, and the Roman historian Tacitus referred to Christians as *Chrestiani* (see Marshall, *The Book of Acts: An Introduction and Commentary* [Grand Rapids: Eerdmans, 1980], 293 n. 1).

18. Tacitus, *The Annals* 13.50; see *Tacitus, The Annals, The Reigns of Tiberius, Claudius, and Nero*, trans. J. C. Yardley (Oxford: Oxford University Press, 2008), 298. The Roman Senate quickly talked Nero out of such rash generosity.

19. James D. G. Dunn, *Romans 9-16*, Word Biblical Commentary (Dallas: Word, 1988), 772.

20. Interpreting the New Testament writings as principally composed for anti-imperial, anti-Roman purposes has recently become a growth industry; for only a few examples of this recent trend, see Richard Horsley, ed., *Paul and Empire: Religion and Power in Roman Imperial Society* (Harrisburg, PA: Trinity Press International, 1997); John Dominic Crossan, *God and Empire: Jesus Against Rome, Then and Now* (New York: HarperOne, 2007). For a level-headed evaluation of this literature, see Scot McKnight and Joseph B. Modica, *Jesus Is Lord, Caesar Is Not: Evaluating Empire in New Testament Studies* (Downers Grove, IL: IVP Academic, 2014).

21. One school of thought understands these "authorities" as invisible, spiritual powers standing behind human activities (cf. Acts 3:17; 13:27-28; Phil. 2:10; Col. 1:16-18). For representatives of this school, see George B. Caird, *Principalities and Powers* (Oxford: Clarendon Press, 1956); Oscar Cullmann, *The State in the New Testament* (New York: Charles Scribner's Sons, 1956), 63-70; Clinton Morrison, *The Powers That Be: Earthly Rulers and Demonic Powers in Romans 13: 1-7*, Biblical Theology 29 (Naperville, IL: A. R. Allenson, 1960); Henry Berkhof, *Christ and the Powers* (Scottdale, PA: Herald Press, 1962); Cyril Powell, *The Biblical Concept of Power* (London: Epworth Press, 1963); Albert van den Heuvel, *Those Rebellious Powers* (New York: Friendship Press, 1965); John Howard Yoder, *The Politics of Jesus: Vicit Agnus Noster* (Grand Rapids: Eerdmans, 1972); Walter Wink, *Naming the Powers* (Philadelphia: Augsburg Fortress, 1985). The difficulty with understanding the authorities in Romans 13 in this way is the "extreme unlikelihood" of the apostle Paul ever instructing Christians to be submissive to these spiritual powers (cf. Rom. 8:37-39; 1 Cor. 15:24-27; Gal. 4:8-11; Col. 2:15); see Dunn, *Romans 9-16*, 760.

22. For an elaboration of this concept, see Yoder, *The Politics of Jesus*, 201-2.

23. G. Delling, "*tassō*," in *Theological Dictionary of the New Testament* (Grand Rapids: Eerdmans, 1972), 8:29.

24. Yoder, *Politics of Jesus*, 208-9.

25. N. T. Wright, "Paul's Gospel and Caesar's Empire," in Horsley, *Paul and Empire*, 172.

26. Robert Jewett, "Response: Exegetical Support from Romans and Other Letters," in Horsley, *Paul and Empire*, 66.

27. Karl Barth, *Community, State, Church* (Eugene, OR: Wipf and Stock, 2004), 139; John Howard Yoder, *The Christian Witness to the State* (Scottdale, PA: Herald Press, 2002), 75.

28. See Cullmann, *The State in the New Testament*, 57; Yoder, *Politics of Jesus*, 198.

29. Technically, the Greek word for sword means a curved knife or short sword; however, in the New Testament the word is used with some flexibility; see Walter Bauer, William Arndt, and F. Wilbur Gingrich, eds., *A Greek-English Lexicon of the New Testament and Other Early Christian Literature* (Chicago: University of Chicago Press, 1957), 497; Wilhelm Michaelis, "*machaira,*" *Theological Dictionary of the New Testament* (Grand Rapids: Eerdmans, 1967), 4:524-27; Joseph H. Thayer, *Greek-English Lexicon of the New Testament* (Grand Rapids: Zondervan, 1969), 393.

30. Following the observations of Louis Swift (*The Early Fathers on War and Military Service* [Wilmington, DE: Michael Glazier, 1983], 91), George Kalantzis notes that there was no "compelling distinction between police work and military campaign in the function of the [Roman] legions. . . . The violence involved in the Roman understanding of 'police work' was equally notorious" (Kalantzis, *Caesar and the Lamb: Early Christian Attitudes on War and Military Service* [Eugene, OR: Cascade, 2012], 189).

31. See Kalantzis, *Caesar and the Lamb*, 118. In *The Crown* (11.2), Tertullian reiterates that disciples who have been taught to turn the other cheek cannot "guard prisoners in chains, administer torture or capital punishment" (Kalantzis, *Caesar and the Lamb*, 123); Lactantius (ca. AD 240-ca. AD 320) also prohibits Christians from serving as judges since "it does not matter whether you kill a man with the sword or with a word since it is killing itself that is prohibited" (*Divine Institutes*, 6.20.16; see Kalantzis, *Caesar and the Lamb*, 182). For additional observations and quotations from the church fathers, see Ronald Sider, *The Early Church on Killing: A Comprehensive Sourcebook on War, Abortion, and Capital Punishment* (Grand Rapids: Baker Academic, 2012), 48-50, 76, 84, 120-21, 167.

32. Kalantzis, *Caesar and the Lamb*, 193.

33. Yoder, *The Christian Witness*, 31.

34. Martin Luther, "Can Soldiers Be Saved?," in *Luther: Selected Political Writings,* ed. and trans. J. M. Porter (Philadelphia: Fortress, 1974), 103. See also *Luther and Calvin on Secular Authority,* ed. and trans. H. Höpfl (Cambridge, UK: Cambridge University Press, 1991), 15.

35. From the Dru edition of Kierkegaard's journals, quoted in Vernard Eller, *Kierkegaard and Radical Discipleship: A New Perspective* (Princeton: Princeton University Press, 1968), 227.

Notes to Chapter Five

1. Richard G. Lee, *The American Patriot's Bible* (Nashville: Thomas Nelson, 2009), available at: http://www.americanpatriotsbible.com.

2. Gregory A. Boyd, "Book Review: The Patriot's Bible (Part 1)," *Christianity Today,* 2009, available at: http://www.christianitytoday.com/pastors/2009/may-online-only /book-review-patriots-bible-part-1.html.

3. http://www.conservapedia.com/Conservative_Bible.

4. Cited in Ronald J. Sider, *Just Politics: A Guide for Christian Engagement* (Grand Rapids: Brazos, 2012), 5.

5. Stanley Hauerwas and William H. Willimon, *Resident Aliens: Life in the Christian Colony* (Nashville: Abingdon, 1989).

6. John H. Elliott, *A Home for the Homeless: A Sociological Exegesis of 1 Peter, Its Situation and Strategy* (Philadelphia: Fortress, 1981), 24.

7. For a discussion of how the Exodus story has been used and misused in American Christianity, beginning with the Puritans and continuing to today, see David S. Gutterman, *Prophetic Politics: Christian Social Movements and American Democracy* (Ithaca, NY: Cornell University Press, 2005). For a broader discussion of Christian nationalism, see Michelle Goldberg, *Kingdom Coming: The Rise of Christian Nationalism* (New York: Norton, 2007); see also Richard T. Hughes, *Christian American and the Kingdom of God* (Champaign: University of Illinois Press, 2009).

8. The Letter to Diognetus is often called an "apology" because the unknown author is writing to Diognetus (also unknown) in order to explain why he has embraced Christianity and has become a follower of Jesus. The letter is typically dated from the mid- to late second century.

9. An accessible translation of the whole of Diognetus chapter 5 can be found in Benjamin H. Dunning, *Aliens and Sojourners: Self as Other in Early Christianity* (Philadelphia: University of Pennsylvania Press, 2009), 65–66; see also *The Apostolic Fathers in English*, trans. Michael W. Holmes (Grand Rapids: Baker Academic, 2006).

10. Note Eph. 2:19, "Therefore you are no longer foreigners and resident aliens, but you are fellow citizens with the saints and the household of God" (my translation). Gentiles living outside the church are described as "foreigners and resident aliens" because they are at home in the world but strangers to the people of God. By implication, when they come to be at home with the church, they will become foreigners and resident aliens to the world.

Notes to Chapter Six

1. See the excellent discussion of this development in James Davison Hunter, *To Change the World: The Irony, Tragedy and Possibility of Christianity in the Late Modern World* (Oxford: Oxford University Press, 2010), 101–31.

2. Cited in Hunter, *To Change the World*, 126–27.

3. Hunter, *To Change the World*, 129. The seven mountains consist of government, education, media, arts and entertainment, religion, family, and business.

4. Hunter, *To Change the World*, 124–25; the quote is by Ralph Reed.

5. John Howard Yoder, *The Priestly Kingdom: Social Ethics as Gospel* (Notre Dame: Notre Dame University Press, 1984), 158: "We should be more relaxed and less compulsive about running the world if we made our peace with our minority situation, seeing this as . . . the unmasking of the myth of Christendom, which wasn't true even when it was believed."

6. Yoder, *The Priestly Kingdom*, 101.

7. See Robert A. J. Gagnon, *The Bible and Homosexual Practice: Texts and Hermeneutics* (Nashville: Abingdon, 2001). See also my review of James V. Brownson, *Bible, Gender, Sexuality: Reframing the Church's Debate on Same-Sex Relationships* (Grand Rapids: Eerdmans, 2013), in *Calvin Theological Journal* 48, no. 2 (2013): 324–28.

8. Jacques Ellul offers an incisive critique of those who engage in "Christian activism" without also presenting, modeling, and emphasizing the importance of genuine

conversion with the cultivation of an inner, spiritual life; see Ellul, *The Politics of God and the Politics of Man,* ed. and trans. Geoffrey W. Bromiley (Grand Rapids: Eerdmans, 1972), 33–40.

9. Scholars such as John Howard Yoder and Stanley Hauerwas refer to this melding of the Christian church with the apparatus and interests of state government as "Constantinianism" or "Christendom." The legacy of Christendom (the term I prefer) dates to the Roman Emperor Constantine's declaration that Christianity was a state-sanctioned religion in the Roman Empire. This is relevant historical background to our discussion; but exploring its history is beyond the scope of this study. For a more thorough analysis along the same lines that I present here, see Stanley Hauerwas, "A Christian Critique of Christian America," in *Christian Existence Today: Essays on Church, World, and Living in Between* (Grand Rapids: Baker, 1988), 171–90, reprinted in *The Hauerwas Reader* (Durham, NC: Duke University Press, 2001), 459–80; Stanley Hauerwas, *After Christendom? How the Church Is to Behave If Freedom, Justice, and a Christian Nation Are Bad Ideas* (Nashville: Abingdon, 1991); see also John Howard Yoder, "The Constantinian Sources of Western Social Ethics" and "Civil Religion in America," both in *The Priestly Kingdom: Social Ethics as Gospel* (Notre Dame: Notre Dame University Press, 1984), 135–47, 172–95; "The Meaning of the Constantinian Shift," in *Christian Attitudes to War, Peace, and Revolution* (Grand Rapids: Brazos, 2009), 57–74. Peter J. Leithart has attempted to refute Yoder's attack on Constantinianism and his endorsement of a pacifistic church as the pre-Constantinian norm in his book *Defending Constantine: The Twilight of an Empire and the Dawn of Christendom* (Downers Grove, IL: IVP Academic, 2010). Although Leithart does offer a necessary trimming of Yoder's sails, I believe that his overall critique ultimately fails because he misrepresents Yoder's argument. For a worthwhile response to Leithart from Yoder's Mennonite compatriots, see *The Mennonite Quarterly Review* 85, no. 4 (2011): 545–655; see also John D. Roth, ed., *Constantine Revisited: Leithart, Yoder, and the Constantinian Debate* (Eugene, OR: Pickwick, 2013).

10. Pacifism does not imply passivity. Jesus was anything but passive as he remained nonviolent. Personally, I am not an advocate of simple nonresistance. I believe that there is such a thing as faithful nonviolent resistance. See John Howard Yoder, *Nevertheless: The Varieties of Religious Pacifism* (Scottdale, PA: Herald Press, 1971).

11. For an example, see George H. C. MacGregor, *The New Testament Basis of Pacifism* (New York: The Fellowship of Reconciliation, 1936).

12. For one example, see the article by John E. Sharp, "Tars, Feathers and Liberty Bonds," *Mennonite World Review,* June 9, 2014, available at: http://mennoworld .org/2014/06/09/columns/tar-feathers-and-liberty-bonds/. Many similar examples could be cited throughout American history.

13. There is no reason to be diverted into the lengthy and complex history of natural law thinking. My own critique of a theology of natural law begins by observing that for any natural law to be truly natural it must be equally accessible, perceptible, and subject to a uniform interpretation by all "natural men"—everywhere and at all times. I do not think it difficult to show that these conditions cannot be met. Furthermore, natural law does not easily comport with Jesus's teaching. How natural is it to turn the other cheek? We have already seen how Calvin works to "naturalize" this part of Jesus's teaching, making the Son of God's instructions subject to whatever seems humanly reasonable.

For a very brief, accessible critique of natural law, see John Howard Yoder, *The Christian Witness to the State* (Scottdale, PA: Herald Press, 2002), 79-83.

14. See Stanley Hauerwas's essays "Can a Pacifist Think about War?" "Whose 'Just' War? Which Peace?" and "Why Gays (as a Group) are Morally Superior to Christians (as a Group)," in *Dispatches from the Front: Theological Engagements with the Secular* (Durham, NC: Duke University Press, 1994), 116-35, 136-52, 153-55; see also Hauerwas, "Peacemaking: The Virtue of the Church," in *Christian Existence Today: Essays on Church, World, and Living in Between* (Durham, NC: Labyrinth Press, 1988), 89-97.

15. Stanley Hauerwas, *Against the Nations: War and Survival in a Liberal Society* (San Francisco: Harper and Row, 1988), 77, 117.

16. One of the best-known exponents of Kuyper's cultural mandate theology is the philosopher Richard Mouw; see, e.g., his books *Politics and the Biblical Drama* (Grand Rapids: Eerdmans, 1976); *He Shines in All That's Fair: Culture and Common Grace* (Grand Rapids: Eerdmans, 2001); *When the Kings Come Marching In: Isaiah and the New Jerusalem* (Grand Rapids: Eerdmans, 2002); *The Challenges of Cultural Discipleship: Essays in the Line of Abraham Kuyper* (Grand Rapids: Eerdmans, 2012). See also Henry R. Van Til, *The Calvinistic Concept of Culture* (Grand Rapids: Baker, 2001 reprint, with a foreword by Mouw). The more recent movement known as "Dominionism" has its roots in the "Christian Reconstructionist" theology of Rousas J. Rushdoony; see his *The Roots of Reconstruction* (Vallecito, CA: Ross House Books, 1991); see also Michael J. McVicar, *Christian Reconstruction: R. J. Rushdoony and American Religious Conservatism* (Chapel Hill: University of North Carolina, 2015). However, Kuyperianism and Dominionism are different ideologies that should not be confused.

17. Mouw, *The Challenges of Cultural Discipleship*, 118.

18. Hunter, *To Change the World*, 95.

19. See Brian Tashman, "Dobson on Obama's Reelection: 'Nearly Everything I Have Stood for These Past 35 Years Went Down to Defeat,'" *Right Wing Watch*, January 7, 2013, available at: http://www.rightwingwatch.org/post/dobson-on-obamas-reelection -nearly-everything-i-have-stood-for-these-past-35-years-went-down-to-defeat/ (italics in original). I have a copy of the original newsletter that Dobson sent out to supporters in my files.

20. See, e.g., the history of evangelical social reform in Donald W. Dayton, *Discovering an Evangelical Heritage* (New York: Harper and Row, 1976).

21. Hunter is absolutely correct, in *To Change the World*, when he says that it is "important to underscore that while the activity of culture-making has validity before God, this work is not, strictly speaking, redemptive or salvific in character. Where Christians participate in the work of world-building they are not, in any precise sense of the phrase, 'building the kingdom of God'" (233). This means that the church needs "to abandon altogether talk of 'redeeming the culture,' 'advancing the kingdom,' 'building the kingdom,' . . . and 'changing the world'. . . . [Such terms imply] conquest, take-over, or dominion, which in my view is precisely what God does not call us to pursue—at least not in any conventional, twentieth- or twenty-first-century way of understanding these terms" (280).

22. Ellul, *The Politics of God*, refers to politics (rightly, in my view) as "the sphere of the greatest affirmation of man's autonomy, of his revolt [against God], of his pretentious attempt to play the role of God" (14). From this perspective, Christianity is *by definition*

antipolitical, which is not to rule out political participation; but it is to remind the disciple called into the political arena of how important it is to adhere consistently to kingdom values. Karl Barth denied the possibility of a Christian political party because the pragmatic means necessary for political success will always compromise the gospel. On the other hand, if the church is a genuine community, there will be no need for a Christian political party since there will be no lack of authentic Christians in politics, obeying the gospel and living as kingdom citizens. See Karl Barth, *Community, State, and Church: Three Essays* (Eugene, OR: Wipf and Stock, 2004), 184–85, 187.

23. Church history is filled with too many examples to list. For one modern story of a miraculous outreach to the orphaned street children of Nairobi, Kenya, by a Christian man who has risked everything for his mission, see Paul H. Boge, *Father to the Fatherless: The Charles Mulli Story* (Pickering, ON: Bayridge Books, 2006); online at: www.mully childrensfamily.org.

24. For example, see: Rod Dreher, "Religious Conservatives: GOP's 'Useful Idiots,'" *The American Conservative*, January 19, 2012, available at: www.theamerican conservative.com/dreher/religious-conservatives-gop-useful-idiots/; or Jeff Fenske, "An Evangelical Manifesto: 'Christians' Have Become 'Useful Idiots' for Political Parties—Creating a Backlash Against Religion," *One Can Happen*, May 4, 2008, available at: https://onecanhappen.wordpress.com/2008/05/04/an-evangelical-manifesto -christians-have-become-useful-idiots/.

Notes to Chapter Seven

1. Victoria Barnett, *For the Soul of the People: Protestant Protest against Hitler* (Oxford: Oxford University Press, 1992), 101, 102.

2. Cited in Stanley Milgram, *Obedience to Authority: An Experimental View* (New York: Harper Perennial, 2009), 2.

3. Mark Van Vugt and Anjana Ahuja, *Naturally Selected: The Evolutionary Science of Leadership* (New York: Harper Business, 2011).

4. For a fuller description of this incident and the issues involved, see Ira Chaleff, *Intelligent Disobedience: Doing Right When What You're Told to Do Is Wrong* (Oakland, CA: Berrett-Koehler, 2015), 113–34.

5. For an analysis of the many similarities—as well as the differences—between 1 Pet. 2:12-17 and Rom. 13:1-7, see John H. Elliott, *1 Peter,* The Anchor Bible (New York: Doubleday, 2000), 493–94.

6. To understand more fully how shockingly countercultural v. 17 is, see Greg Woolf, "Writing Poverty in Rome," in *Poverty in the Roman World*, ed. Margaret Atkins and Robin Osborne (Cambridge, UK: Cambridge University Press, 2006), 91-92; Woolf observes that "impoverishment carried with it the threat of a form of social death." Yet 1 Peter insists that those whom others considered social cadavers are actually in the same class as the emperor. Notice also the implicit undermining of emperor worship contained in Peter's view of social equality.

7. Sandra R. Joshel, *Slavery in the Roman World* (Cambridge, UK: Cambridge University Press, 2010), 119-23.

8. One of the few commentators who perceives the issue at stake is J. Ramsey Michaels, *1 Peter*, Word Biblical Commentary (Waco, TX: Word, 1988), 142.

9. Stanley Hauerwas, *Approaching the End: Eschatological Reflections on Church, Politics, and Life* (Grand Rapids: Eerdmans, 2013), 56 (italics added).

10. Milgram, *Obedience to Authority: An Experimental View*. The newest edition contains an interesting foreword by Philip Zimbardo, the creator of the equally famous Stanford Prison Experiment and author of *The Lucifer Effect: Understanding Why Good People Turn Evil* (New York: Random House, 2008).

11. See Milgram, *Obedience to Authority*, 13–26, for a chilling clinical description of the experiment's details.

12. Milgram, *Obedience to Authority*, 27–31.

13. See Chaleff's description in *Intelligent Disobedience*, 78–81; see also Eleanor Beardsley, "Fake TV Game Show 'Tortures' Man, Shocks France," *NPR.org*, March 18, 2010, available at: http://www.npr.org/templates/story/story.php?storyId=124838091.

14. This is not to endorse behavioral determinism. The individual always retains a will to choose, whether strong or weak, energetic or dormant; thus the individual always remains responsible for his actions.

15. Milgram, *Obedience to Authority*, 54.

16. Milgram, *Obedience to Authority*, 6, 92.

17. Milgram, *Obedience to Authority*, 188.

18. Milgram, *Obedience to Authority*, 145.

19. George Lakoff discusses this in his fascinating analysis of political partisanship in *The Political Mind: A Cognitive Scientist's Guide to Your Brain and Its Politics* (New York: Penguin Books, 2008), 37.

20. Remember Jesus's interpretation of the parable of the sower in Mark 4:14–20 (and parallels).

21. David Gushee, *The Righteous Gentiles of the Holocaust: A Christian Interpretation* (Minneapolis: Fortress, 1994).

22. Gushee, *Righteous Gentiles*, 117–29, 132–36, 141–47, 168.

23. I realize that some skeptics will say that my description of Christian "messaging" actually describes a religious ideology and that the adherents of this ideology are victims of indoctrination and authoritarianism in the same way that the German public had been indoctrinated by Hitler's political authority. Obviously, I disagree with this assessment, but I do not have the space needed to develop an answer here. In one sense, every worldview poses the risk of faith, whether one believes in the tenets of National Socialism or historic Christianity. Consequently, every ideology, whether political or religious, must be able to give an account of itself in public debate on the world stage. I would argue that Christianity is able to do this with sufficient persuasive power that its adherents (at least the thoughtful, self-conscious ones) cannot honestly be described as victims of indoctrination.

24. Richard Steigmann-Gall, *The Holy Reich: Nazi Conceptions of Christianity, 1919–1945* (Cambridge, UK: Cambridge University Press, 2003), 202. A major factor in the church's silence was a particular understanding of Luther's "two-kingdoms" theology. According to this theology, the church had authority in the realm of God's kingdom, which was personal, spiritual, internal, and private. Secular government, on the other hand, was instituted by God to exercise public authority over the kingdom of this world;

therefore, civil authorities were always to be obeyed. In 1933 the prominent German theologian and churchman Otto Dibelius, who had publicly embraced the Nazi party, proclaimed from the pulpit, "We have learned from Martin Luther that the church cannot get in the way of state power when it does what it is called to do. . . . [E]ven when [the state] becomes hard and ruthless . . . it is ruling in God's name!" (*Holy Reich*, 69).

25. Gushee, *Righteous Gentiles*, 162.

26. Of course, some Christians will argue today, as they did during World War II, that Jesus would never ask them to put their family at risk by protecting dangerous strangers such as Jews. I would insist otherwise, while recognizing (without self-righteousness, I hope) that fear and self-interest remain the perpetual opponents of costly discipleship.

27. Steigmann-Gall, *Holy Reich*, 261. This conclusion is not unusual; see Barnett, *For the Soul of the People*, 72.

28. My focus is on confrontation and civil disobedience. I do not mean to suggest that an obedient church will necessarily stop evil movements or direct the course of a nation's history. Yet, I cannot help but be struck by *how few* were the German Christians who had either the perspicacity or the fortitude to stand up in the face of Nazism and say, "No. We will not cooperate with evil."

29. Barnett provides a wealth of postwar reflection from German Christians who were contemplating, by their own admission, where the prewar church had gone wrong. It makes for fascinating and humbling reading (see Barnett, *For the Soul of the People*, 197-309). The first postwar gathering of German Protestant leaders took place in August 1945. Pastor Martin Niemöller had been released from Dachau concentration camp only four months earlier. Never hesitant to speak his mind, he told the assembly: "Our present situation today is not primarily the fault of our people and the Nazis. . . . No, the essential blame rests upon the church; because it alone knew that the road being taken would lead to ruin, and it didn't warn our people, it didn't unveil the injustice that had occurred or—only when it was too late . . . [it] stood more in fear of human beings than of the living God" (198).

30. Peter Haas, *Morality after Auschwitz: The Radical Challenge of the Nazi Ethic* (Philadelphia: Fortress, 1988), 9. I wholeheartedly agree with Haas when he explains how seeing the Holocaust as an utterly unique event strips it of moral relevance for history. Rather, it is a particularly horrendous example of typical social behaviors, for which there are many analogies in history. On the other hand, I wholeheartedly reject Haas's behavioral determinism, where he insists that morality is so shaped by environment as to make one's ethical choices "perfectly predictable" (181). The Holy Spirit "blows wherever it wills" (John 3:8), and how a person responds to that breeze is not always predictable.

31. Milgram, *Obedience to Authority*, 119.

32. Milgram, *Obedience to Authority*, 121.

33. Gushee, *Righteous Gentiles*, 102, 109, 143, 147. For an inspiring example told in detail, see Philip Hallie, *Lest Innocent Blood Be Shed: The Story of the Village of Le Chambon and How Goodness Happened There* (New York: Harper Colophon, 1979). It is the story of how a Protestant pastor, André Trocmé, led his entire village to rescue thousands of Jews during the war.

34. Sebastian Haffner, *Defying Hitler: A Memoir* (London: Phoenix, 2003).

35. Haffner, *Defying Hitler*, 230, 234 (italics added).

36. Space does not allow us to discuss the details of this problem as much as it deserves. The classic work—Christopher R. Browning, *Ordinary Men: Reserve Police Battalion 101 and the Final Solution in Poland* (New York: Harper Perennial, 1998)—offers a fascinating case study of the distressing dynamics involved when group behavior leads fundamentally good people to do horrible things. For broader, more recent research, see Zimbardo, *The Lucifer Effect*, and James Walker, *Becoming Evil: How Ordinary People Commit Genocide and Mass Murder* (Oxford: Oxford University Press, 2007).

37. Augustine, *Confessions*, book 1, chap. 1.1-2.

38. Milgram, *Obedience to Authority*, 188.

39. For a deeper exploration of the ways in which Christian faith is a step into uncertainty, I suggest reading my book *Encountering Jesus, Encountering Scripture: Reading the Bible Critically in Faith* (Grand Rapids: Eerdmans, 2013). Faith is the subjective certainty of that which is objectively uncertain. This may include an interpretation of Scripture or an act of civil disobedience.

40. Haas, *Morality after Auschwitz*, 179 (italics added).

41. Søren Kierkegaard was the great Christian advocate of the need for healthy individualism in both the church and society. His brilliant analysis of the herd mentality is a classic treatment of this subject; see Kierkegaard, *Concluding Unscientific Postscript* (Princeton: Princeton University Press, 1992), 1:544-45; Kierkegaard, *Works of Love* (Princeton: Princeton University Press, 1998), 404-5; and Kierkegaard, *A Literary Review* (New York: Penguin, 2001), 55-101; and the discussion in J. Keith Hyde, *Concepts of Power in Kierkegaard and Nietzsche* (Burlington, VT: Ashgate, 2010), 93-94.

42. Barnett, *For the Soul of the People*, 197. As important as their actions were, the concerns of the Confessing Church were limited. They never publicly objected to Nazi domestic or foreign policy, including Hitler's anti-Semitism.

Notes to Chapter Eight

1. Robert N. Bellah and Philip E. Hammond, *Varieties of Civil Religion* (San Francisco: Harper and Row, 1980), 197; on this point, see also John M. Cuddihy, *No Offense: Civil Religion and Protestant Taste* (New York: Seabury, 1978).

2. Today's church would do well to remember that pre-Constantinian Christianity wholeheartedly rejected civil religion.

3. Oliver O'Donovan asks us to remember an important caveat (which I will discuss more thoroughly at the end of this chapter), namely, that participating in civil religion also suppresses "important possibilities for Christian criticism" of the state and its policies; see O'Donovan, *The Desire of the Nations: Rediscovering the Roots of Political Theology* (Cambridge, UK: Cambridge University Press, 1996), 225. This crucial issue was at the heart of the ancient church's refusal to worship the Roman gods. For a wider discussion of various types of civil religion, see Bellah and Hammond, *Varieties of Civil Religion*, and Robert N. Bellah, *The Broken Covenant: American Civil Religion in Time of Trial* (Chicago: University of Chicago Press, 1992). For Christian critiques of American civil religion, see John Howard Yoder, "Civil Religion in America," in *The Priestly Kingdom: Social Ethics as Gospel* (Notre Dame: Notre Dame University Press, 1984), 172-95;

Stanley Hauerwas, "A Christian Critique of Christian America," in *A Hauerwas Reader* (Durham, NC: Duke University Press, 2001), 459–80; David L. Adams and Ken Schurb, eds., *The Anonymous God: The Church Confronts Civil Religion and American Society* (St. Louis: Concordia Publishing House, 2004).

4. For a discussion of what Eisenhower intended to say, see Patrick Henry, "'And I Don't Care What It Is': The Tradition-History of a Civil Religion Proof-Text," *Journal of the American Academy of Religion* 49, no. 1 (1981): 35–47.

5. For a discussion and critique, see Richard T. Hughes, *Myths America Lives By* (Urbana: University of Illinois Press, 2003); Michelle Goldberg, *Kingdom Coming: The Rise of Christian Nationalism* (New York: Norton, 2006); Richard T. Hughes, *Christian America and the Kingdom of God* (Champaign: University of Illinois Press, 2009); Stephen Backhouse, *Kierkegaard's Critique of Christian Nationalism* (Oxford: Oxford University Press, 2011).

6. The term "German Christians" does not refer to any and all professing Christians in Germany during Hitler's rule, but only to that portion of the German state church that cooperated with the Nazi Party's attempts to co-opt Christianity for its own political purposes. The Confessing Church, which produced the Barmen Declaration, was a portion of German Christianity that stood in opposition to the German Christians. Sebastian Haffner describes seeing a swastika flag flying from every church tower in 1933; see Haffner, *Defying Hitler: A Memoir* (London: Phoenix, 2003), 197.

7. I realize that using the term "nation" may be an anachronism at this stage of history, but it is suitable for my purposes in this chapter.

8. To cite only a few examples: God directs the decision-making of Egypt's Pharaoh (Exod. 9:12; 10:1, 20, 27; 11:10; 14:4, 8, 17) and the Assyrian, Tiglath-Pileser (1 Chron. 5:26); God uses Assyria (2 Kings 17:23; 2 Chron. 33:11; Isa. 7:17–20; 8:7) and Babylon (Ezek. 31:18; 32:28–32) to accomplish his purposes for Israel. God also punishes Pharaoh (Jer. 44:30; Ezek. 29:1–3; 30:20–25), Assyria, and Babylon for the evil they committed (Isa. 10:5, 12, 24; 31:8; Jer. 50:18; Ezek. 32:22; Zeph. 2:13; Zech. 10:11; Micah 5:6).

9. As President Museveni of Uganda did in 2012 by declaring Uganda to be God's new covenant nation.

10. See Exod. 25–26 and Num. 1:50–53 for instructions on how to build the Tabernacle, and 1 Kings 5:17; 6:1–38; 8:6–64; Ezra 1:2–7, for the first and second Temples. Eventual prophetic critiques of Israel will include denunciations of temple sacrifice (Isa. 1:11; Jer. 7:21–26; Hosea 8:13; 9:4); however, their intent was not to abrogate God's previous commands but to condemn Israel's hypocrisy.

11. Hughes, *Myths America Lives By*, 2.

12. The Pilgrim and Puritan settlers in America would be examples of such conservative Bible readers.

13. Robert Bellah argues in favor of reading Israel's story mythologically in this way because it makes the Bible more serviceable to civil religion; see Robert N. Bellah, "Civil Religion in America," in *The Religious Situation 1968*, ed. Donald R. Cutler (Boston: Beacon, 1968), 391, cited by Richard John Neuhaus, "From Civil Religion to Public Philosophy," in *Civil Religion and Political Theology*, ed. Leroy S. Rouner (Notre Dame: Notre Dame University Press, 1986), 98–99.

14. Stephen Grosby, *Biblical Ideas of Nationality: Ancient and Modern* (Winona Lake, IN: Eisenbrauns, 2002), 249.

15. Grosby, *Biblical Ideas of Nationality*, 218.

16. Grosby, *Biblical Ideas of Nationality*, 219.

17. See David W. Bebbington, "Atonement, Sin and Empire, 1880-1914," and Steven Maughan, "Imperial Christianity? Bishop Montgomery and the Foreign Missions of the Church of England, 1895-1915," both in *The Imperial Horizons of British Protestant Missions, 1880-1914*, ed. Andrew Porter (Grand Rapids: Eerdmans, 2003), 14-31, 32-57.

18. For summaries detailing the roots and development of American exceptionalism, see W. S. Hudson, ed., *Nationalism and Religion in America: Concepts of American Identity and Mission* (Gloucester, MA: Peter Smith, 1978); Grosby, *Biblical Ideas of Nationality*, 213-34; for a critique of American exceptionalism, see Gregory Boyd, *The Myth of a Christian Nation: How the Quest for Political Power Is Destroying the Church* (Grand Rapids: Zondervan, 2005); William T. Cavanaugh, *Migrations of the Holy: God, State, and the Political Meaning of the Church* (Grand Rapids: Eerdmans, 2011), 88-108; John D. Wilsey, *One Nation Under God? An Evangelical Critique of Christian America* (Eugene, OR: Wipf and Stock, 2011).

19. Hudson, *Nationalism and Religion*, 23; for many similar quotes, see Todd Gitlin and Liel Leibovitz, *The Chosen Peoples: America, Israel and the Ordeals of Divine Election* (New York: Simon and Schuster, 2010), 65-145. Roger Williams (1603-1683) was one of the few Puritan leaders to disagree with the mythological use of Israel's story, rejecting the idea of America as the new Israel, insisting that the Exodus story be read literally as real history, describing God's dealings with ancient Israel only; see Hughes, *Myths America Lives By*, 32. The cumulative effect of Williams's various dissenting opinions was banishment from the Massachusetts Colony. He moved on to found Providence, Rhode Island, the first place in America to legislate both the freedom of religion and the separation of church and state.

20. Cited in S. Backhouse, *Kierkegaard's Critique of Christian Nationalism* (Oxford: Oxford University Press, 2011), 87.

21. The text says: "I will restore your judges as in days of old, your counselors as at the beginning. Afterward you will be called the City of Righteousness, the Faithful City. Zion will be redeemed with justice." See Susannah Heschel, *The Aryan Jesus: Christian Theologians and the Bible in Nazi Germany* (Princeton: Princeton University Press, 2008), 190.

22. Believing this is not a surrender to the bogeyman of relativism. It is simply to affirm the goodness of all God's creation. Sin pervades the world, but it has not destroyed the world's essential goodness. And, trust me, French bread never tastes as good anywhere else as it does in France.

23. For a more extended discussion of God's tendency to fulfill his promises in ways that are completely unexpected, see my discussion of Jesus as "the-messiah-no-one-expected" in *Encountering Jesus, Encountering Scripture: Reading the Bible Critically in Faith* (Grand Rapids: Eerdmans, 2013), 15-45.

24. The church as the true Israel is made especially clear in Paul's letters (e.g., Rom. 3-5; 2 Cor. 3-4; Gal. 3-6; Phil. 3; Titus 1), where Paul is arguing against a group sometimes known as the "Judaizing party." The latter insisted that, for Gentile believers, faith in Jesus is not enough to enter into right relationship with God. They must also be circumcised and keep some version of the Old Testament law before entering fully into the new covenant.

25. Revelation delights in using numerology and *gamatria*, different symbolic ways of using numbers, a common device in the ancient world and apocalyptic literature. These numbers were never intended to be taken literally.

26. From his book *Political Theology* (1922), cited and discussed in Cavanaugh, *Migrations of the Holy*, 96.

27. See the discussions of these examples in Geiko Müller-Fahrenholz, *America's Battle for God: A European Christian Looks at Civil Religion* (Grand Rapids: Eerdmans, 2007), 150-53; Anatol Lieven, *America Right or Wrong: An Anatomy of American Nationalism*, 2nd ed. (Oxford: Oxford University Press, 2012), 131-34.

28. For insightful discussions of this dimension of civil religion, see Carol Marvin and David W. Ingle, *Blood Sacrifice and the Nation: Totem Rituals and the American Flag* (Cambridge, UK: Cambridge University Press, 1999); Jonathan H. Ebel, *G. I. Messiahs: Soldiering, War, and American Civil Religion* (New Haven: Yale University Press, 2015).

29. Cavanaugh, *Migrations of the Holy*, 54.

30. For a particularly disturbing example of this blindness in an Army chaplain, see John McDougall, *Jesus Was an Airborne Ranger: Find Your Purpose Following the Warrior Christ* (Colorado Springs, CO: Multnomah, 2015).

31. Cited in Marvin and Ingle, *Blood Sacrifice*, 106. For many different versions of this saying, see: http://www.quoteinvestigator.com/2015/04/24/war/.

32. Ebel, *G. I. Messiahs*, 42.

33. See Stanley Hauerwas and William H. Willimon, *Resident Aliens: Life in the Christian Colony* (Nashville: Abingdon, 1989), 35, 62.

34. Jean-Jacques Rousseau, *The Social Contract*, trans. Maurice Cranston (New York: Penguin, 1968), book 4, chap. 8.

35. Carlton J. H. Hayes, *Nationalism: A Religion* (New York: Macmillan Company, 1960), 102-5; William T. Cavanaugh, *Theopolitical Imagination: Discovering the Liturgy as a Political Act in an Age of Global Consumerism* (London: T & T Clark, 2002), 35-46.

36. The faithful exceptions have been those in the "free-church" tradition, such as the Mennonites and Quakers.

37. Heschel, *The Aryan Jesus*, 81, 114.

38. Richard Steigmann-Gall, *The Holy Reich: Nazi Conceptions of Christianity, 1919-1945* (Cambridge, UK: Cambridge University Press, 2003), 149.

Notes to Chapter Nine

1. This has not always been my position; I found myself migrating into the pacifist camp via my research and thinking for this book.

2. Augustine's argument (see pp. 38-39 and 50, above) that Jesus's apparently pacifist teachings were only intended to train Christian hearts, not to determine Christian actions—thereby enabling disciples to kill their enemies lovingly, without prejudice—is a horrible intrusion of Augustine's neo-Platonic philosophical background attempting to muzzle Jesus's clear intentions. Augustine's unwarranted distinction between a person's spirit/attitude, on the one hand, and his or her body/actions, on the other, is characteristic of Greek thought, not Scripture. The brilliant man from Hippo may be a saint for some, but he was not infallible.

3. Tertullian (ca. AD 160–225), *Apology* 37.

4. When applied properly, just-war theory can help to minimize or even to eliminate war. If its criteria were taken seriously by all parties to a conflict, the possibility of war and its ramifications would be greatly reduced. Just-war thinking is not a method for justifying a desired conflict, which is the way it is typically abused in American discourse; see John Howard Yoder, *When War Is Just: Being Honest in Just War Thinking* (Minneapolis: Augsburg, 1984); see also John Howard Yoder, *Christian Attitudes to War, Peace and Revolution* (Grand Rapids: Brazos, 2009); Daniel Bell, *Just War as Christian Discipleship: Recentering the Tradition in the Church Rather Than the State* (Grand Rapids: Brazos, 2009).

5. *Magi* is the Greek word for magicians and astrologers who knew how to access the spiritual powers of the universe. Medieval embarrassment over Jesus's receiving homage from such pagans began their transformation into wise men and then kings in the Western tradition.

6. See *The Acts of the Military Martyrs* (ca. AD 260–303) and the discussion provided by George Kalantzis, *Caesar and the Lamb: Early Christian Attitudes on War and Military Service* (Eugene, OR: Cascade, 2012), 154–69. Roy Davies, a specialist in the history of the Roman army, refers to *The Acts of the Military Martyrs* as a reliable source of information on Roman military practice at the time; see Davies, *Service in the Roman Army* (New York: Columbia University Press, 1989), 13.

7. Phillip Wynn, *Augustine on War and Military Service* (Minneapolis: Fortress, 2013), 33–34.

8. Kalantzis, *Caesar and the Lamb*; Ronald J. Sider, *The Early Church on Killing: A Comprehensive Sourcebook on War, Abortion, and Capital Punishment* (Grand Rapids: Baker Academic, 2012).

9. Peter J. Leithart, *Defending Constantine: The Twilight of an Empire and the Dawn of Christendom* (Downers Grove, IL: IVP Academic, 2010), however, attempts to keep the debate alive. He focuses his energy on refuting Yoder's claims for early Christian pacifism by arguing that the early church did not behave in a uniformly pacifist manner. But Leithart confuses uniformity of practice with uniformity of teaching. He says: "We have little evidence one way or another but the sparseness of the evidence is crucial. How can we conclude anything about 'what all Christians thought and did' when we are relying on tiny fragments of extant evidence? . . . Yoder must discover a moment in the church's history in which the church was universally opposed to violence and war" (Leithart, *Defending Constantine*, 259, 293). But proving a universal behavior is not the point here. At issue is the fact that *all* Christian teaching prior to Constantine uniformly forbids disciples from engaging in violence and killing. Leithart tries to evade the significance of this observation by pointing out that the extant written evidence is "sparse" and, by implication, may represent a small, minority position. Kalantzis aptly replies by noting that "such arguments ignore the unfortunate fact of history that, if we discount the diverse literary record because it might be representing the views of only a 'small, articulate minority,' we would have very little left of the Christian story, faith, and practice—let alone of Greek or Roman history" (*Caesar and the Lamb*, 45).

10. He cites Athenagoras, *Plea* 345; Tertullian, *Spectacles* 2; *Patience* 3; *Modesty* 12; Minucius Felix, *Octavius* 30; Origen, *Matthew* and *Against Celsus*, 3.7, 8.73; Cyprian, *Donatus* 6, 7; *Patience* 14; and letters 55 and 56; Archelaus, *Disputation* 2; Arnobius of Sicca,

Pagans 1.6, 2.1; Lactantius, *Divine Institutes* 1.18; 3.18; 5.8-10; 6.6, 20; *Apostolic Tradition* 16. See Sider, *The Early Church*, 168 n. 34.

11. Sider, *The Early Church*, 171. The twenty-eight references are listed in note 59. For similar observations, see Kalantzis, *Caesar and the Lamb*, 52. Richard B. Hays, *The Moral Vision of the New Testament* (San Francisco: HarperCollins, 1996), 317-46, offers an excellent discussion of this passage and its relevance today. Note that none of these ancient writers agrees with Augustine's attempts to spiritualize Jesus's teaching so that disciples are allowed to kill as long as the circumstances and motivations are righteous.

12. Kalantzis, *Caesar and the Lamb*, 7.

13. George R. Watson, *The Roman Soldier* (London: Thames and Hudson, 1969), 143.

14. Leithart notes, correctly, that Origen allows for the righteousness of the Roman wars for which the church prays rather than fights. He admits: "The force of the passage is pacifist, of course, and that should not be missed" (*Defending Constantine*, 269). I would add that we should not forget Paul's convictions expressed in Romans 12-13: God institutes government to perform actions that disciples must avoid. We should also remember that Origen was a man of his age; there is thus no reason to share his assumptions about the virtues of Roman war-making.

15. See Kalantzis, *Caesar and the Lamb*, 62-63, 102-3, 105, 119-20, 122-24, 151, 157-60, 175-76, 182, 193; Sider, *The Early Church*, 26, 43, 58, 67, 70, 121-23, 153, 156, 171, 175-80.

16. Kalantzis, *Caesar and the Lamb*, 42-45, 52-55, 58-59, 88-91, 103, 135-36, 145-47, 163, 171, 175, 179, 182, 193; Sider, *The Early Church*, 23-29, 31, 45-47, 68, 76, 84, 101, 106-7, 110, 168-71, 177, 192-93.

17. Kalantzis, *Caesar and the Lamb*, 62, 64-66, 92-93, 154, 160-69, 191-92; Sider, *The Early Church*, 62, 71, 92, 120-23, 171. The Roman military oath was called a *sacramentum,* which religiously bound the soldier to the emperor, as the empire's high priest, and to the Roman gods. Christian baptism and the Eucharist were each an alternative *sacramentum* obligating a Christian soldier to renounce his military oath. A soldier's participation in the church thereby became an overt act of civil disobedience.

18. See Kalantzis, *Caesar and the Lamb*, 62-63, 193, 200; Sider, *The Early Church*, 91, 120, 123. Eventually, Christian soldiers who had killed were allowed to remain in (or be readmitted to) the church after a period of penance (*Canons of Hippolytus* 14; ca. AD 336-40) or after a three-year exclusion from the sacraments (Saint Basil of Caesarea, *First Canonical Epistle*, Canon 13; post-AD 370). Note that these measures are post-Constantinian when Christian military service became widely accepted.

19. For one such discussion, see Wes Howard-Brook, *Empire Baptized: How the Church Embraced What Jesus Rejected, 2nd-5th Centuries* (Maryknoll, NY: Orbis, 2016).

20. *Letter 185: Augustine to Boniface* (ca. AD 417), para. 24: The Christian use of force was legitimate once "the church receives power through God's generosity and at the appropriate time, *because of the king's religion and faith*" (italics added); see E. M. Atkins and R. J. Dodaro, eds., *Augustine: Political Writings* (Cambridge, UK: Cambridge University Press, 2001), 188. Augustine is endorsing the use of force to compel schismatics back into the one church. It is also the clear presupposition behind his acceptance of Christians entering the emperor's army.

21. Kayla Williams (with Michael E. Staub), *Love My Rifle More Than You: Young and Female in the U.S. Army* (New York: Norton, 2005), 43.

22. On the trauma and guilt created by killing at close range with an edged weapon, see Lt. Col. Dave Grossman, *On Killing: The Psychological Cost of Learning to Kill in War and Society* (New York: Back Bay Books, 2009), 114–30. Grossman refers to this as "an intimate brutality." His book is now required reading at West Point, the Air Force NCO Academy, the FBI Academy, the DEA Academy, and numerous other military academies and institutions.

23. Williams, *Love My Rifle*, 15.

24. Williams, *Love My Rifle*, 246–51.

25. There is no evidence that women are any worse at learning to kill than men are, "which may or may not be comforting" (Grossman, *On Killing*, xiv).

26. Grossman, *On Killing*, 3–4.

27. S. L. A. Marshall, *Men against Fire* (Gloucester, MA: Peter Smith, 1978). The revised edition of *On Killing*, 5–37, updates the debate with extensive confirmation of Marshall's conclusions.

28. Grossman, *On Killing*, 28.

29. Grossman, *On Killing*, 36.

30. Joanna Bourke, *An Intimate History of Killing: Face to Face Killing in 20th Century Warfare* (New York: Basic Books, 1999), 67, 73; for a detailed discussion of the techniques and logic of basic training, see chap. 3, "Training Men to Kill," 57–90; see also Ann Jones, *They Were Soldiers: How the Wounded Return from America's Wars—The Untold Story* (Chicago: Haymarket Books, 2013), 94–97.

31. Grossman, *On Killing*, 36.

32. Grossman, *On Killing*, 82; see Grossman's discussion of "The Guilt of Killing," 86–92; "Killing and Physical Distance," 97–137; "The Greatest Trap of All: To Live with What Thou Hast Wrought," 224–29; and "The Killing Response Stages," 233–47.

33. Jonathan Shay, *Achilles in Vietnam: Combat Trauma and the Undoing of Character* (New York: Scribner, 1994), 197. Researchers are increasingly raising the likelihood of *permanent* alterations in brain chemistry among those who suffer from PTSD and other combat trauma, meaning that these veterans may never be completely free of their psychological problems. Church leaders like Kenneth Copeland and David Barton, who blithely insist that good Christians will never suffer from PTSD, demonstrate an appalling depth of ignorance, arrogance, and cruelty; see Rob Shryock, "Right-Wing Evangelicals Claim 'Good Christians' Can't Get PTSD," *Alternet*, December 1, 2013, available at: http://www.alternet.org/belief/why-right-wing-evangelicals-claim-good-christians-cant-get-ptsd. I have also seen the online video recording their outlandish claims.

34. Shay, *Achilles in Vietnam*, 33.

35. Shay, *Achilles in Vietnam*, 83 (italics in original).

36. Shay, *Achilles in Vietnam*, 93.

37. See Rita N. Brock and Gabriella Lettini, *Soul Repair: Recovering from Moral Injury after War* (Boston: Beacon Press, 2012).

38. I am obviously extending the implications of Chaplain Keiser's thoughts even further by asserting that military training, by definition, violates the conscience.

39. Michael Vincent, "More Soldiers Dying from Suicide Than Combat," *ABC*

.net, November 11, 2013, available at: http://www.abc.net.au/news/2013-11-12/more -us-soldiers-dying-from-suicide-than-combat/5085070; for more on the shocking rise in veteran suicide rates and their participation in dangerous behaviors, see Jones, *They Were Soldiers*, 97–116.

40. Williams, *Love My Rifle*, 13; see also Madeline Morris, "In War and Peace: Rape, War and Military Culture," in *War's Dirty Secret: Rape, Prostitution, and Other Crimes against Women*, ed. Anne Llewellyn Barstow (Cleveland: Pilgrim Press, 2000). Morris's study indicates that the models of masculinity encouraged by military culture are of the very kind that "have been found to be related to heightened levels of rape propensity" (*War's Dirty Secret*, 181, 184–87). According to the US Defense Department, 26,000 rapes and sexual assaults were committed in 2012 within the US military; that amounts to 71 assaults every day against military personnel—both women and men. See also the shocking documentary film *The Invisible War*, written and directed by Kirby Dick, produced by Tanner King Barklow and Amy Ziering. One federal official has dismissed the problem of sexual assault in the US military by calling rape "an occupational hazard" for military women.

41. See Brock and Lettini, *Soul Repair*.

42. Tim O'Brien, *The Things They Carried* (New York: Broadway Books, 1990), 68–69.

Notes to Chapter Ten

1. "Robber Barons" is a term of derision that refers to nineteenth-century industrialists such as J. P. Morgan, Andrew Carnegie, and John D. Rockefeller, who used unscrupulous measures such as monopoly controls, price-gouging, and violence against union organizers to enrich themselves at the expense of working people.

2. I wonder how many readers can remember the presidential primary debate between Ronald Reagan and George H. W. Bush, in which candidate Bush, soon to become Reagan's vice president, labeled his opponent's trickle-down theory "voodoo economics"? It certainly has come to bewitch the American marketplace and its advocates today.

3. Paul Craig Roberts, *The Failure of Laissez Faire Capitalism and Economic Dissolution of the West* (Atlanta: Clarity Press, 2013), 81.

4. There is an important and growing body of literature that analyzes this problem and the dangers it holds for society. See, e.g., James Lardner and David A. Smith, eds., *Inequality Matters: The Growing Economic Divide in America and Its Poisonous Consequences* (New York/London: Demos, 2005); Larry M. Bartels, *Unequal Democracy: The Political Economy of the New Gilded Age* (Princeton: Princeton University Press, 2008); Matt Taibbi, *The Divide: American Injustice in the Age of the Wealth Gap* (New York: Spiegel and Grau, 2014).

5. Roberts, *The Failure of Laissez Faire Capitalism*, 98.

6. Thomas Piketty, *Capital in the Twenty-First Century*, trans. Arthur Goldhammer (Cambridge, MA: Belknap Press, 2014). Piketty concludes: "Once a fortune is established, the capital grows according to a dynamic of its own" (440). In a market economy based on private property, "the private rate of return on capital, r, can be significantly higher for long periods of time than the rate of growth of income and output, g. . . . The

inequality r>g implies that wealth accumulated in the past grows more rapidly than output and wages. . . . The consequences for the long-term dynamics of the wealth distribution are potentially terrifying" (571).

7. Roberts, *The Failure of Laissez Faire Capitalism*, 134.

8. Marian MacDorman, T. J. Mathews, Ashna D. Mohangoo, and Jennifer Zeitlin, "International Comparisons of Infant Mortality and Related Factors: United States and Europe, 2010," *National Vital Statistics Reports* 63, no. 5 (September 24, 2014), available at: https://www.cdc.gov/nchs/data/nvsr/nvsr63/nvsr63_05.pdf.

9. Roberts, *The Failure of Laissez Faire Capitalism*, 150.

10. Roberts, *The Failure of Laissez Faire Capitalism*, 144.

11. Thucydides, *History of the Peloponnesian War*, book 5.

12. See Redmond Mullin, *The Wealth of Christians* (Maryknoll, NY: Orbis, 1984), 25–39; Justo L. Gonzalez, *Faith and Wealth: A History of Early Christian Ideas on the Origin, Significance, and Use of Money* (New York: HarperSanFrancisco, 1990), 20–27; Luke Timothy Johnson, *Sharing Possessions: What Faith Demands* (Grand Rapids: Eerdmans, 2011), 127–33.

13. There is no reason to think that all Jerusalem disciples were poor. It is safe to assume that a wide spectrum of economic levels was represented among the many pilgrims who responded to Peter's speech on the Day of Pentecost (Acts 2:41). Josephus describes the great wealth and property accumulated by priestly families in the capital city (*Life* 63), and Acts 6:7 lets us know that "a large number of priests" had come to faith in the resurrected Jesus.

14. The book of Acts provides ample evidence to show that the ancient church did not practice "communism." It did not forbid private property. It did not demand communal ownership. The context makes clear that when Luke says, "The believers had everything in common," he means that every believer was willing to share whatever they had with anyone else who needed it more than they did. This included a willingness to liquidate private property in order to make the proceeds available to others. This is not communism but a radical kind of *communalism*, where all thoughts of ownership are conditioned by the overriding virtue of generosity, exactly the opposite of the typical Western conviction where the rights of private ownership reign supreme.

15. For a good analysis of how these two stories relate within the story line of Acts, see Aaron J. Kueker, "The Spirit and the 'Other,' Satan and the 'Self': Economic Ethics as a Consequence of Identity Transformation in Luke-Acts," in *Engaging Economics: New Testament Scenarios and Early Christian Reception*, ed. Bruce W. Longenecker and Kelly D. Liebengood (Grand Rapids: Eerdmans, 2009), 81–103.

16. The dangers of "cheap grace," that is, the mistaken belief that one can follow Jesus on the cheap, are explored by Dietrich Bonhoeffer in his classic book *The Cost of Discipleship*, trans. R. H. Fuller (New York: Macmillan, 1963), 45–60.

17. This statement is not to be confused with Zionism or certain Christian theological claims about the modern state of Israel (see chapter 8, above).

18. On the details of Israel's extensive social welfare system, see Steven A. Kaufman, "A Reconstruction of the Social Welfare System of Ancient Israel," in *The Shelter of Elyon: Essays on Ancient Palestinian Life and Literature in Honor of G. W. Ahlstrom*, ed. W. Boyd Barrick and John R. Spencer, JSOT Sup. 31 (Sheffield, UK: JSOT Press, 1984), 277–86; M. Douglas Meeks, *God the Economist: The Doctrine of God and Political Economy*

(Minneapolis: Fortress, 1989), 83-97; Moshe Weinfeld, *Social Justice in Ancient Israel and the Ancient Near East* (Jerusalem: Magnes, 1995); Samuel L. Adams, *Social and Economic Life in Second Temple Judea* (Louisville: Westminster John Knox, 2014), 88-109, 172-73.

19. For a good explanation of the apparent tension here, see Norman K. Gottwald, "Abusing the Bible: The Case of Deuteronomy 15," *Review & Expositor* 111, no. 2 (2014): 196-98.

20. Notice that neither the Old Testament nor Jesus ever suggests that there can be "unworthy poor" who do not deserve our help.

21. See Craig L. Blomberg, *Neither Poverty nor Riches: A Biblical Theology of Possessions* (Downers Grove, IL: InterVarsity, 1999), 42-49.

22. Meeks, *God the Economist*, 87.

23. A. Rahel Schafer, "Rest for Animals? Nonhuman Sabbath Repose in Pentateuchal Law," *Bulletin for Biblical Research* 23, no. 2 (2013): 167-86.

24. This important caveat is relevant to contemporary Zionism. Israel was never given a blanket promise to possess the land. It was always conditioned by Israel's obedience to the covenant, which includes just and humane treatment for fellow inhabitants, such as the Palestinians.

25. R. Mullin, *Wealth of Christians*, 15-24; Gonzales, *Faith and Wealth*, 15-16; Timothy J. Gorringe, *Capital and the Kingdom: Theological Ethics and Economic Order* (Maryknoll, NY: Orbis, 1994), 119.

26. See Jacob Jervell, *Luke and the People of God: A New Look at Luke-Acts* (Minneapolis: Augsburg, 1972), 50-74. However, Jervell does not specifically refer to the Old Testament social welfare laws.

27. Craig Blomberg argues, correctly I believe, that this reference to "the poor" should be taken literally rather than figuratively; see Blomberg, *Christians in an Age of Wealth: A Biblical Theology of Stewardship* (Grand Rapids: Zondervan, 2013), 116.

28. Recall the discussion of 1 Corinthians 6:1-11 in chapter 3, above.

29. See also Blomberg, *Neither Poverty nor Riches*, 194-95. Blomberg aptly elaborates by observing that Paul recognizes that "there are extremes of wealth and poverty which are intolerable in the Christian community." Thus Paul's "insistence on the right of all to a fair share."

30. Walter Pilgrim, *Good News to the Poor: Wealth and Poverty in Luke-Acts* (Minneapolis: Augsburg, 1981); David Seccombe, *Possessions and the Poor in Luke-Acts* (Linz: Fuchs, 1983); Thomas E. Schmidt, *Hostility to Wealth in the Synoptic Gospels* (Sheffield: JSOT, 1987); Christopher M. Hays, *Luke's Wealth Ethics: A Study in Their Coherence and Character* (Tübingen: Mohr Siebeck, 2010).

31. Comprehensive surveys of the biblical material may be found in Blomberg's *Neither Poverty nor Riches* and his *Christians in an Age of Wealth*; see also Ben Witherington, *Jesus and Money: A Guide for Times of Financial Crisis* (Grand Rapids: Brazos, 2010).

32. For a more recent example, see Peter H. Sedgewick, *The Market Economy and Christian Ethics* (Cambridge, UK: Cambridge University Press, 1999), 125-27. Sedgewick's description of Miroslav Volf's political theology (196-99) shows Volf falling into the same mistake.

33. Stanley Hauerwas, *The Peaceable Kingdom: A Primer in Christian Ethics* (Notre Dame: University of Notre Dame Press, 1983), 99, 101-3.

34. Blomberg, *Christians in an Age of Wealth*, 196-212.

35. The problems are exacerbated by the shockingly low levels of charitable giving in the American church. On average, each churchgoer in American gives only 2 percent of her or his annual income to charitable causes, including the church she or he attends. A study conducted in the late 1990s discovered that 15 percent of America's Christians contributed 80 percent of the money given to charity, while 20 percent gave away nothing at all. See Blomberg, *Christians in an Age of Wealth*, 23–25.

36. J. D. Trout, *The Empathy Gap: Building Bridges to the Good Life and the Good of Society* (New York: Viking Penguin, 2009), 40.

37. Helpful summaries of practical steps to be taken by every Christian appear in Blomberg, *Christians in an Age of Wealth*, 137–44, 173–247, and Witherington, *Jesus and Money*, 141–69; see esp. Witherington's section entitled "Deprogramming Ourselves from a Lifestyle of Conspicuous Consumption and Self-Gratification."

38. See Blomberg's chapter entitled "The Church as Steward," in *Christians in an Age of Wealth*, 219–42.

39. Blomberg, *Neither Poverty nor Riches*, 132.

40. Witherington, *Jesus and Money*, 154–55.

41. See Ronald Sider, *Rich Christians in an Age of Hunger: Moving from Affluence to Generosity* (Nashville: Thomas Nelson, reprint 2015); Ronald Sider, *Just Generosity: A New Vision for Overcoming Poverty in America* (Grand Rapids: Baker, 1999); Peter Greer and Phil Smith, *The Poor Will Be Glad: Joining the Revolution to Lift the World Out of Poverty* (Grand Rapids: Zondervan, 2009); Luke Timothy Johnson, *Sharing Possessions: What Faith Demands*, 2nd ed. (Grand Rapids: Eerdmans, 2011); Blomberg, *Christians in an Age of Wealth*, 173–93.

42. For a spectrum of critiques on capitalism, from both religious and nonreligious perspectives, see Donald A. Hay, *A Christian Critique of Capitalism* (Nottingham: Grove Books, 1975); Daniel Bell Jr., *The Cultural Contradictions of Capitalism* (New York: Perseus, 1976); Robert L. Heilbroner, *The Nature and Logic of Capitalism* (New York: Norton, 1985); Walter L. Owensby, *Economics for Prophets: A Primer on Concepts, Realities, and Values in Our Economic System* (Grand Rapids: Eerdmans, 1988); Craig M. Gay, *With Liberty and Justice for Whom? The Recent Evangelical Debate over Capitalism* (Grand Rapids: Eerdmans, 1991); Ronald H. Preston, *Religion and the Ambiguities of Capitalism* (Cleveland: Pilgrim Press, 1991); Jeremy Seabrook, *The Myth of the Market: Promises and Illusions* (New York: Black Rose Books, 1991); Timothy J. Gorringe, *Capital and the Kingdom: Theological Ethics and Economic Order* (Maryknoll, NY: Orbis, 1994); Peter H. Sedgwick, *The Market Economy and Christian Ethics* (Cambridge, UK: Cambridge University Press, 1999); William T. Cavanaugh, *Being Consumed: Economics and Christian Desire* (Grand Rapids: Eerdmans, 2008); Daniel Bell Jr., *The Economy of Desire: Christianity and Capitalism in a Postmodern World* (Grand Rapids: Baker, 2012).

43. See Michael Novak, *The Spirit of Democratic Capitalism* (New York: Touchstone, 1982). His section "A Theology of Democratic Capitalism" (333–60) is a good example of how to use Scripture to bolster one's ideology rather than reading it for instruction and understanding. His section describing Christian discipleship as the archetype of a competitive lifestyle is downright painful to read.

44. F. A. Hayek, *The Road to Serfdom: Texts and Documents; The Definitive Edition* (Chicago: University of Chicago Press, 2007).

45. Unfortunately, these are brief notations that remain undeveloped in both works.

In discussing poverty as a threat to the economy and polity of democratic capitalism, Novak says, "Social welfare programs fit the logic of democratic capitalism and have a legitimate claim on it" (*The Spirit of Democratic Capitalism*, 218). In *The Road to Serfdom*, Hayek observes that "a wooden insistence" on laissez faire principles damages society (71); "the marketplace sometimes requires certain kinds of government action," as in consumer protection, limited working hours, labor safety rules, "certain" public, social services and environmental protections, regulating monopolies (86–89), and government health insurance (148)!

46. A great deal of capitalist thought in America today draws its inspiration from the dog-eat-dog social Darwinism of the atheist philosopher Ayn Rand; see Gary Weiss, *Ayn Rand Nation: The Hidden Struggle for America's Soul* (New York: St. Martin's, 2012). Weiss concludes that "the Republican party has become more the party of Ayn Rand than the party of Teddy Roosevelt or Abraham Lincoln" (248). Rand was an important mentor to Alan Greenspan, who served as chairman of the Federal Reserve of the United States from 1987 to 2006 and was consciously guided by Randian principles. Republican representative Paul Ryan, Speaker of the House, former vice-presidential candidate, and confessing Christian, has declared Rand's novel that extols self-serving individualism, *Atlas Shrugged*, to be one of his favorite books. He makes it required reading for all of his staff and interns. The fact that American evangelicalism can continue uncritically to endorse such economic policies is additional testimony to the enfeebled, if not downright apostate, condition of the American church. Weiss has rightly condemned the plot lines of Rand's two novels, *The Fountainhead* and *Atlas Shrugged*, as "staggeringly immoral" (249).

47. Adam Smith, *An Inquiry into the Nature and Causes of the Wealth of Nations* (Chicago: University of Chicago Press, 1976), 2:323–26; cited in Bell, *The Economy of Desire*, 139.

48. Cited in Bell, *The Economy of Desire*, 198.

Notes to Chapter Eleven

1. Terry Eagleton, *Reason, Faith, and Revolution: Reflections on the God Debate* (New Haven: Yale University Press, 2009), 27.

2. Eagleton, *Reason, Faith, and Revolution*, 55.

3. Cited in Joshua J. Whitfield, *Pilgrim Holiness: Martyrdom as Descriptive Witness* (Eugene, OR: Cascade, 2009), 29.

4. Stanley Hauerwas, *Approaching the End: Eschatological Reflections on Church, Politics, and Life* (Grand Rapids: Eerdmans, 2013), 56.

5. Rupert Shortt, *Christianophobia: A Faith under Attack* (Grand Rapids: Eerdmans, 2012).

6. Shortt, *Christianophobia*, xx.

7. The bibliography on this subject is too vast to list here. For one classic example, see Tim LaHaye and David Noebel, *Mind Siege: The Battle for Truth in the New Millennium* (Nashville: Thomas Nelson Workbook, 2000).

8. For a recent treatment of this history and the compromises involved, see Wes

Howard-Brook, *Empire Baptized: How the Church Embraced What Jesus Rejected, 2nd–5th Centuries* (Maryknoll, NY: Orbis, 2016).

9. Christopher Bryan, *Render to Caesar: Jesus, the Early Church, and the Roman Superpower* (Oxford: Oxford University Press, 2005), 50–51; see also 41–47, 62–64, 126–27. W. D. Davies came to the same conclusion thirty years ago: see *The Gospel and the Land: Early Christianity and Jewish Territorial Doctrine* (Berkeley: University of California Press, 1974), 352–53.

10. Michelle Goldberg, *Kingdom Coming: The Rise of Christian Nationalism* (New York: Norton, 2006), 17–21.

11. Goldberg, *Kingdom Coming*, 18.

12. Michael Weinstein, a 1977 honor graduate of the Air Force Academy whose family is Jewish, founded the Military Religious Freedom Foundation (MRFF) in order to combat religious prejudice in America's armed forces. The organization has been nominated six times for the Nobel Peace Prize. Mr. Weinstein's son, who also attended the Academy, has his own stories confirming the anti-Semitic, Christian abuse of power at the Academy. For extensive testimony to these and other problem situations throughout the country, see the MRFF website at www.militaryreligiousfreedom.org. Mr. Weinstein and his family receive frequent death threats for the work they do through the MRFF. Michael's wife, Bonnie Weinstein, has published a shocking book that includes a selection of hate mail that they have received over the years, a great deal of it sent by people *professing to be Christians*. In fact, many letter-writers explicitly root their hate and vitriol in their Christianity. It makes for horrendous reading. The book is entitled *To the Far Right Christian Hater: You Can Be a Good Speller or a Hater, But You Can't Be Both*. It is available at the MRFF website and Amazon.

13. George Yancey and David A. Williamson, *So Many Christians, So Few Lions: Is There Christianophobia in the United States?* (London: Rowman and Littlefield, 2015). (Hereafter, page references to this work appear in parentheses within the text.) Unfortunately, this study does not offer specifics about the extent of animosity toward Christians in the United States. Nevertheless, what is most useful for our purposes are the reasons given by respondents to explain their hostility toward the Christian religion.

14. I realize that some people are offended by Jesus Christ in particular while warmly embracing other religious viewpoints. Jesus warns his disciples not to be surprised when they encounter this kind of targeted hostility. In this case, the only legitimate basis for a Christian's complaint would be in a situation where the believer experiences religiously based discrimination that violates his or her civil liberties and equal treatment under the law. There may be such cases—I can think of hiring practices in certain academic institutions, for instance (see *So Many Christians*, 97, 124–25, 140)—but few of the examples cited by the Religious Right in their reports on the culture wars meet these criteria. Once again, complaints about this type of animosity are simply complaints about the Christian life.

15. It is important to understand that the word "conservative" is not being used as a theological term here. The problem in the minds of this study's respondents is not *theological* conservatism but *political* conservatism, i.e., Republican politics.

16. Critics may object by saying that such attitudes could exist without revealing themselves in this type of sociological study. While this is possible, it cannot excuse us from ignoring what the respondents clearly do say about the basis of their hostility.

17. Of course, Christian conservatives/Republicans have not cornered the market on betraying the gospel. Liberal, progressive Christians have their own ways of making equally dangerous mistakes, usually taking the forms of universalism, denying human sinfulness and the need for redemption, or viewing Jesus's death on the cross as an exemplary but not an atoning sacrifice. Nevertheless, there are no "liberal" Christian organizations with anything like the political or financial clout wielded by groups like the Christian Coalition, the Family Research Council, or the American Family Association, to name only a few.

18. Some people abuse the term "church militant" by using it to justify their physical and psychological aggression against anyone they define as an enemy of the faith. I once heard a pastor speak this way while delivering an anti-Muslim public lecture. He boasted about the fact that he and his elders carried handguns to every church function in order to protect their flock.

19. In my opinion, one of the most profound clarifications of this distinction between the "church militant" and the "church triumphant" appears in Søren Kierkegaard's *Practice in Christianity*, part III, section v (Princeton: Princeton University Press, 1991), 201-32. Kierkegaard warned about participating in a Danish state church that proclaimed Christianity's worldly triumph: "As long as this world lasts and the Christian Church in it, it is a militant Church. . . . But woe, woe to the Christian Church when it will have been victorious in this world, for then it is not the Church that has been victorious but the world. Then the heterogeneity between Christianity and world has vanished, the world has won, and Christianity has lost" (223). "Only the Church militant is truth. . . . In this world it is the militant Church that is related to Christ in his abasement. . . . This is the truth, the Church triumphant and established Christendom are untruth" (232).

20. Morna Hooker, "Interchange and Suffering," in *Suffering and Martyrdom in the New Testament: Studies Presented to G. M. Styler by the Cambridge New Testament Seminar*, ed. William Horbury and Brian McNeil (Cambridge, UK: Cambridge University Press, 1981), 70-83.

21. The apostle Peter shares the same view of Christian suffering. In 1 Peter 3:13, he says, "Rejoice that *you participate in the sufferings of Christ*, so that you may be overjoyed when his glory is revealed" (italics added).

22. This particular example of Jesus's reversal of human values is brilliantly conveyed in John's Gospel by his use of the word *hupsoō* ("lift up" or "exalt"; see John 3:14; 8:28; 12:32, 34). The word becomes a double entendre that refers to the moment Jesus is hoisted onto the cross as also being the point of exaltation to his throne. Jesus is crowned at his execution.

23. Hooker, "Interchange and Suffering," 83. Unfortunately, space forbids a more extensive treatment of Hooker's arguments. Her article will repay whatever time readers may devote to finding and studying it for themselves.

24. In reality, 2 Corinthians is the fourth letter that Paul sent to Corinth; but it is only the second letter that is extant.

25. For good, secondary overviews of Kierkegaard's wisdom on suffering for Christ, see David J. Gouwens, *Kierkegaard as Religious Thinker* (Cambridge, UK: Cambridge University Press, 1996), 162-85; Sylvia Walsh, *Living Christianly: Kierkegaard's Dialectic of Christian Existence* (University Park: Pennsylvania State University Press, 2005), 113-48.

26. Though the theme of suffering appears in many of Kierkegaard's works, the

works most extensively dealing with Christian suffering are *Practice in Christianity*, trans. and ed. Howard V. Hong and Edna H. Hong (Princeton: Princeton University Press, 1991); *Upbuilding Discourses in Various Spirits*, trans. and ed. Howard V. Hong and Edna H. Hong (Princeton: Princeton University Press, 1993), Part III, "The Gospel of Sufferings, Christian Discourses," 213–341; and *Christian Discourses*, trans. and ed. Howard V. Hong and Edna H. Hong (Princeton: Princeton University Press, 1997), Part II, "States of Mind in the Strife of Suffering," 93–159.

27. Kierkegaard observed: "Christianity is a madness . . . it must appear as a madness to the sensate [sensible] person. . . . Christianity came into the world as the absolute, not, humanly speaking, for comfort; on the contrary, it continually speaks about how the Christian must suffer or about how a person in order to become and remain a Christian must endure sufferings that he consequently can avoid simply by refraining from becoming a Christian" (*Practice in Christianity*, 62–63).

28. Sometimes enemies become friends once we begin to love them. Maybe they were never truly enemies in the first place, but only different from us.

29. Paul and James may also have Christian suffering in mind, but their advice describes the spiritual character that can be formed in any situation.

30. Kierkegaard, *Practice in Christianity*, 108–9 (italics in original).

31. Kierkegaard offers a good exposition of these texts in *Upbuilding Discourses in Various Spirits*, 217–29, under the heading "What Meaning and What Joy There Are in the Thought of Following Christ."

32. This task of knowing God's will is not as mystical as many people want to make it. In terms of God's will for my life, 99.9 percent of it is laid out for me in Scripture: be an obedient citizen of the kingdom of God as taught and modeled by Jesus and applied to the early church throughout the other books of the New Testament. When life as an obedient kingdom citizen becomes my daily habit, the more idiosyncratic decisions about career options, and so on, become more straightforward.

33. Kierkegaard, *Upbuilding Discourses in Various Spirits*, 298–99 (italics in original).

34. For a closer look at the role of offense in Christian faith and the relationship of both to reason, see my book *Encountering Jesus, Encountering Scripture: Reading the Bible Critically in Faith* (Grand Rapids: Eerdmans, 2013).

35. Kierkegaard, *Practice in Christianity*, 114–15.

Notes to Chapter Twelve

1. I marveled the next day when every major news broadcast described how the violent mass of protesters had turned against the police in an unprovoked attack, causing officers numerous injuries. I was reminded of the standard US critique of Soviet news outlets spouting state propaganda during the Cold War. I had been in the center of it all, and the truth was exactly the opposite of what the public was being told by the mainstream media.

2. Richard Burridge, *Imitating Jesus: An Inclusive Approach to New Testament Ethics* (Grand Rapids: Eerdmans, 2007), 71–79, 81, 152–54, 179–81, 220–25, 279–83, 339–46, 408–9.

3. *Lares* were protective spirits who watched over the home; *penates* were the spirits

of the ancestors. Each of them was represented by a small image kept near the hearth or on the dining table during meals, and every Greco-Roman family had them. In the course of doing business, I am sure that Paul was as hospitable, honest, and gracious toward these idolatrous shoppers—and just as willing to sell them a tent—as he was toward fellow members of his local churches.

4. A Rorschach test asks people to identify what they see in a series of ink blots; the answers are then subjected to psychological analysis.

5. See the interesting discussion in Victoria Barnett, *For the Soul of the People: Protestant Protest against Hitler* (Oxford: Oxford University Press, 1992), 88–98.

6. See Richard Steigmann-Gall, *The Holy Reich: Nazi Conceptions of Christianity, 1919-1945* (Cambridge, UK: Cambridge University Press, 2003), 176, 185. After the war, Niemöller and many of those who had sided with him deeply regretted their lack of vision and condemned the Confessing Church's indifference to anti-Semitism as their failure to fully appreciate the meaning of the gospel. Niemöller spent the last seven years of Nazi rule in concentration camps for opposing Hitler in other ways. He is probably best known for his postwar poem of lament confessing his mistake:

> First they came for the Socialists, and I did not speak out—
> Because I was not a Socialist.
>
> Then they came for the Trade Unionists, and I did not speak out—
> Because I was not a Trade Unionist.
>
> Then they came for the Jews, and I did not speak out—
> Because I was not a Jew.
>
> Then they came for me—and there was no one left to speak for me.

7. For people who are convinced that human life begins at conception, opposition to abortion is a necessary, principled position. But other political positions of the Religious Right that bind them to the Republican Party require closer scrutiny.

8. Reinhold Niebuhr, *An Interpretation of Christian Ethics* (London: SCM, 1948), 51.

9. Reinhold Niebuhr, *Christianity and Power Politics* (New York: Charles Scribner's Sons, 1940), 9.

10. See the website http://www.7culturalmountains.org/.

11. T. S. Eliot, *The Idea of a Christian Society* (New York: Harcourt, Brace, 1940), 56, 97.

12. When Jesus says that his yoke is "light" and "easy," he is contrasting Christian discipleship with the current Jewish ideal of living under "the yoke of Torah." Jesus's yoke is light because he is the Truth who brings disciples into a gracious relationship with the Father. The way of Torah is no longer light since it has been superceded in the coming of Jesus.

Select Bibliography

A wealth of literature is available to anyone seeking additional information on the topics explored in *I Pledge Allegiance*. Although each chapter concludes with a brief list of books for further reading, neither the titles found in those lists nor those contained in a chapter's notes exhaust all the research comprising the background to this book. Thus, for the industrious reader, I have included this additional bibliography of titles that I found useful but, for one reason or another, failed to make it into the notations or chapter lists for further reading. Remembering that "useful" is not synonymous with "agreeable," there is always important, heuristic value in wrestling with ideas and arguments that differ from our own.

Adams, Ian. *The Logic of Political Belief: A Philosophical Analysis of Ideology*. Savage, MD: Barnes & Noble, 1989.

Anderson, Benedict. *Imagined Communities: Reflections on the Origins and Spread of Nationalism*. London: Verso, 2006.

Backhouse, Stephen. *Kierkegaard's Critique of Christian Nationalism*. Oxford: Oxford University Press, 2011.

Bammel, Ernst, and C. F. D. Moule, eds. *Jesus and the Politics of His Day*. Cambridge: Cambridge University Press, 1984.

Barth, Karl. *The Call to Discipleship*. Translated by G. W. Bromiley, edited by K. C. Hanson. Minneapolis: Fortress, 2003.

Beavis, Mary Ann. *Jesus and Utopia: Looking for the Kingdom of God in the Roman World*. Minneapolis: Fortress, 2006.

Bell, Daniel M. *Just War as Christian Discipleship: Recentering the Tradition in the Church Rather Than the State*. Grand Rapids: Brazos, 2009.

Benson, Bruce Ellis, and Peter Goodwin Heltzel, eds. *Evangelicals and Empire: Christian Alternatives to the Political Status Quo*. Grand Rapids: Brazos, 2008.

Brimlow, Robert W. *What about Hitler? Wrestling with Jesus's Call to Nonviolence in an Evil World*. Grand Rapids: Brazos, 2006.

Buttry, Daniel L. *Christian Peacemaking: From Heritage to Hope*. Valley Forge: Judson, 1994.

Cadoux, Cecil John. *The Early Church and the Word: A History of the Christian Attitude to Pagan Society and the State Down to the Time of Constantinus*. Edinburgh: T. & T. Clark, 1925.

Cahill, Lisa Sowle. *Love Your Enemies: Discipleship, Pacifism, and Just War Theory*. Minneapolis: Fortress, 1994.

Cavanaugh, William T. *Theopolitical Imagination: Discovering the Liturgy as a Political Act in an Age of Global Consumerism*. London: Bloomsbury T. & T. Clark, 2002.

Chappell, Paul K. *Peaceful Revolution: How We Can Create the Future Needed for Humanity's Survival*. Westport, CT: Easton Studio, 2012.

Cromartie, Michael, ed. *Caesar's Coin Revisited: Christians and the Limits of Government*. Grand Rapids: Eerdmans, 1996.

Cuddihy, John Murray. *No Offense: Civil Religion and Protestant Taste*. New York: Seabury, 1978.

Cullmann, Oscar. *The State in the New Testament*. New York: Charles Scribner's Sons, 1956.

Diamond, Sara. *Facing the Wrath: Confronting the Right in Dangerous Times*. Monroe, ME: Common Courage Press, 1996.

Dooley, Mark. *The Politics of Responsibility: Kierkegaard's Ethics of Responsibility*. New York: Fordham University Press, 2001.

Eagleton, Terry. *Ideology: An Introduction*. London/New York: Verso, 1991.

Eller, Vernard. *Kierkegaard and Radical Discipleship: A New Perspective*. Princeton: Princeton University Press, 1968.

Ellul, Jacques. *Anarchy and Christianity*. Translated by Geoffrey W. Bromiley. Grand Rapids: Eerdmans, 1991.

Ferguson, Everett. "Early Christian Martyrdom and Civil Disobedience." *Journal of Christian Studies* 1, no. 1 (Spring 1993): 73–83.

Forrester, Duncan B. *Christian Justice and Public Policy*. Cambridge: Cambridge University Press, 1997.

Fritzsche, Peter. *Germans into Nazis*. Cambridge, MA: Harvard University Press, 1998.

Giddens, Anthony. *The Nation-State and Violence*. Berkeley: University of California Press, 1987.

Gorringe, Timothy J. *Capital and the Kingdom: Theological Ethics and Economic Order*. Maryknoll, NY: Orbis, 1994.

Griffin, David Ray, John B. Cobb Jr., Richard A. Jalk, and Catherine Keller. *The American Empire and the Commonwealth of God: A Political, Economic, Religious Statement*. Louisville: Westminster John Knox, 2006.

Haidt, Jonathan. *The Righteous Mind: Why Good People Are Divided by Politics and Religion*. New York: Vintage Books, 2012.

Hamel, Gildas. *Poverty and Charity in Roman Palestine, First Three Centuries C.E.* Berkeley: University of California Press, 1990.

Harrington, Daniel, and James Keenan. *Jesus and Virtue Ethics: Building Bridges between New Testament Studies and Moral Theology*. Lanham, MD: Rowman & Littlefield, 2002.

Hastings, Adrian. *The Construction of Nationhood: Ethnicity, Religion and Nationalism.* Cambridge: Cambridge University Press, 1997.

Hauerwas, Stanley. *After Christendom? How the Church Is to Behave If Freedom, Justice, and a Christian Nation Are Bad Ideas.* Nashville: Abingdon, 1991.

———. *Against the Nations: War and Survival in a Liberal Society.* San Francisco: Harper & Row, 1988.

———. *Character and the Christian Life: A Study in Theological Ethics.* San Antonio: Trinity University Press, 1975.

———. *Christian Existence Today: Essays on Church, World, and Living in Between.* Grand Rapids: Brazos, 2001.

———. *Dispatches from the Front: Theological Engagements with the Secular.* Durham, NC: Duke University Press, 1994.

———. *In Good Company: The Church as Polis.* Notre Dame: Notre Dame University Press, 1995.

Hayes, Carleton J. H. *Nationalism: A Religion.* New York: Macmillan, 1960.

Henry, Maureen. *The Intoxication of Power: An Analysis of Civil Religion in Relation to Ideology.* Dordrecht, The Netherlands: D. Reidel, 1979.

Heschel, Susannah. *The Aryan Jesus: Christian Theologians and the Bible in Nazi Germany.* Princeton: Princeton University Press, 2009.

Hinlicky, Paul R. *Before Auschwitz: What Christian Theology Must Learn from the Rise of Nazism.* Eugene, OR: Cascade Books, 2013.

Hornus, Jean-Michel. *It Is Not Lawful for Me to Fight: Early Christian Attitudes toward War, Violence, and the State.* Translated by Alan Kreider and Oliver Coburn. Scottdale, PA: Herald Press, 1980.

Hudson, Wynthrop S., ed. *Nationalism and Religion in America: Concepts of American Identity and Mission.* Gloucester, MA: Peter Smith, 1978.

Jewett, Robert, and John Shelton Lawrence. *Captain America and the Crusade against Evil: The Dilemma of Zealous Nationalism.* Grand Rapids: Eerdmans, 2003.

Joireman, Sandra F., ed. *Church, State, and Citizen: Christian Approaches to Political Engagement.* Oxford: Oxford University Press, 2009.

Kateb, George. *Patriotism and Other Mistakes.* New Haven: Yale University Press, 2006.

Kierkegaard, Søren. *The Point of View.* Translated and edited by Howard V. Hong and Edna H. Hong. Princeton: Princeton University Press, 1998.

Kurlansky, Mark. *Non-Violence: The History of a Dangerous Idea.* New York: Random House, 2006.

Lakoff, George. *Moral Politics: How Liberals and Conservatives Think.* 2nd ed. Chicago: University of Chicago Press, 2002.

———. *The Political Mind: A Cognitive Scientist's Guide to Your Brain and Its Politics.* New York: Penguin Books, 2008.

———. *Thinking Points: Communicating Our American Values and Vision.* New York: Farrar, Straus and Giroux, 2006.

Lasserre, Jean. *War and the Gospel.* Translated by Oliver Coburn. Scottdale, PA: Herald Press, 1962.

Lieven, Anatol. *America Right or Wrong: An Anatomy of American Nationalism.* Oxford: Oxford University Press, 2012.

Lifton, Robert Jay, and Greg Mitchell. *Hiroshima in America: Fifty Years of Denial*. New York: G. P. Putnam's Sons, 1995.

Lovin, Robin W. *Christian Realism and the New Realities*. Cambridge: Cambridge University Press, 2008.

Malina, Bruce J. *The Social Gospel of Jesus: The Kingdom of God in Mediterranean Perspective*. Minneapolis: Fortress, 2001.

Marvin, Carolyn, and David W. Ingle. "Blood Sacrifice and the Nation: Revisiting Civil Religion." *Journal of the American Academy of Religion* 64, no. 4 (Winter 1996): 767-80.

————. *Blood Sacrifice and the Nation: Totem Rituals and the American Flag*. Cambridge: Cambridge University Press, 1999.

McKnight, Scott. "Ethics of Jesus." In *Dictionary of Jesus and the Gospels*, edited by Joel B. Green, Jeannine K. Brown, and Nicholas Perrin. Downers Grove, IL: IVP Academic, 2013.

McMahan, Jeff. *Killing in War*. Oxford: Clarendon Press, 2009.

Müller-Fahrenholz, Geiko. *America's Battle for God: A European Christian Looks at Civil Religion*. Grand Rapids: Eerdmans, 2007.

Nadelson, Theodore. *Trained to Kill: Soldiers at War*. Baltimore: Johns Hopkins University Press, 2005.

Nelson-Pallmeyer, Jack. *Saving Christianity from Empire*. New York: Continuum, 2005.

Neufeld, Thomas R. Yoder. *Recovering Jesus: The Witness of the New Testament*. Grand Rapids: Brazos, 2007.

O'Donovan, Oliver. *The Desire of the Nations: Rediscovering the Roots of Political Theology*. Cambridge: Cambridge University Press, 1996.

————. *Resurrection and the Moral Order: An Outline for Evangelical Ethics*. Grand Rapids: Eerdmans, 1986.

Ogletree, Thomas W. *Hospitality to the Stranger: Dimensions of Moral Understanding*. Philadelphia: Fortress, 1985.

O'Leary, Cecilia Elizabeth. *To Die For: The Paradox of American Patriotism*. Princeton: Princeton University Press, 1999.

Pieterson, Lloyd. *Reading the Bible after Christendom*. Harrisonburg, VA: Herald, 2012.

Pilgrim, Walter E. *Uneasy Neighbors: Church and State in the New Testament*. Minneapolis: Fortress, 1999.

Plamenatz, John. *Ideology*. New York: Praeger, 1970.

Polner, Murray, and Thomas E. Woods Jr., eds. *We Who Dared to Say No to War: American Antiwar Writing from 1812 to Now*. New York: Basic Books, 2008.

Press, Eyal. *Beautiful Souls: Saying No, Breaking Ranks, and Heeding the Voice of Conscience in Dark Times*. New York: Farrar, Straus and Giroux, 2012.

Preston, Ronald H. *Religion and the Ambiguities of Capitalism*. Cleveland: Pilgrim Press, 1991.

Rhee, Helen. *Loving the Poor, Saving the Rich: Wealth, Poverty, and Early Christian Formation*. Grand Rapids: Baker, 2012.

Rouner, Leroy S., ed. *Civil Religion and Political Theology*. Notre Dame: Notre Dame University Press, 1986.

Sedgewick, Peter H. *The Market Economy and Christian Ethics*. Cambridge: Cambridge University Press, 1999.

Shanks, Andrew. *Civil Society, Civil Religion*. Oxford: Blackwell, 1995.

Shriver, Donald W. *Honest Patriots: Loving a Country Enough to Remember Its Misdeeds*. Oxford: Oxford University Press, 2005.

Smith, Anthony D. *Nationalism: Theory, Ideology, History*. Cambridge, UK: Polity, 2010.

Sobrino, Jon. *The True Church and the Poor*. Maryknoll, NY: Orbis, 1984.

Storkey, Alan. *Jesus and Politics: Confronting the Powers*. Grand Rapids: Baker Academic, 2005.

Stringfellow, William. *Conscience and Obedience: The Politics of Romans 13 and Revelation 13 in Light of the Second Coming*. Eugene, OR: Wipf and Stock, 1977.

———. *An Ethic for Christians and Other Aliens in a Strange Land*. Waco, TX: Word, 1973.

Tal, Uriel. *Religion, Politics and Ideology in the Third Reich: Selected Essays*. London/New York: Routledge, 2004.

Tinder, Glenn. *The Political Meaning of Christianity, the Prophetic Stance: An Interpretation*. New York: HarperCollins, 1991.

Trocmé, André. *Jesus and the Nonviolent Revolution*. Translated by Michael H. Shank and Marlin E. Miller. Scottdale, PA: Herald Press, 1973.

Westen, Drew. *The Political Brain: The Role of Emotion in Deciding the Fate of the Nation*. New York: Public Affairs, 2007.

Wheeler, Sondra Ely. *Wealth as Peril and Obligation: The New Testament on Possessions*. Grand Rapids: Eerdmans, 1995.

Wilsey, John D. *American Exceptionalism and Civil Religion: Reassessing the History of an Idea*. Downers Grove, IL: IVP Academic, 2015.

Wogaman, J. Philip. *Christian Perspectives on Politics*. Philadelphia: Fortress, 1988.

Wright, N. T. *How God Became King: The Forgotten Story of the Gospels*. New York: HarperOne, 2012.

Yoder, John Howard. *Christian Attitudes to War, Peace, and Revolution*. Edited by Theodore J. Koontz and Andy Alexis-Baker. Grand Rapids: Brazos, 2009.

———. *Discipleship as Political Responsibility*. Translated by Timothy J. Geddert. Scottdale, PA: Herald Press, 2003.

———. *For the Nations: Essays Evangelical and Public*. Grand Rapids: Eerdmans, 1997.

———. *Karl Barth and the Problem of War*. Nashville: Abingdon, 1970.

———. *Nevertheless: The Varieties of Religious Pacifism*. Scottdale, PA: Herald Press, 1971.

———. *The Pacifism of Karl Barth*. Scottdale, PA: Herald Press, 1968.

———. *The Politics of Jesus*. Grand Rapids: Eerdmans, 1972.

———. *The Priestly Kingdom: Social Ethics as Gospel*. Notre Dame: University Press, 1984.

———. *What Would You Do? A Serious Answer to a Standard Question*. Scottdale, PA: Herald Press, 1992.

———. *The War of the Lamb: The Ethics of Nonviolence and Peacemaking*. Edited by Glen Harold Stassen, Mark Thiessen Nation, and Matt Hamsher. Grand Rapids: Brazos, 2009.

Index of Names and Subjects

Index of Scripture References